A Visual History of Modern Britain

Edited by
Professor Jack Simmons

The Town

Geoffrey Martin

Vista Books

© Geoffrey Martin 1961

First published by
VISTA BOOKS
Longacre Press Ltd., 161–166 Fleet St., London, EC4
Printed in Great Britain by
Taylor Garnett Evans & Co. Ltd, London & Watford

Author's Note

A book of this kind attracts several obligations for each of its pictures, and many more for those that are considered but not included. The list below conceals more courtesies from those whom I have troubled with enquiries than I can hope to acknowledge, and though I have particular pleasure in thanking Mr. J. F. Whitehead of Appleby, Mr. Kenneth Smith, the Librarian of Carlisle, and Mr. A. A. C. Hedges, the Librarian of Great Yarmouth, for much willing help, that is only a token of my gratitude to a great many private owners, institutions and their officials. I am indebted to Dr. Esmond de Beer for lending me photographs of the drawings from the Van der Hem Atlas, and to Mr. P. H. Hulton, the editor of the Walpole Society's facsimile of the drawings, for his friendly advice. Sir John Summerson readily interrupted his own work to lend me his print of the picture of Covent Garden, and my colleague Mr. Norman Scarfe, whose work I interrupt continually, drew my attention to the pictures of Bury St. Edmunds and Newmarket, and lent me his own photographs of them. Mr. Graham Beynon pursued the Aberavon mace for me, and Miss Isobel Jones was kind enough to read and discuss parts of the text. The General Editor, Professor Jack Simmons, has given me, characteristically, unfailing and unstinted help. My wife, who has suffered every word and picture here and untold thousands besides, without losing hope or charity, could not have expended more care on a book of her own than she has on this.

G.M.

Contents

Author's Note	2
List of Illustrations	3
Editor's Introduction	8
The Medieval Town	9
Reformation and Revolutions	21
The Modern Town	43
Illustrations	85
Bibliographical Note	213
Index	215

List of Illustrations

The author and the publishers wish to thank the Trustees of the British Museum for permission to reproduce those pictures marked by the abbreviation B.M. The items marked M.O.W. and R.C.H.M. are supplied by the Ministry of Works and the Royal Commission on Historical Monuments, and are reproduced by permission of the Controller of Her Majesty's Stationery Office; those marked N.B.R. are from the National Buildings Record.

1 Caernarvon, by John Boydell, 1750. (By courtesy of the National Library of Wales.)
2 Stirling. (Scotsman Publications Ltd.)
3 York, City Walls. (Walter Scott (Bradford) Ltd.)
4 Southampton, Bar Gate, by Thomas Shotter Boys, 1853. (By courtesy of the Laing Art Gallery, Newcastle-upon-Tyne.)
5 Winchelsea. (Aerofilms Ltd.)
6 Wells, Vicars' Close. (Reece Winston.)
7 St. Albans, houses, c. 1380. (B.M. MS. Cotton Nero D.VII.)
8 House from the Holkham Picture Bible. (B.M. Add. MS. 47680; photograph: Courtauld Institute of Art.)
9 Norwich, Market Place, by John Sell Cotman, c. 1807. (Tate Gallery.)
10 Shepton Mallet, Old Shambles in 1882. (N.B.R.)
11 Selby, Market Place. (*The Times*.)
12 Dalton-in-Furness, Market Place, c. 1810. (Block by courtesy of Barrow-in-Furness Public Library.)
13 Chichester, Market Cross. (N.B.R.)
14 Carlisle, Toll Board. (By courtesy of Carlisle Corporation.)
15 Great Yarmouth, Tollhouse, c. 1890. (By courtesy of Great Yarmouth Public Library.)
16 York, the Ouse from Lendal Bridge. (Walter Scott (Bradford) Ltd.)
17 York, Gildhall. (Walter Scott (Bradford) Ltd.)
18 King's Lynn, King John's Cup. (By courtesy of the Mayor and Corporation of King's Lynn.)
19 Bristol, initial letter of charter, 1347. (By courtesy of Bristol Corporation.)
20 Aberavon, Borough Mace, c. 1500. (Brian Lucas, Port Talbot.)
21 Bristol, the Mayor's Oath, from Robert Rickart's *Kalendar*. (By courtesy of Bristol Corporation.)
22 Thaxted, Gildhall. (N.B.R.)
23 Ludlow, misericord from St Lawrence's Church. (N.B.R.)
24 Leicester, glass panel, c. 1500. (Leicester Museums.)
25 Northleach, brass of John Taylour, c. 1490. (N.B.R.)

26 Wells, Market Place. (From J. Britton, *Architectural Antiquities of Great Britain*, 1807–1827.)
27 Oxford, Merton College, front quadrangle. (N.B.R.)
28 Oxford, New College, misericord. (R.C.H.M.)
29 Bristol, St. Mary Redcliffe. (Reece Winstone.)
30 Bristol, St. Mary Redcliffe, William Canynges' effigy. (A. F. Kersting.)
31 Glastonbury, George Hotel. (N.B.R.)
32 Pilgrim's badge, St. Thomas of Canterbury. (London Museum.)
33 Pilgrim's badge, Walsingham. (London Museum.)
34 Dunstable, St. Fremund's shrine, *c.* 1450. (B.M., Harleian MS. 2278.)
35 Carlisle, initial letter of charter, 1315. (By courtesy of Carlisle Corporation.)
36 Melrose Abbey. (M.O.W., Scotland.)
37 Siege coins, Scarborough and Newark, *c.* 1645. (British Museum.)
38 Gloucester, New Inn. (J. Britton, *Architectural Antiquities*.)
39 London, by Antonius van den Wyngaerde, *c.* 1560 (detail). (Ashmolean Museum, Oxford.)
40 Norwich, St. Andrew's Hall. (N.B.R.)
41 Boston, Old School House. (N.B.R.)
42 Ipswich, Cardinal's College Gate. (R.C.H.M.)
43 Cambridge, Trinity College, the Great Court. (R.C.H.M.)
44 Coventry, Butchers' Row, *c.* 1850. (N.B.R.)
45 Edinburgh, the Old College. (By courtesy of Edinburgh Public Library.)
46 Robert Rollock, Principal of Edinburgh College. (By permission of the Scottish National Galleries.)
47 Warwick, Leycester Hospital. (*The Times*.)
48 Carlisle, silver racing bells. (By courtesy of Carlisle City Museum.)
49 Richmond, Yorks., standing salt. (By courtesy of the Worshipful Company of Goldsmiths.)
50 Finsbury, Charterhouse, tomb of Thomas Sutton. (R.C.H.M.)
51 Lincoln, bakers' marks from the minutes of the Common Council, 1523. (W. T. Jones.)
52 Newcastle-upon-Tyne, town hutch. (By courtesy of Newcastle City Library.)
53 London, St. Andrew Undershaft, monument of John Stow. (R.C.H.M.)
54 John Heywood, *The Four Prentises of London*, 1615, title page. (Bodleian Library.)
55 Wymondham, Market House. (N.B.R.)
56 Chester, the Rows. (N.B.R.)
57 Bristol, a Nail. (Reece Winstone.)
58 Chester, Bishop Lloyd's house, Watergate Street. (N.B.R.)
59 Great Yarmouth, a Row. (By courtesy of A. Rainer-Todd, Great Yarmouth.)
60 Denbigh, High Street. (By courtesy of Professor Jack Simmons.)
61 London, Covent Garden. (By courtesy of the Earl of Pembroke.)
62 London, Lincoln's Inn Fields, 1741. (London Museum.)
63 Glasgow, Tolbooth steeple, *c.* 1890. (Mansell Collection.)
64 Edinburgh, Gladstone's Land. (R.C.H.M. Scotland.)
65 Aberdeen, Provost Skene's house. (By courtesy of Aberdeen Art Gallery and Museum.)
66 Denbigh, Sir Hugh Middleton's cup. (By courtesy of the Worshipful Company of Goldsmiths.)
67 Chester, Bridge Gate and water tower, *c.* 1660. (B.M., Harleian MS. 2073.)
68 Amwell, Herts., source of the New River. (B.M., Potter Collection.)
69 London, broadsheet of the Plague, 1666. (London Museum.)
70 London, the Great Fire, 1666. (London Museum.)
71 London, Wren's Plan, 1666. (London Museum.)
72 London from the Thames, *c.* 1750. (N.B.R.)
73 Bath, the King's Bath, by Willem Schellinks, 1662. (By courtesy of the Osterreichische Nationalbibliothek, Vienna.)
74 Tunbridge Wells, by Johannes Kip, 1718. (By courtesy of Tunbridge Wells Public Library.)
75 Chatham, by Jacob Esselens, 1660. (By courtesy of the Osterreichische Nationalbibliothek.)
76 Harwich, Dockyard Crane, *c.* 1667. (A. H. Smith.)
77 Whitehaven, by Matthias Reed, 1738. (By courtesy of Whitehaven Museum.)
78 Bury St. Edmunds, *c.* 1700. (By courtesy of Moyses Hall Museum, Bury St. Edmunds.)
79 Marlborough, the Mace, 1652. (By courtesy of the Worshipful Company of Goldsmiths.)
80 Thetford, Sword of State, *c.* 1675. (By courtesy of the Worshipful Company of Goldsmiths.)

81 Lostwithiel, Silver Oar, 1670. (By courtesy of the Worshipful Company of Goldsmiths.)
82 Bruton, Sexey's Hospital. (N.B.R.)
83 Liverpool, Old Blue Coat School. (N.B.R.)
84 Southwold, South Green. (Reece Winstone.)
85 Fulham, London, Sun Fire Mark. (By courtesy of the Sun Insurance Office Ltd.)
86 Blandford Church. (A. F. Kersting.)
87 *Enthusiasm Displayed*, by Robert Pranker, after John Griffiths, c. 1750. (B.M., King's Library.)
88 Carmarthen, St. Peter's Church, mayoral pew. (N.B.R.)
89 Poole, Skinner Street Congregational chapel. (N.B.R.)
90 Great Yarmouth, St. George's Church. (N.B.R.)
91 Bath, Dr. Oliver and Mr. Peirce. (By courtesy of the Royal National Hospital for Rheumatic Diseases, Bath.)
92 Richard Nash. (National Portrait Gallery.)
93 Bath, the Circus. (N.B.R.)
94 Bath, Queen Square. (N.B.R.)
95 Bath, Royal Crescent. (N.B.R.)
96 Bath, Royal Crescent, by Thomas Shepherd, 1801. (N.B.R.)
97 Bath, Upper Assembly Rooms, by Thomas Malton, Jr. (By courtesy of the Laing Art Gallery, Newcastle-upon-Tyne.)
98 Bath, Taking the Waters, by Thomas Rowlandson. (B.M., Dept. of Prints and Drawings.)
99 Bristol, Theatre Royal. (N.B.R.)
100 Colchester, mayor's theatre ticket. (By courtesy of the Worshipful Company of Goldsmiths.)
101 London, Covent Garden, 1763. (B.M., King's Library.)
102 Newmarket, by ? Peter Tillemans. (By courtesy of John Pattison, Esq., Great Hautboys House, Coltishall, Norfolk.)
103 Vauxhall, Spring Gardens, 1766. (B.M., Dept. of Prints and Drawings.)
104 Fleet Prison Enquiry, studio of William Hogarth, 1729. (National Portrait Gallery.)
105 Industry and Idleness, No. 10 by William Hogarth. (B.M., Dept. of Prints and Drawings.)
106 The Harlot's Progress, No. 4, by William Hogarth. (B.M., Dept. of Prints and Drawings.)
107 Execution of Earl Ferrers, 1760. (B.M., Dept. of Prints and Drawings.)
108 An Election Entertainment, by William Hogarth, 1755. (B.M., Dept. of Prints and Drawings.)
109 Appleby, 1754. (By courtesy of J. F. Whitehead, Esq.)
110 Westminster Election, 1796, by Robert Dighton. (London Museum.)
111 Queenborough, the poll book, 1754. (Kent Record Office, by permission of the Mayor and Corporation of Queenborough.)
112 Bristol, Clare Street, c. 1770. (By courtesy of British Railways, Southern Region.)
113 Port Glasgow, 1768. (Mitchell Library, Glasgow.)
114 Scarborough, by John Settrington, 1735 (detail). (B.M., King's Library.)
115 Portsmouth Point, by Thomas Rowlandson, 1782. (By courtesy of the City of Portsmouth Libraries and Museums Committee.)
116 The Cockpit, by William Hogarth. (B.M., Dept. of Prints and Drawings.)
117 Denbigh, cockpit. (N.B.R.)
118 Great Yarmouth, *The Dutch Fair*, by George Vincent, 1820. (By courtesy of Great Yarmouth Public Libraries Committee.)
119 Chester, Gild Banner. (By courtesy of Chester Corporation.)
120 Dalkeith, Incorporated Trades Badge. (By courtesy of the National Museum of Antiquities of Scotland.)
121 Liverpool, Town Hall. (N.B.R.)
122 Westminster Bridge, by Antonio Canaletto, c. 1747 (detail). (Reproduced by gracious permission of Her Majesty The Queen.)
123 London, the Adelphi. (From B. Pasterini, *The Works in Architecture of the Brothers Adam*.)
124 London, Somerset House. (N.B.R.)
125 Inveraray, Burgess Ticket, 1749. (Scottish Record Office.)
126 Wolverhampton, silver tea kettle, 1750. (By courtesy of Wolverhampton Corporation.)
127 Coventry, Lammas Day, by David Gee, 1830. (By courtesy of Coventry Libraries and Museums Committee.)
128 Bridlington, shop front. (N.B.R.)
129 Cheltenham, 1 Montpellier Walk. (N.B.R.)
130 Worcester, the Severn Bridge. (From Valentine Green, *The History of Worcestershire* 1796.)
131 Salisbury, Bishop's Gildhall, 1788. (By courtesy of the Salisbury, S. Wilts. and Blackmore Museum.)
132 Tremadoc, the Square. (N.B.R.)

133 Edinburgh, the Cowgate. (By courtesy of Edinburgh City Library.)
134 Edinburgh, the High School. (By courtesy of Edinburgh City Library.)
135 Edinburgh, St. George's Church. (By courtesy of Edinburgh City Library.)
136 Edinburgh, Charlotte Square. (J. L. A. Evatt.)
137 Edinburgh, Moray Place. (By courtesy of G. J. Kennedy, Esq.)
138 Edinburgh, Moray Place. (By courtesy of Edinburgh City Library.)
139 Edinburgh, the University. (By courtesy of Edinburgh City Library.)
140 Edinburgh from Calton Hill, by Thomas Miles Richardson. (By courtesy of the Laing Art Gallery, Newcastle-upon-Tyne.)
141 Edinburgh from the Mound, c. 1850. (By courtesy of Edinburgh City Library.)
142 Edinburgh, Dean Bridge. (Scotsman Publications Ltd.)
143 Bristol, Clifton Suspension Bridge. (Aerofilms Ltd.)
144 Brighton, H.R.H. The Prince Regent, 1818. (By courtesy of Brighton Public Library.)
145 Weymouth, Ladies in the Assembly Rooms, 1774. (Victoria and Albert Museum.)
146 Brighton, the Pavilion. (By courtesy of Brighton Public Library.)
147 Brighton, the Chain Pier. (From J. M. W. Turner, *Picturesque Views on the South Coast of England*, 1826.)
148 Hove, Brunswick Square. (N.B.R.)
149 Beaumaris, Victoria Terrace. (N.B.R.)
150 Cheltenham, Queen's Hotel. (By courtesy of Trust Houses Ltd.)
151 Berwick-on-Tweed, epitaph of Capt. George Younghusband, R.N. (N.B.R.)
152 London, Regent Street, c. 1825. N.B.R.)
153 London, Park Crescent. (A. F. Kersting.)
154 London, Cumberland Terrace, Regent's Park. (N.B.R.)
155 London, Regent's Park, c. 1835. (B.M., Dept. of Prints and Drawings.)
156 London, Macclesfield Bridge, Regent's Park. (N.B.R.)
157 Edinburgh, Holyrood House. (Scotsman Publications Ltd.)
158 London, Buckingham Palace, c. 1828. (London Museum.)
159 Dunwich, 1754. (From Thomas Gardner, *Historical Account of Dunwich*.)
160 Tregony, *Freedom and Purity of Election*, 1820. (B.M., Dept of Prints and Drawings.)

161 Manchester, *A View of St. Peter's Place*, 1819. (Block by courtesy of the John Rylands Library, Manchester.)
162 Nottingham, burning of the Castle, 1832. (By courtesy of Nottingham Public Library.)
163 Newcastle-under-Lyme, The Mock Mayor, 1833. (E. Harrison & Son, Newcastle-under-Lyme.)
164 Boston, the borough regalia. (By courtesy of Boston Corporation.)
165 Thomas Burbidge. (Leicester Museums.)
166 Leicester, Hall Book, 1836. (Leicester Museums.)
167 Exeter, water carriers. (From *Cholera in Exeter*, 1832.)
168 Exeter, burning infected clothing. (From *Cholera in Exeter*, 1832.)
169 Coventry, The Provident Friendly Dispensary. (N.B.R.)
170 Manchester, Chartist Strike, 1842 (*Illustrated London News*, 20 August 1842.)
171 Newport, Monmouthshire, Chartist Revolt, 1839. (By courtesy of Newport Museum and Art Gallery.)
172 Newcastle-upon-Tyne, *Demolition of houses*, by William Nicholson. (By courtesy of the Laing Art Gallery, Newcastle.)
173 Newcastle-upon-Tyne, Grainger Street. (N.B.R.)
174 Newcastle-upon-Tyne, *Grainger Street*, by Thomas Miles Richardson. (By courtesy of the Laing Art Gallery, Newcastle.)
175 Newcastle-upon-Tyne, High Level Bridge, c. 1850. By W. Boozey.
176 Sheffield, by William Ibbitt, c. 1850. (By courtesy of Sheffield City Library.)
177 Rothesay, c. 1825. (Mitchell Library, Glasgow.)
178 Torquay, c. 1840. (By courtesy of Professor Jack Simmons.)
179 Tenby, c. 1835. (By courtesy of the National Library of Wales.)
180 Oban. (Scotsman Publications Ltd.)
181 Douglas, I.O.M., c. 1890. (By courtesy of the Manx Museum.)
182 Manchester, Town Hall, 1877. (By courtesy of Manchester City Library.)
183 Harwich, Pier. (A. H. Smith.)
184 London, St. Mary Magdalene, Paddington. (N.B.R.)
185 Appleby, Boroughgate, 1853. (By courtesy of J. F. Whitehead, Esq.)
186 Gorbals, Main Street, c. 1860. (Mansell Collection, London.)

187 Glasgow, Clothes Market, c. 1890. (Mansell Collection.)
188 Merthyr Tydfil, Queue at a Pawnshop. (*Illustrated London News*, 13 February 1875.)
189 Glasgow, Saltmarket. (Mansell Collection.)
190 Whitehall, People's Mission Hall, c. 1870. (By courtesy of the Salvation Army.)
191 Slum Children's Picnic, c. 1900. (By courtesy of the Salvation Army.)
192 Saltaire, c. 1860. (By courtesy of Bradford City Library.)
193 Sir Titus Salt, c. 1870. (From *Historical Notes on Bradford Corporation*, 1881.)
194 Aberdeen, Queen Victoria opening the water supply. (*Illustrated London News*, 27 October 1866.)
195 Lake Vyrnwy, Montgomery. (By courtesy of Liverpool Corporation.)
196 London, City extension of the L. C. & D. Railway. (*Illustrated London News*, 28 April 1864.)
197 Barrow-in-Furness, steam tram, c. 1890. (By courtesy Barrow Public Library.)
198 Birmingham, Bull Ring. (N.B.R.)
199 London, Piccadilly Circus. (By courtesy of British Railways, Southern Region.)
200 Appleby, Boroughgate, 1897. (By courtesy of Appleby Corporation.)
201 Kirkcaldy Fire Brigade, 1898. (James R. Smith & Son, Kirkcaldy.)
202 Westminster, Millbank Gardens, 1905. (By courtesy of London County Council.)
203 Wandsworth, Tooting Bathing Lake, 1906. (By courtesy of London County Council.)
204 The Upper Rhondda Fawr. (H. Tempest (Cardiff) Ltd.)
205 Liverpool Waterfront. (By courtesy of Alfred Holt & Co.)
206 Liverpool Landing Stage, c. 1890. (N.B.R.)
207 Reading, Food Queue, c. 1916 (Imperial War Museum.)
208 Brighton, Earl Beatty unveiling the War Memorial, 7 October 1922. (Radio Times – Hulton Picture Library.)
209 Leeds, Quarry Hill Flats. (C. H. Wood (Bradford) Ltd.)
210 London, a steam lorry under escort during the General Strike, 1926. (Thomson News Services Ltd.)
211 Wigan, a street corner in the 1930s. (Radio Times – Hulton Picture Library.)
212 Nottingham, Kenton Square, 1931. (By courtesy of the Medical Officer of Health, Nottingham.)
213 Wembley, West Ham United supporters, 1923. (Radio Times – Hulton Picture Library.)
214 Marks and Spencer's shop, Bedford, c. 1932. (By courtesy of Marks and Spencer & Co., Ltd.)
215 The Gaumont Palace Cinema, Birmingham, c. 1945. (By courtesy of Circuits Management Association Ltd.)
216 Kentmere, the market-day omnibus. (By courtesy of Janet Martin.)
217 London, Elephant and Castle Underground Station. (Imperial War Museum.)
218 London, Barrage Balloon. (Fox Photos. Ltd.)
219 London, Oxford Street, 1940. (Fox Photos. Ltd.)
220 Plymouth, Royal Parade. (*Western Morning News*.)
221 Plymouth, Woolster Street. (Tom Molland, Ltd.)
222 Cwmbran, Two Locks. (By courtesy of Cwmbran Development Corporation.)
223 Glenrothes, Woodside. (By courtesy of Glenrothes Development Corporation.)
224 Crawley, Queen Square. (By courtesy of Crawley Development Corporation.)
225 Corby, Woodnewton Way Infants' School. (By courtesy of Corby Development Corporation.)
226 Birmingham, Elmdon Airport. (By courtesy of British European Airways.)
227 Liverpool, Mersey Tunnel Entrance. (By courtesy of the Roads Campaign Council.)
228 Colchester, Opening of the Oyster Fishery. (F. J. Armes.)
229 Colchester, Silver Oyster-Gauge. (By courtesy of the Worshipful Company of Goldsmiths.)
230 Hawick, Common Riding. (By courtesy of the *Hawick Express*.)
231 Kendal, Call Stone. (*Westmorland Gazette*.)
232 Kirkwall, Ball Game. (W. S. Hewison, Kirkwall.)
233 London, Lord Mayor's Show, 1959. (*The Times*.)

Editor's Introduction

The purpose of this *Visual History* is to provide, largely by means of pictures, an account of the social history of modern Britain. The attempt is no novelty in itself; but some of the principles on which it is based are new. They must be explained if the scope, and the limitations, of the series are to be understood.

The use of a text based both on pictures and on words requires, I hope, no justification. For the document, the picture, and the object in a museum are all important alike in helping us to understand the life of the past, and they need to be treated together if they are to reveal their full significance.

It is an essential part of the plan of the *Visual History* that the illustrations should be authentic, not conjectural. They comprise therefore either pictures contemporary with the scenes and events they portray or photographs of contemporary objects. Reconstructions, however ingenious or convincing, are excluded. In most fields, contemporary pictures begin to become available from the fifteenth century onwards. The main weight of this work therefore falls on the past 500 years, though one or two subjects can usefully be treated from a somewhat earlier date.

It is a corollary of this principle that the pictures chosen should be from England, Wales, or Scotland. In many previous pictorial histories—including one of the best of them, *The Life and Work of the People of England,* by Dorothy Hartley and Margaret Elliot—Continental pictures were freely admitted, often without any indication that they came from abroad. On occasion the use of foreign examples may be absolutely necessary; but such cases will be rare, and each will be specifically noted in the caption attached to the picture.

In selecting the pictures, a special effort has been made to exploit the great collections of material that are assembled in the museums, galleries, and libraries of Britain outside London. Inevitably, such great London collections as those of the British Museum and the National Buildings Record must be heavily drawn upon; but the vast body of pictures and museum objects to be seen today in the English provinces, in Wales and in Scotland, has been very little studied by historians. I hope that this series of books may do something to reveal the astonishing wealth of material that has been accumulated, over the past century and more, in these places; especially since now, with modern techniques of display, much of it is so delightfully presented.

The plan of the *Visual History* is not based, like most of its predecessors, on a division by period. Instead, it is divided by subject. Though each volume is self-contained, it will gain from being read in conjunction with the rest. Some important subjects will inevitably cut across the division adopted for the series as a whole. Thus the evolution of local government will be treated both in the volume on *The Town* and in that on *Government*; the history of trade will be discussed, from different aspects, in *The Town*, in *Transport*, and in *Industry*. Such cross-references will, I hope, be valuable in themselves, helping to emphasise the inter-dependence of all parts of the whole great theme: the evolution of modern Britain.

J.S.

The Medieval Town

Towns are living things: they are both places, and the sum of the people who live in them. As long as they have existed they have attracted people most potently. In the Middle Ages towns grew and survived because the heavy mortality within their walls was balanced by newcomers willing to risk their lives there; and the lure of the modern city's lights has grown with their stridency. Settlers come and townsmen stay to buy and sell, or to seek human company and share the comforts of a wealthy community; and because wealth can command power they are much concerned with public affairs: townsmen usually govern themselves, while their towns house national or regional governments. In unsettled times towns have to be fortresses; they are always markets, and usually places on which traffic naturally converges; but although one or another of their features may overshadow the rest, like the walls of Caernarvon ⟨1⟩*, the market-place of Kelso, or the great river at Liverpool ⟨205⟩, essentially towns shelter people. That is what "town" means, for originally a *tun* was a homestead, and to this day the word is used in that sense in the North of England, like *toun* in the old Scots tongue, in the names of single farms.

Although the English town has a native name, unlike the French *ville* and the German *Stadt*, which have a Latin ancestry, we have to look to Latin, and beyond Latin to Greek, to talk about the qualities which mark the town dweller. An urbane man is one polished by urban society; the *urbs* or city bestows a grace upon him that cannot be acquired from mere country living, although he may deplore the brashness of his barbarian cousin, the townee ⟨54⟩, whose manners are also strange to the countryside. If he be urbane, he is bound to be civil, and he is entitled to be called civilised, but these are words that carry us into the Hellenic world. Civilised life was life in the Roman *civitas*, a word that translated the Greek *polis*, or city-state, the institution in which European civilisation began.

* The numbers in diamond brackets, e.g. ⟨1⟩, refer to the illustrations on page 85 onwards.

THE TOWN

Because the city-state once dominated the Mediterranean it now dominates the European vocabulary of public affairs and, inevitably, our thinking about the history of towns. The Greek cities, particularly in the great age of Athens, were intellectually and aesthetically dazzling. Rome turned the city-state into an empire that tied the Solway Firth to the headwaters of the Euphrates, and when Rome could no longer hold what she had taken, Byzantium inherited the Greek patrimony in the eastern Mediterranean and lived on it splendidly for a thousand years. Each of these great cultures was ruled by the city. The Greeks set their mark on the Mediterranean and the Black Sea through their trading colonies. Rome secured her interests by planting cities where they would not grow spontaneously, and feeding them on Mediterranean values. Byzantium fought to hold territories rather than to acquire them, for her empire was the oldest and richest part of Rome's, but once again the empire was identified with the city that lay at its heart, and that survived to show barbarian Europe what a city should be.

These facts make it difficult to discuss early town life in Europe, and particularly that in Britain. Not only did the richest medieval towns barely match their ancient predecessors in size and lustre, but their accomplishments were first belittled by the revival of classical art and learning after the Middle Ages, and then swamped by the great industrial changes that have created a new society in the last two hundred years. Those changes restored town life to its old pre-eminence, albeit with an unwashed face ⟨176⟩, and they began in Britain, the least thoroughly Romanised of the western Roman provinces. As industrial society emerged and spread over Europe and North America, the period since the collapse of Rome seemed more than ever an interlude: nineteenth-century Manchester ⟨182⟩, twentieth-century Chicago, are closer to the great cities of antiquity than were either medieval Manchester, or the self-consciously Classical towns of Colonial and Revolutionary America.

Yet the modern British city grew out of the medieval town. Medieval London is a familiar ghost, but there was also a medieval Glasgow and a medieval Manchester; and Manchester looked back to a Roman settlement. Although British towns were relatively small before the eighteenth century, they were very numerous, and in England they lay so thick upon the ground that even now there are very few towns that cannot point to some urban features in their history before the Industrial Revolution. In all Britain, perhaps only South Wales ⟨204⟩ exemplifies that sudden change from a rural to an industrial urban society that is widely believed to have been characteristic of northern England, while in England itself many of the towns had Roman predecessors. The Romans bequeathed some excellent town-sites to Britain, and as later men were prepared to live on them, unabashed by comparison with the talented dead, they created in time an urban culture more imposing than even Rome had known. The beginning of such a movement is no less interesting, and certainly no less strange, than its outcome.

Britain was Roman ground from A.D. 43 until the early fifth century. When the Romans arrived they found no recognisable towns, and after securing their military needs they began to set up model communities. The first of these was raised beside the seat of the chief British kings, and its walls and streets still govern the plan of modern Colchester. Other towns of the same type followed at Lincoln, Gloucester and York. These privileged cities were supplemented by cantonal capitals, which urbanised or superseded British tribal centres, and by small markets which grew at road and river-crossings, or by military stations. There was no special magic in Roman planning; the largest town in the province was London, which grew spontaneously on foreign trade and never received formal privileges of self-government; while some of the cantonal capitals, like those at Silchester and Wroxeter, decayed and never recovered. The raids by Picts, Scots and Anglo-Saxons in the later years of Roman rule provoked an elaborate system of defences in which the small towns received special attention, but many of the larger, including London, were still populous and busy. *Aquae Sulis*, the spa now known as Bath, flourished very late, serving an urban and cosmopolitan society of a kind that disappeared with the Roman Empire and was rediscovered, like the Roman baths themselves, in another age.

The fate of the towns under the invading English is uncertain. Some few, like Canterbury, served as capitals of new petty kingdoms, and London seems to have kept its trade, but many others succumbed to violence and political disorganisation. The British in the west and north were forced into districts where for military and geographical reasons there were no towns, and although they stayed in touch with the Mediterranean world they preserved no Roman municipal traditions. Neither did the English, but their conversion to Christianity brought bishops' households and a new importance to sites like Dorchester-on-Thames, deliberately chosen for their Roman associations; and trade with the Continent created new communities. By the eighth century there was a busy harbour at Southampton, while Ipswich manufactured a distinctive pottery that was widely distributed in East Anglia. Similar manufacturing centres appeared soon afterwards at Thetford, Stamford and St. Neots.

The crisis of the Scandinavian invasions not only unified the English kingdoms but also jolted the English town into existence, selecting those markets that were defensible, those fortresses that could command trade, and investing the hardiest of them with a precise status. In the last century of the Old English state the fortified towns or *burhs* had a distinctive public role, housing mints and markets, and often serving as the capitals of the shires that the West Saxons imposed tidily upon districts reconquered from the Danes. The Normans strengthened and enriched the towns, although their castle-building and military government left some marks that were still visible in Domesday Book, twenty years after the Conquest. French and Flemish colonies appeared at places like Norwich and Nottingham, and Jews settled in about a dozen of the largest towns. Anglo-Norman lawyers distinguished the privileged townsman as a *burgess*, dweller in a borough; and burgesses in Domesday mark new boroughs as well as old, clustering round the abbey gates at Bury St. Edmunds or Abingdon, or by castles like Quatford on the Severn or Rhuddlan in Denbighshire.

In the twelfth century municipal liberties were extended by direct bargaining with the king. Powerful communities like the Londoners or the men of the Cinque Ports, who ranked formally as *barones* as though they were military tenants innocent of the trade that enriched them, offered ready money or specialised services in return for the beginnings of self-government. Other towns copied their example as best they could, and most freely in Richard I's and John's reigns, when the king's needs were the towns' opportunities. The boroughs' great objects at this time were to replace the king's reeve with their own nominated magistrates, usually two bailiffs, and through them to render the king's dues directly to the royal exchequer ⟨233⟩, depriving the sheriff of any surplus that might be collected.

Meanwhile boroughs in the sense of privileged trading communities appeared in Wales and Scotland. In central and southern Wales merchants and artisans gathered round the invading Normans' castles and were granted communal liberties and low rents. Montgomery and Cardiff became the capitals of shires on the English model. In the later twelfth century a Welsh revival brought Cardigan and other lordships under native rule again, and confirmed the Marches, as the debatable lands were called, in that equivocal semi-detached state that made them so powerful a force in English politics. The boroughs and castles were interdependent and survived violent changes of ownership, while in the north, where Anglo-Norman influence was indirect, similar institutions developed spontaneously under Welsh rule. At places like Nevin and Pwllheli, or Llanvaes in Anglesey, there were small ports that the princes of Snowdonia protected and favoured with privileges.

The Scottish burgh was distinguished as royal when it was founded by the king, and as a burgh of regality or of barony when it was the licensed foundation of one of his subjects, according to the power that the founder commanded on his own estates. The great majority of medieval burghs were royal, and the earliest seem to be the work of David I (1124-53). At a few places, including Edinburgh and Stirling, David probably granted burghal status to existing communities, but many were deliberate creations, like the burgh of Canongate which he made in 1136 for Holyrood Abbey, between the abbey precinct and "my burgh" of Edinburgh. At Dingwall, founded in 1227, ten years' remission of rent was offered to new settlers, while at St. Andrews and Glasgow, where the bishops had licence to charter burghs in the twelfth century, there are references to new building.

The burghs were largely settled by Englishmen and Flemings, attracted by favourable terms in the same way that Norman knights were drawn to David's service. The burgesses enjoyed a monopoly of trade in a prescribed area—Inverness claimed the whole land to the north, and reviled the upstart Dingwall and Wick—and were generally organised in a gild, a religious sodality of very remote origin that bound its members by ritual drinking and feasting, and that was particularly associated in Britain with municipal institutions. The burghs were simple in plan with wooden houses and earthen walls. At Edinburgh a single street ran along the crest of the ridge from the castle-gates toward Holyrood, widening at the Lawnmarket. Stirling has a very similar site ⟨2⟩ and plan, and Elgin, which has changed much less, has kept the lanes that ran behind the burgage plots. Inverness is laid out on the river-line, a fact that adds greatly to the attractiveness of the modern town. By comparison the English boroughs were bigger and more numerous, but in sum their buildings were not much more impressive. The larger towns each had several parish churches by the eleventh century, and their numbers soon increased: York ultimately had forty-one and London more than a hundred, but they were usually not large until the later Middle Ages ⟨29⟩, and the most commanding buildings were the cathedral ⟨3⟩ and monastic churches ⟨11⟩. Town walls were often rebuilt in stone ⟨3⟩, unless there were serviceable Roman defences, as at Colchester, but the houses were wooden, with rare exceptions such as survive at Lincoln and Bury St. Edmunds. Stone houses are often attributed to Jews, a recollection of that community's wealth and need for security that is reasonable, even if the attribution cannot be proved; the citizens of Oxford bought a Jew's house for their town hall when the Jews were expelled from England in 1290.

London was much the largest and most powerful English town, and by the end of the twelfth century Westminster, almost a suburb of London tenuously joined by the great houses along the river-strand, had displaced Winchester as the normal seat of the king's court and treasury, and so of the government. In the thirteenth century London kept its place effortlessly as other towns grew, buying themselves free of the sheriff's authority, and often replacing their bailiffs with the single magistrate called a mayor

⟨21⟩, an importation from the communes of the great continental towns. Some of London's features, such as its foreign communities—the Hanseatic merchants in their *Komptor* by the Thames, called the Steelyard ⟨39⟩ from its great weighbeam, or the Italian bankers who handled papal subsidies, and replaced the Jews as royal financiers—were reflected in other towns, but generally the urban jam was thinly and unevenly spread. Edward I's campaigns in Wales enriched Chester, and York housed the Exchequer and other government offices when the king made war on Scotland. The border fortress of Carlisle was valuable in war ⟨35⟩ and in peace, and so were the Cinque Ports, which owed their power as much to their joint fishing-expeditions during the North Sea herring season as to their naval services. Meanwhile new boroughs appeared in great numbers; there were more than seventy in Devon before the sixteenth century, and twenty-three in the district that is now called Lancashire. A few such places, like Lynn on the Bishop of Norwich's estate by the Wash, grew to a substantial size, but most were no more than a troop of enfranchised tenants and a licensed market. Occasionally their lords regretted even those concessions: the abbot of Cirencester hounded the borough there out of existence, and both Warrington and Manchester had their privileges challenged in the fourteenth century, and were degraded to the status of manors. Oxford and Cambridge succumbed to a different misfortune, becoming the seats of universities which provided them, alone outside the capital, with what would now be called a residential population, but which stifled their municipal government for centuries ⟨27, 28⟩.

The most striking new towns in the thirteenth century were those that Edward I established in Wales, especially during and after his campaign of 1282, when the great fortresses of Caernarvon ⟨1⟩, Conway and Beaumaris were raised to secure Snowdonia. Like the new boroughs at Criccieth, Harlech and Bere in Merioneth, chartered in 1285, they were intended to be administrative centres, and were settled by Englishmen to whom their political and commercial privileges were confined. But they were also compulsory markets for their districts, and the Welsh came to settle in them in such numbers that the burgesses found themselves under civil siege as well as an occasional military one. Outside Wales Edward's efforts were less successful. Winchelsea, then perhaps the chief port on the Channel, was rebuilt on a new site between 1280 and 1288 when the old town was washed away, but New Winchelsea was wasted by plague in the fourteenth century, and then abandoned by the sea that devoured its predecessor ⟨5⟩. Newton in Dorset, planned in 1286, progressed no further than the occupation of a few plots which were soon abandoned again. Hull, one of the towns most readily associated with Edward's name, was only developed by him, in succession to the decayed Humber port of Ravenser Od, from an existing port.

One last scheme illustrates the strength and the weakness of Edward's government very well. In 1296 he issued writs to twenty-four towns, including London, to send men skilled in making a new town to confer with him at Bury St. Edmunds. Evidently disappointed by the outcome of this conference, he ordered a new assembly to meet at Harwich, revealing that it was to discuss the future of Berwick-on-Tweed, captured from the Scots in 1296. A third meeting was then called at Berwick itself, but like its predecessors it produced no obvious result. Berwick was opened to Englishmen and chartered in 1302, but Edward did not need a publicly recruited committee to endorse that policy. His hopes for Berwick must have outrun his means and perhaps his subjects' willingness to co-operate.

The deliberations over Berwick came at the end of the first rapid expansion of town life in Britain. The population of Europe, after growing for three hundred years, was checked sharply in the fourteenth century, and the institutions that had grown with it, especially the towns, were severely tested. Town life had recaptured something of its old richness, at something of the old cost. The friars who spread through Europe in the thirteenth century were particularly concerned with conditions in towns. The older religious orders did no parochial work, and some of the smaller parish churches in the towns had fallen into disuse for want of adequate endowments. The friars found ample work both in England and Scotland, which became a separate province of the Franciscan order; Norwich and Newcastle each had four friaries, Edinburgh and Chester had three. As they came late, they had to take what sites there were. At Bristol the Carmelites found themselves surrounded by the city's brothels, and the Bristolians' noisy enthusiasms so disturbed the friars' devotions that they had to appeal to the municipal authorities to clear the neighbourhood.

The records of friaries often include licences to make new water-conduits from springs outside the town, and this involved elaborate negotiations. The fountain in the Great Court of Trinity College, Cambridge ⟨43⟩ taps a pipe laid by the Franciscans, and there were similar works in London, Bristol, Colchester and many other towns. Shortage of water was one of the problems that drove the bishops of Salisbury down from Old Salisbury to the Avon, and resources elsewhere that were adequate in the eleventh century may have seemed less copious or less convenient in the thirteenth. It looks as though the friars, finding the more populous towns short of water after two centuries of growth, had to contrive their own supply.

From the thirteenth century the older towns' strength lay in trade rather than in industry. In the century after the Conquest the towns of the eastern lowlands from York to London—with a few exceptions the largest in England—housed a substantial weaving industry, from which some cloth was exported with the raw wool that was the staple of the Midland fairs. Flemish immigration stimulated the trade, as it did in Scotland, but probably at the price of conflict between the gilds merchant and the cloth workers such as occurred in some Scottish burghs. Then in the thirteenth century the industry seemed to decline; and it was once supposed, improbably enough, that weaving disappeared in England until Edward III re-introduced it with more Flemings. What in fact happened was that cloth-making moved from the older towns into country districts, and this movement was encouraged, if it was not begun, by the introduction of water-driven machinery to full cloth. In the country the industry was unhampered by gild regulations, and was helped by the markets and small boroughs that landlords had hopefully set up. Northleach in Gloucestershire, given a market and a fair in 1227, became a town of wealthy merchants in the fifteenth century ⟨25⟩, while Kendal in Westmorland and Leeds in the West Riding, which also had chartered burgage tenements and markets, gathered in cloth from the uplands around them.

The new rural industry benefited the old towns in East Anglia, which were mostly ports, but the Midland boroughs were more severely affected. Early in the fourteenth century trade began to contract all over Europe, and the incipient depression was enormously aggravated by the bubonic plague, the Black Death, which entered England at Melcombe in Dorset in the summer of 1348, raged through the country for two years, and remained endemic until the seventeenth century. The plague did great damage in the towns, and although normal life began again as rapidly as it always does after such disasters, the economic effects were serious and prolonged. On the other hand, the great toll of deaths meant a general shortage of labour, and despite the Statute of Labourers (1351) and all attempts to enforce it men went where the wages were highest. The attractions of town-life were great enough to mitigate its hazards, and some of the towns, at least, recovered and maintained their position. Indeed, though they lacked the Scottish burghs' power to restrain the movement of industry, many of the free boroughs gained new political strength in the disturbed century that followed the plague.

One exception to the general slackening of trade was the growth of the English cloth industry. The fine wool that had earlier gone to Flanders was diverted to English weavers, and by the sixteenth century the proportion of wool exported had declined to a small fraction of the country's output, while English cloth, though still often dyed abroad, commanded the markets that the Flemings had once held. The chief manufacturing centres were in the Cotswolds and East Anglia, where great parish churches mark the former wealth of what are today only villages, and there are similar signs of prosperity in Somerset ⟨10⟩, where in the Wife of Bath's day Bath was better known for woollens than for waters. Totnes in Devon rebuilt its parish church entirely between 1432 and 1460, a period covering several years of depression in national trade, while in the Midlands Coventry's wealth, exemplified in its churches and in the Holy Trinity gildhall, showed that the benefits of trade were not exclusively for *parvenu* towns. There were other sources of prosperity too. Newcastle had its trade in coal, which probably expanded in the fifteenth century; Bristol enjoyed a rich overseas trade, and St. Mary, Redcliffe, crowned with a clerestory at the sole expense of a wealthy merchant, William Canynges the younger ⟨30⟩, is the finest of the many churches that were completed or rebuilt there in the fifteenth century ⟨29⟩. But trade fluctuated until the century was far advanced, and townsmen everywhere lost no chance of emphasising their collective poverty whenever national taxes were negotiated.

Yet it was at this time that municipal privileges were rounded off in England by charters of formal incorporation, and that the boroughs' duty to send representatives to Parliament came to be regarded as a privilege rather than a burden; two rights that are among the principal distinctions of the modern town. Formal incorporation, which recognises the right of a community to act collectively, as though it were a single person, was a sophisticated legal device, and in England it was evolved for the benefit of the towns. In a sense the burgesses of a borough had acted collectively from its inception, but they could not claim to do so in law, as when, for example, they incurred debt or wished to acquire property. The early charters conferred privileges upon the burgesses, their heirs and successors, but public service was hazardous when there was no doctrine of communal responsibility, and a town's officers could and did suffer individually for collective faults. An incorporate borough in England came to have five essential qualities: it had a fictitious personality in law, and therefore could sue and be sued as though it were a responsible individual; it was able to acquire land; it could hold property in perpetuity; it had a common seal to authenticate its actions; and it had power to make by-laws. Some of these points were granted or assumed before the full doctrine of incorporation evolved. Common seals appeared very early; the burgesses of Gloucester made one in 1200, when they were allowed to elect their own reeves, and the citizens of Oxford acknowledged a communal obligation to Osney Abbey in 1191 under their common seal. By-laws were also agreed upon more often than they were offered to higher authority for confirmation, although London produced an enormous list of articles for the King's Great Seal in 1321, and other boroughs took the same precaution from time to time.

The real movement toward incorporation began in the fourteenth century, when two towns that were anxious about their status were made "communities" by royal charter. In 1345 the men of Coventry ended a long struggle against the prior who was lord of half their town by securing a royal charter that acknowledged the burgesses of the whole town as a "community". In 1348 Hedon, its trade threatened first by Ravenser and then by Hull, sought to strengthen its position by solemnly reasserting its privileges, which were recited in the charter after the incorporating clause.

These concessions to secondary boroughs were followed, after the upheaval caused by the plague, by an effective incorporation of Bristol in 1373, when the city was removed from its two counties and made a county in its own right, with its own sheriff and other appropriate royal officers. This privilege was extended to York in 1396, to Newcastle-upon-Tyne in 1400, to Norwich in 1404 and Lincoln in 1409. Henry V's wars and Henry VI's long minority checked such innovation, but in 1440, a year after Plymouth was incorporated by Act of Parliament—a terse recognition of the growing importance of that harbour—Hull received the first full charter of incorporation, upon which all subsequent grants were based. Towns could still, like Bristol, be erected into counties; Canterbury received such a grant in 1461 after being incorporated in 1448, and Coventry became a county in 1451, although that was an addition to incorporation, not a refinement of it.

The new doctrine was important in law, for the idea of collective responsibility lies behind all later advances in commercial organisation, but for a long time it was the municipal corporation's political significance that attracted attention. In practice, incorporation often rather confirmed than created a borough's status, and the forms of municipal government had in many cases already hardened before they were officially made perpetual. With the relatively small population of towns the closed councils of twenty-four or forty-eight probably did not permanently exclude many of the ambitious, and although later common property might be abused, the burgesses at large were at this stage chiefly concerned with their collective rights in the common land of the borough, and particularly with the right of grazing between harvest and seed-time ⟨127⟩. What mattered politically was the form that the parliamentary elections took, and that was often still undetermined in the fifteenth century, when we find the first positive signs of outside interest in the boroughs' representation. At Coventry the burgesses seem to have had a voice in the elections from the beginning, while at Nottingham the electoral body changed almost from Parliament to Parliament. Some royal charters specified parliamentary representation, although there are also instances of towns being relieved of the burden. Ludlow was given two members in 1461, and a number of others towns were called upon to return for the first time, including Gatton, in 1453, and Grantham in 1467. Anxious references in the Paston letters to electoral prospects in Norwich or Yarmouth, and wheedling or peremptory missives among borough muniments, show plainly that new winds were blowing.

INCORPORATION: RIGHTS AND OBLIGATIONS

Parliaments were not held very frequently, and for most towns were remote events, except when some cause took them out of London and into the provinces: as when the Lancastrian kings moved troublesome assemblies to Coventry or Leicester, in the heart of their Midland estates. Townsmen were usually intent upon more prosaic affairs. Whatever their individual fortunes, the towns had established themselves, and their real importance lay in their traditions of self-government and collective action. Their courts, often developed far beyond the simple comprehensive assemblies of earlier centuries, and fortified by a correspondingly elaborate system of records—rolls and registers of acts and precedents—dispensed the law of the land, modified by a vast accumulation of local custom; and in safeguarding the rights of married women to property, and the interests of minors, the towns were in advance of contemporary practice. The financial officers, usually called chamberlains and appointed from year to year, accounted for substantial sums from a variety of sources, and if some of the money was spent upon display, much of it went to discharge communal responsibilities. The age set great store by maintaining appearances, and the mace borne before the mayor ⟨21⟩—a dignity specifically granted to Faversham in 1406—or more rarely the sword of state ⟨80⟩, was a necessary mark of authority. Besides these expenses, and the equally important ritual feasting ⟨18⟩ that bound the townsmen together, there appear more sober accounts. Money was distributed weekly to the poor at Southampton, and corn on major festivals at Lydd, while towns like Exeter and Hereford managed hospitals and almshouses, besides funds bequeathed to the municipality by private citizens.

The provisions for maintaining decent order in the towns were much like those of rural manors, particularly when the courts turned their attention to the town lands, but they were imposed and administered in the name of the community by its own officers. The assizes of bread and ale, usually regarded as a source of income through penal fines rather than a guide to standards of quality, were supervised by the mayor or bailiffs in person, as was the national assize of measures, for which in England as in Scotland the towns kept specimen lengths and weights. A free borough also had stocks and pillory, the ducking-stool for frauds and scolds, and even gallows, for apart from displaying the dismembered bodies of traitors occasionally distributed by the king, boroughs had a summary jurisdiction over some thefts, and the taking of human life in public was a great feature of government in Britain until the later nineteenth century. Beyond these matters the general duties of watch and ward were especially enjoined on the boroughs, and although they were generally not disturbed by the civil wars of the fifteenth century—except for Stamford, sacked in 1461 by the Lancastrian army—the towns' contribution to the country's armed forces, both in money and men, was considerable.

Another institution that the medieval town shared with the countryside, and yet modelled after its own fashion, was the gild ⟨22⟩. Associated from the earliest times with municipal duties, the gilds enriched the towns in every way. Occasionally their work was of lasting importance, as when the craft gilds, under municipal supervision, fashioned the rules of apprenticeship, of which the London code was nationally applied by the Elizabethan Statute of Apprentices. Gild plays, like the celebrated Coventry cycle, were the chief stock of the English drama that flowered marvellously in the sixteenth century; and earlier they may have helped to preserve the literary uses of the vernacular tongue when it was supplanted by Latin for administrative purposes, and by Norman-French in polite society. Feast-day processions and pageants were another long-lived bequest ⟨119⟩.

Even in the fourteenth century a substantial proportion of Londoners were literate, and owned not only private memoranda books, but books of romances, and in the next century there appear commercial schools teaching writing, accountancy and French. By that time French was a commercial rather than a social accomplishment, for the French veneer on the upper classes was wearing thin, and in London at least the distinction between the wealthy merchant and the landed gentleman was soon blurred, if indeed it had not always been. Merchants bought country seats, won titles, married their daughters into the gentry, and adopted coats of arms. The trappings of gentility were always admired, and the habit, especially prevalent among provincial merchants, of using personal marks ⟨30⟩ for heraldic as well as for business uses, reflects their attraction. The late medieval merchant understood his communal responsibilities, but his personal ambition turned rather to national than to urban society.

In Scotland the contrast between town and country life was more rigorously maintained, although burghal exclusiveness was modified from the late fifteenth century as burghs of barony multiplied. Inside the burghs two general rules applied. The first was that the governing bodies were exclusive, receiving parliamentary sanction in 1469 from an Act that prohibited popular interference in elections, and provided that a new council should be elected each year by the existing one. At the same time the municipalities, representing the old gilds merchant, fought successfully to control the craft gilds. From 1425 to 1427 the crafts were able to elect their own inspectors of work and, apparently, to fix prices and wages, but the policy was then abandoned, and the gilds had to seek recognition as corporate bodies under "seals of cause", uttered by the municipalities, or by the superior in a burgh of barony. Their officers were allowed to inspect work but not to meddle with prices or contracts, and the gild members were excluded from municipal office, which they could attain only by renouncing their crafts and becoming merchants, that is general traders, tied to no interest. The Convention of Royal Burghs, a body that emerged in the sixteenth century, was similarly closed to ordinary gildsmen, as were parliamentary seats, and the Convention reacted with scandalised dismay in 1574 when it was discovered that the "alledgit proveist of Haddingtoun" was a shoemaker, elected by an unholy conspiracy of the crafts.

The merchants who enforced their monopoly were principally engaged in foreign trade, which like the English trade in wool, which was directed through Calais, was concentrated on a staple town—Veere in Zeeland. There was also a wine trade with Bordeaux—Froissart refers casually to English, Welsh, and Scottish ships at that port in 1372—and this trade, unlike the English, was not affected by the French conquest of Gascony in the 1450s. Down to the Reformation Scotland's relations with France were cordial, and claret remained the drink of Edinburgh's "rascal multitude" after their English fellows had taken to beer. Claret drinkers or no, the Scots were poor, and the sum of their exports and of the trade in foreign luxuries that came into the country made no great show by the standards of London and Bristol, but the burghs were not a negligible force in the kingdom. One significant luxury that the economy supported was the trio of universities founded before 1500—St. Andrews in 1411, Glasgow in 1450, and Aberdeen in 1494. All three were under close episcopal supervision, but they were essential to the culture fashioned in the next century, which brought the burghs into their own.

Reformation and Revolutions

As Europe's trade and population expanded again in the later fifteenth century, the continent's political and commercial pattern changed. The kingdom of France absorbed Aquitaine and Brittany, checking the English trade with Bordeaux, and opposing a potentially hostile coastline to Devon and Cornwall. Calais stayed English until 1558, and kept the wool staple, but the focus of the international cloth trade was now Antwerp. Columbus's discovery of Cuba in 1492 was less immediately important than Vasco da Gama's voyage round the Cape in 1498, which opened the far Eastern spice trade to the Portuguese; their ships began to carry spices direct to Antwerp, and in 1503 a cargo arrived in the Thames. Then Charles V succeeded to the thrones of Spain and the Holy Roman Empire, including the Netherlands, while in America the conquest of Mexico unimaginably enriched his possessions. American gold heightened the excitements of the new trade in Antwerp, ruining Spain's own economy and confusing half Europe's minds with dreams of ease and empire.

In England these changes stimulated and re-orientated the country's trade. The English Channel became one of the principal thoroughfares of Europe, essential to Spain as her link with Flanders, and jealously watched by France. When Henry VIII's matrimonial policies made an enemy of the Emperor, Catherine of Aragon's nephew, the south coast mattered even more. Scotland's friendship with France kept Berwick-on-Tweed and Carlisle primarily fortresses, but the Tudors' Welsh blood and benign Welsh policy relaxed the tension in North Wales; the Snowdonian boroughs were first opened to Welshmen as burgesses in 1507, and then were given parliamentary seats when Henry VIII united Wales and England. By that time only three of the boroughs were of any economic importance: Beaumaris, the only one to be formally incorporated (1562), Caernarvon and Conway. All had a modest sea trade, as well as markets and fairs, and Beaumaris, which was already shipping roofing slate and Lancashire woollens to Ireland, was a port of call for ships from Spain as well as coasting vessels. The ports of South Wales had some trade in coal, although this was still small. The chief beneficiary of Tudor rule in Wales was Ludlow in Shropshire, which was made the seat of the Council in the Marches of Wales, and enjoyed the advantages of a provincial capital, such as the Council in the North brought to York.

York declined in the later Middle Ages, falling from first or second place among medieval provincial cities to fourteenth in the subsidy returns of the 1520s. In 1539, however, the King's Council in the North was established there after the suppression of the rising called the Pilgrimage of Grace. It had a predecessor in a council of Richard III's, and performed the functions of the Privy Council in a troubled area remote from London, being at once a court of justice and department of state. Its court was effective and popular, and the Council's presence did much to restore York's fortunes, but the city benefited less from the current boom in the cloth trade than did London and the southern ports. Even Kendal merchants sent their cloth to Southampton, and Blackwell Hall in London was a depot for every major manufacturing area in the country. Despite checks from Wolsey's foreign policy, the trade in broadcloth continued to expand until over-production and a devaluation of the coinage ruined it in 1551.

One of the imports that balanced the cloth trade was religious dissent. English Bibles were smuggled into the eastern ports from the Netherlands in the 1520s and distributed among merchants and some artisans. The Reformation in England in Henry VIII's reign was shaped by royal policy and enacted by Parliament, but its course was applauded by many townsmen. After John Wycliffe's party was suppressed in the universities at the end of the fourteenth century, and at large more severely in the fifteenth century, it continued to exist secretly, particularly among the literate laity in the towns. The book trade at Norwich harboured some heretics and London provided a number of martyrs, mostly artisans, but including in the 1490s the mother-in-law and the widow of Sir John Yonge, a city alderman and grocer. Lollard beliefs were diffuse, but they anticipated most Protestant teachings, and in addition to Lollardy there was strong anti-clerical feeling, especially in London and other towns, which made men more receptive to reforming opinions.

The dissolution of the monasteries between 1536 and 1540 was of less moment to the towns than to the countryside, although it must often have dislocated trade. The burgesses of Bury St. Edmunds and St. Albans enjoyed no immediate access of freedom when the royal commissioners moved in; and monastic cathedrals such as Durham and Exeter kept their old status and their old inmates under new names. Six new cathedrals were instituted: Bristol, Chester, Gloucester, Oxford, Peterborough, and Westminster—which was dissolved in 1550. Peterborough Cathedral, under the dean and chapter, enjoyed the same power over the manorial borough outside the precinct wall that the abbot and convent had exercised from its beginnings. In a few instances townsmen collectively bought monastic churches: Tewkesbury was allowed to save its splendid church from destruction; and St. Albans, incorporated in 1551, received the abbey church (now the cathedral) for parochial use. In many places the churches and other buildings were unroofed. Reading Abbey became a royal residence for a time, and stone from the church was used to rebuild St. Mary's church in the town. The only clear evidence of industrial use comes from Malmesbury, where a clothier called William Stumpe bought the domestic buildings and concentrated his cloth-workers in them, presenting the abbey church to the town; but at Ipswich the corporation rehoused the town grammar school in the Dominican friary, and Norwich used the Blackfriars' church as a civic hall ⟨40⟩.

The dissolution of gilds and chantries in 1547 was felt more widely. Henry VIII frowned on changes in doctrine, but Protestant views had spread; Cambridge University was deeply affected by Lutheran teaching, and the English Bibles distributed to the churches under Cromwell's ministry excited theological speculation among the laity. In 1547 Edward VI's minority brought the extreme Protestants into power, and the doctrinal reformation began which produced Cranmer's *Book of Common Prayer* and, after reaction in Mary's reign, the Elizabethan settlement. In the first year of the new reign the government confiscated endowments of masses for the dead and all other commemorative prayers. The doctrinal implications of this policy were probably widely accepted in the towns, but its

THE TOWN

effects were disconcerting, for the municipal and craft gilds were deeply involved in religious observances, and there were few, if any, charitable endowments that the Act did not affect. It had been plain for some time that such a measure was likely, and towns with a corporate governing body were able to protect themselves to some extent. The right of presenting priests to chantries was often invested in the corporation, as at Scarborough, where the bailiffs and commonalty held the advowsons of all the chantries in St. Mary's church. As early as 1539 the bailiffs of Colchester successfully petitioned the King for permission to convert the endowments of two wealthy chantries in their gift to the use of a grammar school, and in 1547 the common council of Lincoln made haste to take up the gild and other religious funds in the city before the new laws could take effect. Two towns at least were disappointed by the government's timidity, for the original Act included collegiate churches in its scope, and the townsmen of Oxford and Cambridge thought it hard that, when so much else was going down, some of their own troublesome lodgers should not be dispersed. But Oxford had already had its answer when the monastic lands there were distributed to the colleges of the university, and Henry, never at a loss for an improving word, had rejected the town's application with gratuitous advice.[1] At Cambridge the university was inspected by commissioners of its own contriving, whose report held no comfort for the town.

The towns most affected by the confiscation were those in which the gilds sustained the real community. Birmingham, a small market town, owed most of its urban qualities to the gild of Holy Cross, which maintained the town's main roads and bridges, and had a gildhall dignified by a striking clock. Coventry paid the Crown more than £1,300 for a perpetual lease of the Corpus Christi and Holy Trinity gild lands, but the smaller towns could not drive bargains of that kind and were reduced to anxious petitioning. Sheffield won a charter of incorporation from Queen Mary in 1554 for the twelve Capital Burgesses and Commonalty of the Town and Parish, who maintained urbanity on an income of seven guineas. Birmingham managed to keep its gildhall and an endowment to support a grammar school, but much property went to private owners, who were not all philanthropists. Burford lost all its gild lands, except what was saved for a grammar school, and the burgesses had to buy back the rest by private negotiation to maintain their charities.

The places that had drawn wealth from the cloth trade had special need of such contrivances, for the second phase of the English Reformation was

---

[1] "I judge no land better bestowed than that which is given to our universities. . . . As you love your welfares . . . follow no more this vein, but content yourselves with that you have already, or else seek honest means to increase your livelihood."

fought out against a background of economic catastrophe. The market in Antwerp collapsed in 1551, and for more than a decade successive governments, Protestants and Roman Catholic, followed a consistent economic and social policy. In 1552 the quality of cloth was regulated by statute, and broadcloth-making was forbidden to anyone not apprenticed, or of seven years' experience in the trade. But the best hope of controlling the industry was to restore the towns' authority, and in 1553 Mary's government exempted the corporate towns from the second Act, and restricted the size of rural clothiers' establishments in 1555. This legislation was crowned in Elizabeth's reign by the Statute of Artificers (1563), which sought to make it more difficult for a man to become a lawyer or a merchant than to follow the plough or some honest trade, for fear that there should be none but gentlemen in England. The fear was ill founded, but the code did something to help the corporate towns.

Meanwhile the towns had done something to help themselves. Poor relief had been a subject of national legislation since 1536, but most of the work was repressive, with flogging for the able-bodied beggar, and only voluntary contributions to maintain the infirm poor. King's Lynn issued lead badges "engraved with a rose and an E and an R" (for Edwardus Rex, this being 1547) whereby the deserving poor "may be knowen from other". Wanderers of all kinds aroused suspicion; at Lincoln a London butcher was put into the stocks, although he said that he sought to visit his grandmother: men have told more unlikely stories. Then the depression in the 1550s defined the problem, and the towns solved it. London bought the old hospital of St. Thomas in Southwark and received the royal palace of Bridewell ⟨106⟩ from the King to use as poorhouses, and began to levy a compulsory poor-rate to maintain the work. Norwich, Ipswich and Colchester did the same between 1555 and 1557, and the practice spread until it was written into the national system of poor relief crowned by the Elizabethan statutes of 1597 and 1601. A municipal levy to support municipal work was a simple idea, but a fruitful one, and the ground for it had been a long time preparing.

The towns that inaugurated the poor law were within easy reach of each other, and conferred about it informally. There was no body like the Scottish Convention of Royal Burghs to bring them together, and the government was increasingly distracted by its religious and foreign policies. Mary's desire to restore the Roman Catholic religion and to please her husband, Philip of Spain, brought about the deaths of three hundred Protestants, and caused a hopeless war that lost Calais. The war was a wretched and expensive failure; the executions stiffened the Protestant faith, and, because they were attributed to Philip's advisers, helped to discredit Roman Catholicism as an alien creed. Towns saw more of the holocaust than did the countryside, because Protestant beliefs had a better hold on them—Hadleigh in Suffolk seemed, in John Fox's words, "in respect of scriptural knowledge rather a university of the learned than a town of clothmaking or labouring people"—and because the authorities wished to terrify as many people as possible. The fires were usually lit in spaces outside the walls, like Smithfield in London or Boughton Spital at Chester, but Bishop Hooper was burned in St. Mary's Square before the cathedral at Gloucester, for greater example.

Although Mary's policies failed, the forms and ceremonies of the Elizabethan settlement were closer to Rome than the Edwardian reforms had left them. The injunctions in the time of Edward VI to strip the churches of images and other liturgical furnishings were widely obeyed, but the material was replaced very quickly in Mary's reign, and not always removed under Elizabeth. Zealots in the seventeenth century and later restorers found a great deal to destroy in the churches, and besides purely religious ceremonies there were many other practices, some of them very old, which were offensive to extreme Protestant taste but were regarded with general affection. In some instances they were pagan ceremonies ⟨232⟩ which the Church had tolerated. Maypole dances and evergreen decorations in the streets at Christmas fell into that category, but the Church was often more directly involved, as it was with gild plays and mummings. At Chester the city's elaborate processions and plays continued until 1572, although a play of the Assumption was abandoned in Edward VI's reign, and the texts of others were altered. In 1571 "the Whitsun plays were played to the dislike of many, because they savoured somewhat of popish teaching", and between 1572 and 1574 Puritan feeling checked the performances, but they began again and were gradually transformed into the spectacle called the Midsummer Show, held on the Roodee, with which the Puritans were no better pleased. One very odd and tenacious ceremony was the observance at Congleton in Cheshire of the patronal feast of St. Peter ad Vincula—St. Peter's Chains. Before the Reformation a fast was proclaimed on St. Peter's Eve, when a runner passed about the town wearing a harness of bells called the Chains. Both proclamation and running survived the abolition of the fast; the proclamation became a ribald joke, and the Chains were sounded until the ceremony dissolved in riot early in the nineteenth century. It was not possible to abolish holidays overnight, and their accompanying ceremonies lived on. This was particularly noticeable at fairs, where trade kept older festivals alive, and some race-meetings may have developed in this way. There was racing on the Roodee at Chester on Shrove Tuesday for a silver bell, and a pair of race-bells have survived at Carlisle from the sixteenth century ⟨48⟩.

Carlisle was a garrison town, and the races may have been held under the governor's patronage. At the other end of the frontier Berwick-on-Tweed was strengthened early in Elizabeth's reign with walls and emplacements designed for artillery warfare. The new work makes Berwick the last English walled town, but the threat against which it was raised was even then diminishing, for by 1560 Scotland was a Protestant country, newly liberated from the French troops of its Regent, Mary of Guise, and joined with England by common fears and interests for the first time in its history. The Scottish Reformation was a revolutionary movement but it was a revolution helped after 1558 by the existence of a Protestant England and by the rivalries of the great Catholic powers, Spain and France, who would each rather see the other's satellites turn Protestant than stay satellites.

The Scottish settlement was more Calvinist than was the English, and the gap between the two Churches widened with time until the final victory of Presbyterianism in 1688. The nobles' proprietary interest in the kirk lands left a very slender endowment for the reformed religion, and as the new system took shape the towns dominated it. Instead of a country gentleman like the Anglican parson, the Scottish minister emerged as a learned townsman who carried the adamantine urbanity of Geneva into his parish. The most significant municipal enterprise in sixteenth-century Scotland was the founding of Edinburgh University in 1583 ⟨45⟩. It was the first civic university in Britain, and was established by the city council with, no doubt, the Universities of Strasbourg and Geneva in mind. In 1581 the council chose a site at Kirk O'Field, south of the city, built upon it, and appointed the first professor in 1583, making him principal in 1586 ⟨46⟩. From 1614 to 1640 the university was inspected annually by a committee representing the city, its ministers, and the Advocates, who with other corporate benefactors endowed the chair of humanities in 1597.

In general, the century was kind to Scottish towns, and the eighty-odd burghs of barony founded between 1500 and 1600 mark an increase in trade as well as seignorial ambitions and royal complaisance. The royal burghs thought they would be ruined, and burghs of all kinds looked inimically upon "pure chapmen that beris their pakkis upoun their bakkis" and infringed burghal rights; but the Crown even sanctioned rural markets and fairs, and began to license them without creating new burghs round them. Even so, the burghs were able to extend their privileges; the fishing industry was brought under their control in 1573, and in 1592 craftsmen were forbidden to work in the suburbs of free burghs where they might escape supervision and taxation. This rule was held not to apply to seignorial lands, and the Edinburgh suburb of Portsburgh sheltered several chartered crafts until it was sold by its superior to the city in 1648 and became, like the Canongate and Leith, a burgh of barony with Edinburgh its corporate lord. Despite the burghs' querulous defence of their privileges there was, at least for the while, business enough for everyone. The later sixteenth

THE TOWN

century saw the rapid spread of mining and carrying in Lothian and Fife, where the string of coastal burghs from Tranent through Dysart to Anstruther thrived on coal, fish and salt.

There was less borough-making in England, except in a parliamentary sense, and there were widespread complaints about taxation, yet individual wealth and comfort was increasing, and much new building was going on in towns. This was still of the kind that the modern eye classifies as antique —half-timbering and plasterwork, or stone with a minimum of dressing, with windows, doors and chimneys treated casually and not as part of a formal composition. Most merchants' houses stood end-on to the street, and if they differed from their medieval predecessors it was probably in being bigger and yet more compactly disposed; three storeys were common, as in New Street in booming Plymouth, with more private rooms above the street, although the shop still occupied the front of the ground floor. Shrewsbury and York preserve the feeling of sixteenth-century towns: uneven, looming buildings ⟨44⟩, too solid to be called ramshackle, and canyons like the Shambles. Market places, in particular, were often built up after being open in the Middle Ages. By the seventeenth century Birmingham had made a warren of its triangular market place by raising buildings over the permanent stalls, and there is a rectangular block, divided by narrow lanes, at the end of Ludlow market which must have grown up in the same way.

Streets and market places developed in a haphazard fashion; their original lines slowly modified by minor adjustments and encroachments. Only two towns, Chester and Great Yarmouth, developed a distinctive street architecture, and the origins of the quite different features which both places call Rows are characteristically obscure. In the main streets of Chester the ground floors of the buildings are set behind an arcade, which supports a public walk, lined with shops at the first-floor level ⟨56, 58⟩. The Rows were taking this form in the fourteenth century, but they were extended in the sixteenth century and later, and even in 1700 not all the houses projected over the upper walks. Short arcades were probably a common feature of the larger towns ⟨60⟩, and many houses projected so far as to need, and pay rent for, supporting pillars in the street. It is the upper level of shops that makes Chester's Rows unique in Britain.

The Rows at Yarmouth ⟨59⟩ took shape late in the sixteenth century, upon what was almost certainly an earlier plan. The main streets of the town run north and south of a sinuous line shaped by the curve of the river, with nearly 150 narrow alleys crossing them. The narrowest of these herring-bone-like passages was only twenty-seven inches wide at its straitest point, and most were less than a hundred feet apart. Except for the market place and churchyard, and the site of a friary, all at the north end of the town, the whole space inside the walls was covered with buildings with only a sprinkling of yards and gardens, for by the end of the sixteenth century the plots divided by the Rows were covered with small back-to-back houses that faced on to the Rows. The evidence suggests that a general rebuilding in flint and brick began then, and was largely accomplished in the seventeenth century. When it was completed, Yarmouth must have been by far the most densely built town outside the City of London.

The Rows' narrow openings protected them from the bitter east winds of a Yarmouth winter, and their plan argues a regard for economy and security uncommonly clear-headed by English standards. Yarmouth was a fishing-port, with a river-haven that was finally made secure by Dutch engineers who began work in 1566, after five earlier attempts had failed. The town stretched along the river bank, sheltering a long quay, and itself protected to the east by a wall, looking across the sandy Denes to the North Sea. Inside the walls was a market place, at what might be called the landward end, by the church. That apart, the rest of the space was used for houses, with gardens at first, but later packed side by side; safe from the wind and from human enemies; after the last rebuilding, safe from fire; and sparing newcomers, even into the nineteenth century, the hazards and miseries of suburban life.

While the Dutch tamed the Yare, Chester watched the Dee silting, and in 1571 there was talk of Chester's pitiful decay, which "without help will assuredly grow to utter ruin and beggary". Yet other evidence suggests an enterprising and reasonably well-found city. Like Lincoln, Chester bought up conduits when the religious houses were suppressed, and later had a municipal supply of water piped to the High Cross, turned on morning and afternoon. In 1601 John Tyrer introduced a more elaborate scheme with a water tower over the Bridge Gate, a development hardly foreseen in 1571 ⟨67⟩. Even in adversity, a city like Chester maintained its attraction and its credit; elsewhere there were more obvious grounds for confidence. Liverpool handled the Irish flax that had once come to Chester, and there was a linen industry in Lancashire that about 1600 began to make fustian, with Mediterranean cotton. In the south-east a new invasion of Flemish immigrants, Protestant refugees from the Spanish Netherlands, brought the manufacture of the fashionable and profitable New Draperies to Colchester and Norwich. Since the 1550s overseas trade had settled down to new markets in Holland and Germany, restricted at first but greatly improved by peace with Spain in James I's reign.

During the sixteenth century the membership of the House of Commons increased by more than half, from nearly 300 to 462, and 135 of the new Members came from boroughs. Yet at the end of Elizabeth's reign there were four times as many gentlemen in the House, men of the quality of the knights of the shire in medieval Parliaments, as there were townsmen duly qualified by residence in the cities and boroughs that they represented. The change was foreshadowed in the fifteenth century, but the towns then often held off the nobility and gentry. In the later Tudor reigns they succumbed, and in Elizabeth's time only a handful, led by London and including Bristol, could point to a consistent record of Members freely chosen from their own numbers. These were places in which the leading townsmen were themselves of more than knightly means; most boroughs with two seats accepted calls on one of them, and not infrequently on both.

Such patronage was not uniform, nor consistently exercised. The Earl of Derby's influence protected one of Liverpool's seats from the Chancellor of the Duchy of Lancaster, and so enabled the burgesses to return their fellow and hero, Alderman Ralph Sekerston. The Earl of Leicester, who lorded it over Denbigh from his castle, was an inveterate collector of High Stewardships, but had uneven success in influencing elections in the towns under his care. The number of purely proprietary boroughs was very small: Gatton, already a huddle of cottages, and Newton in Lancashire, where the right of nominating the two members was sold in 1594 with the barony of Newton, were examples, but there were not many more. The sixteenth century saw three small boroughs in the Isle of Wight, Newtown, Newport and Yarmouth, enfranchised at the instance of a new Governor-General, Sir George Carey, who by 1601 wrote to Yarmouth asking the burgesses to send a sealed blank for their return "as heretofore you have done". The Cinque Ports struggled against their Warden, who was also the returning officer, and the Lancashire boroughs fell into the Duchy's net unless other hands grasped them, but in most places even powerful interests were not immortal, and might change from year to year. By 1600 Cornwall had twenty-one enfranchised boroughs, many of which were a by-word for corruption in later centuries ⟨160⟩, but which returned a strange variety of members to Tudor Parliaments. At any time some new patron might intervene, as the Earl of Essex did ubiquitously during his short career; all that was certain was that no seat from this time forth could go begging.

In the constitutional struggles of the seventeenth century the gentry's predominance in the House of Commons was very important, but it was an accidental predominance, and not the result of a political conspiracy. Towns might be annoyed or embarrassed by the clamour of prospective Members or patrons, but they usually found that they were no worse served by influential outsiders. On their side the Members looked upon their constituents' interests as a necessary charge, and a reasonable price to pay for their new felicity. What patrons and Members alike sought was esteem, and it was the Stuarts' misfortune that esteem attached to membership of a tax-granting assembly. To sit in Parliament was to be in London and at the heart of affairs, and that was a distinction that no man of pretension could afford to deny himself.

The only occupation that Tudor governments regarded with unqualified approval was arable husbandry, and the growth of London implied all that was most distasteful to them. It drew workmen from the countryside and the gentry from their estates, encouraged extravagant spending on imported materials and devoured the country's food. All this had been true of medieval London in some degree, but since the sixteenth century London's growth has been a source of continuous wonder and alarm, each century supposing that it had reached the limits of human toleration. By 1600 London's population had probably reached 150,000, and in the next century, despite the Plague of 1665 which killed twice as many people as the largest provincial city contained, it increased threefold. Under the Tudors the rate of growth was modest, but disturbing enough, and it was marked by severe overcrowding in and around the walled medieval city. A royal proclamation in 1583 forbade new building in London or within three miles of its gates, and the letting of any house to more than one family. The provision was repeated in a statute of 1592, but both building and sub-letting continued.

The most striking new work in the sixteenth century was west of the City, along the river, where the town houses of medieval bishops were reft from their successors to make palaces for the nobility. The properties of Llandaff, Chester and Worcester were swallowed by Somerset House; Essex House came to the Earl of Essex from his step-father Leicester, who had it indirectly from the Bishop of Exeter. Apart from these changes on the river front and the Strand, and some new building at Whitehall Palace, lately Cardinal Wolsey's York House, there was undramatic but substantial work about the City wall, with sites like St. Mary's Hospital (St. Mary Spittle) built over with "many fair houses for receipt and lodging of worshipful persons", and, more frequently, tenement houses and tightly packed cottages. By 1600 the City's suburbs stretched more than a mile east of the Tower, in a tangle of wharves and shipyards, and beyond Holborn and the Temple to the west, perhaps to within three-quarters of a mile of the Middlesex gallows at Tyburn ⟨107⟩, now Hyde Park Corner.

Within these bounds London lived its own life, ruled by the officers of the great City companies. The City was a fortress of trade and industry, at the heart of the capital, but the least changing part of it. The dissolution of the monastic houses diminished the Church's interest. St. Paul's and its churchyard were places of public resort, and the citizens looked upon the cathedral very much as their own property. Sir William Paulet made a great house of the Austin Friary in Broad Street, but more and more the aristocracy settled in the west, toward and in Westminster; when great merchants like Sir Thomas Gresham bought country estates, they kept their town houses, and those houses were different in size rather than in kind from their neighbours. The City's public buildings hardly matched its wealth. The Guildhall had not been altered since the fifteenth century, except that its kitchens were enlarged in Henry VII's reign, and the Lord Mayor had no official residence until the eighteenth century, being lodged in the livery companies' halls for his year of office. The Goldsmiths, a powerful and wealthy company, had "a proper hall, but not large"; the Drapers' was a "very large and spacious" house, but it had been built by Thomas Cromwell and bought by the Company. Sir Thomas Gresham built the Royal Exchange on a spacious Flemish model, but had to recruit its first tenants by private blandishments; the citizens preferred to huddle closer together rather than display their wealth, and the multiplication of houses on London Bridge ⟨39⟩ was architectural excitement enough for them.

By the beginning of the seventeenth century London had three theatres —the Curteyn and the Theatre in Shoreditch, and the famous Globe on the south bank—but, unlike Edinburgh, no university. Sir Thomas Gresham's college of public lecturers had no regular students, and the law schools of the Inns of Court were only neighbours to the City. The citizens did not lack pride, but their corporate traditions were often unspoken and informal. Undertakings like the New River ⟨68⟩, which brought the City its first supply of pure water, were left to individuals; and when the corporation laid out formal walks and paths in Moorfields, London's first public park, it did so on ground that had been kept open by many lawless forays from the City before it was bequeathed in 1605 to public use. It is not surprising that the revolution in architecture and planning that marks the end of the medieval tradition began outside the City itself, or, indeed, that the City is still distinguished from the great town called London.

The new movement began in Charles I's reign, when the square called Covent Garden ⟨61⟩ was laid out for the Earl of Bedford behind his house in the Strand, and houses were built on a regular plan in Lincoln's Inn Fields and Great Queen Street. These operations were supervised by the Commissioners for Buildings, a body set up by Charles I with the sanguine intention of ordering London's development, and Covent Garden was planned by Inigo Jones, who had already devised the Banqueting Hall at Whitehall for James I. Jones's scheme was the first of its kind in Britain, a *piazza* bounded on the south by the Earl's garden, and on the north and east by houses with regular façades, shaped to a classical order, and linked by arcades which also came to be known nonsensically as *piazzas*, a name still applied to their successors. On the west side was a church, St. Paul's, which like the rest of the work has been rebuilt and swamped by the market. The Earl had probably envisaged a more modest plan, but needed the King's licence to sanction the houses that he had already built along Drury Lane. He had the consolation of patronising an entirely new architectural fashion.

Lincoln's Inn Fields were Crown property, formerly monastic land, but they traditionally served the Inns of Court as a playground, as Moorfields did the City. In 1617 the Inns asked that the fields should be laid out like Moorfields, but the lease fell into the hands of a private speculator, William Newton, who offered to increase his rent by building houses. The King could not resist the double temptation of ready money and another chance of imposing an urbane model upon London's builders. Newton had his licence before the Inns could protest, and built houses on the west and south sides of the fields, and in Great Queen Street ⟨62⟩. The Commission saw to it that the work conformed to a regular pattern: a classical order rising from the first floor and supporting an eaves cornice, no gables, with the ornamentation sparing and in classical taste. Newton was harried by the Inns, who petitioned the House of Commons to stop his building in 1641; the Civil War would have checked it in any case, but its combination of court patronage, foreign taste and intrusive commercialism made it offensive to the lawyers, who were radical only in politics. Like Covent Garden, Newton's houses came into their own after the war: at first the political crisis obscured their significance. In 1642 London's economic and political importance was barely matched by its social influence, but it was ready to grow rapidly as a centre of fashion in a wealthier society.

One kind of provincial town had similar potentialities: the spas, as medicinal wells came to be called after Spa in Belgium. Bath was well known in the Middle Ages, and the Poor Law of 1572 named Bath and Buxton as places to which the sick poor might legitimately travel. The waters at Bath passed to the town after the abbey was dissolved, and the corporation repaired and improved the baths ⟨73⟩; at Buxton the earls of Shrewsbury patronised and promoted St. Ann's Well. Both were only health resorts, but they provided amusements for their patients, including plays by London companies at Bath, and walking-galleries, the origin of the seaside promenade, at Buxton. A visit from James I's queen, Anne of Denmark, in 1613 brought Bath further patronage, and the appearance of new spas shows a general interest in and demand for them. The Harrogate waters were discovered in the sixteenth century, Tunbridge Wells in 1606 ⟨74⟩, Epsom about 1620, and Scarborough by "a discreet Gentlewoman . . . physically addicted" about 1626. Tunbridge Wells was advanced by a visit from Henrietta Maria, but in 1640 there was no permanent accommodation at the site, although a promenade—the Pantiles—had been laid out, and there were resting-rooms, charging a half-crown subscription. Epsom had occasional horse races under James I's patronage, but so had Newmarket Heath in Suffolk ⟨102⟩, where there were no mineral waters. Significantly the spas were not specially condemned by the Puritans; their frivolity was still subdued.

Tunbridge Wells and Epsom were close to the capital, and, like markets offering more ordinary commodities, they attracted London's money. So did coal from Newcastle, fruit and vegetables from Kent and Essex market gardens, and corn and cattle from the Midlands. The coal trade apart, London's demands were not felt as widely in the early seventeenth century as they were a century later when Daniel Defoe found no district unaffected by them, but they maintained some prosperity in southern England during the depression that enfolded Charles I's reign. It was a depression mainly in the cloth trade, but its effects there were uneven: the Suffolk broadcloth towns fossilised, while Leeds grew modestly with a new church, St. John's in Briggate; and cotton-weaving spread in Lancashire. The Cotswold and Wiltshire industries did well, and Chipping Campden, a wool market rather than a manufacturing town, took on much of its present handsome shape under the patronage of its merchant-lord, Sir Baptist Hicks. Once again it was the older incorporate towns that complained most, harried by plague and the burden of their public duties, envious of London's effortless growth, and aware that they no longer controlled the country's most vigorous industry.

The religious and political discontents that swelled into the Civil War sounded in the towns, but were not necessarily associated with depression. Devon was a great Puritan county, but its towns and seaports were among the busiest in the country, fed on the cloth trade and Atlantic traffic, and their grievances touched royal exactions and trading monopolies. In most political matters it is unprofitable to distinguish towns from countryside, for the gentry's association with the boroughs often made them speak with one voice in Parliament. Three of the Five Members whom Charles I tried to arrest in January 1642 as his chief enemies in the Commons represented south-western boroughs: Pym sat for Tavistock, Holles for Dorchester, and Strode for Bere Alston; but like their fellows, Hampden and Hazlerigg, they were members of landed families and they had only nominal interests in their constituencies. As traders depend upon orderly government, they are not usually avid for political change, and the King might have found more allies than he did in the towns. Actions of *Quo warranto* that forced boroughs to defend their charters in court or pay for new ones were not a long-sighted way of raising funds, and Charles was too proud to make friends as Elizabeth made them. The towns still offered loyal greetings and even plate to the Stuarts in their progresses—

James I had a 45-ounce gold cup and £100 from Coventry in 1617—but they no longer had the honeyed thanks that Elizabeth bestowed: "It is the best [speech] that I ever heard: you shall have my hand", and "I have laid up in my breast such good will, as I shall never forget Norwich." A crown was well worth such care.

Puritanism was an older discordance; the unresolved debates of Edward VI's reign revived in Elizabeth's, and soon threatened the Anglican Church. Puritanism appealed to merchants and artisans from the beginning, and amateur theology throve in the towns, with abundant opportunities for discussion. The excitements of Elizabeth's reign, when Roman Catholicism was backed by a powerful foreign enemy, made many people critical of Anglican compromises, and those who favoured more reforms were called Puritans. Then and later the word covered many opinions, but at first the Presbyterians were at the heart of the opposition, until they were matched by the forerunners of later dissenting movements, notably Congregationalists and Baptists. All Puritans emphasised the importance of preaching, and this accorded well with civic traditions: the mayors of London attended the sermons at St. Paul's Cross in great state, and the only part of St. Mary's hospital at Bishopsgate to survive the Dissolution was the churchyard cross, where the City fathers attended special courses of Easter sermons. Most town churches were poor and disorganised in the later sixteenth century, and municipalities often appointed general preachers of their own: men chosen for their skill with a sermon, who were more likely than not to be Puritan. Lincoln city council was torn in the 1580s over preaching and sabbatical observances, and those who derided the city preachers and encouraged May games were suspected of being Papists. Some of them may have been, but the strictest of their opponents were unmistakably Puritans, whom the Anglican Church came to regard as an equally formidable enemy. Lincoln had a series of Puritan preachers in the early seventeenth century, one of whom, John Smith, founded a Baptist congregation and eventually fled to Amsterdam.

The town libraries that appeared in the sixteenth century could also serve the Puritan cause; the Earl of Huntingdon founded a library at Leicester for that purpose, and William Smart of Ipswich left his collection of books for the use of the Ipswich general preachers, who were not chosen for their Anglican orthodoxy. The reformed grammar schools were another object of Puritan attention, and here again some of the least conformable divines were among the most effective teachers, such as Thomas Parker of Newbury, who later took the town's name to Newbury, Massachusetts. But the disputes of the 1630s did not always prefigure the patterns of the war; it was the Scots, not the English, who went to war for religion, and when religious war in Scotland provoked political crisis and war in

THE TOWN

England not all those who had challenged the King were pleased to have their challenge accepted.

The war found the towns deeply divided, but in the early stages at least the dominant party in the manufacturing towns opposed the King. London stood consistently for Parliament, and the eastern counties banded together in an association that stifled all royalist sympathies except in King's Lynn. Yorkshire was mainly royalist territory; the clothing towns of the West Riding, Bradford, Halifax and Leeds, were parliamentarian, but were reduced in 1643, and only Hull, with its valuable docks and armoury, held out against the King. Manchester resisted the King and beat off a brief siege in the first year of the war, while in the debatable lands of the Midlands, Coventry and Birmingham were strongly parliamentarian and Birmingham was a valuable source of arms. The Severn basin was mainly royalist territory, but Puritan Gloucester obdurately spoiled the scene; Bristol began the war on Parliament's side, but fell to Prince Rupert in 1643, and remained the King's chief strength for more than a year. In the south-west, at least to the Tamar, the towns resisted the King, although, in Exeter as in Bristol, they contained substantial royalist minorities. Plymouth, like the other Channel ports, was a Puritan stronghold.

Territorially the war was spasmodic and confused; there were no consistent frontiers, and even the destination of Birmingham's swords depended on the manufacturers' sympathies rather than on the military control of the district. Most sieges were short and did comparatively little damage, although Scarborough endured as many as seven ⟨37⟩, and Colchester suffered severely from a twelve-week siege during the royalist risings in 1648 known as the Second Civil War. At Denbigh the threat of operations against the royalist garrison of the castle moved some of the townspeople to leave the new market at the foot of the hill and return to the safety of the medieval town-walls, but the migration lasted no longer than the emergency ⟨60⟩.

Civilians on both sides grew impatient as the war dragged on; the men of Bridgnorth, loyal to the King at first, blamed their royalist garrison for the damage done when the town was taken in 1646, just as the eastern towns paid less and less willingly for Parliament's uncontrollable army. When the war was done and the King dead, the republicans found themselves on the defensive, and Cromwell's government was reduced to manipulating the corporations, either by new charters, as at Reading and Colchester in 1656–7, or by direct interference, as when Major-Generals Whalley and Berry imposed a new town clerk on Lincoln in 1655. The war hindered rather than destroyed trade, but the towns were slow to recover. At Berwick-on-Tweed the military governor built a new church which still survives, one of the very few built during this time, and in response to demands for a northern university a short-lived college was founded at Durham. In Scotland, which was united with England after General Monck's campaign in 1651, vigorous military government in the Highlands and free trade with the English colonies brought several years of prosperity. The garrisons and their keep were resented, and the experiment did not last long, but when the old restrictions were reimposed in 1660 there was a new incentive to develop Scottish trade and manufacture.

The Stuarts' return coincided with a marked expansion of trade and industry, beginning the movement that in the next two centuries made Great Britain the chief industrial and commercial power in the world. Its effects were masked for a time by the political legacies of the Civil War, and by the final catastrophe of the bubonic plague. Of all political problems, the most vexed and confused was the religious settlement, and some important social issues waited upon it. The Anglican Church had survived its tribulations, but it no longer had any large claims to comprehensiveness; its opponents were divided, though too numerous to ignore. Presbyterianism, apparently so powerful before the war, was now spent politically; the Independents, whom the army had brought into power, had prevented a Presbyterian settlement, but were not united and were challenged on their own ground by the Quakers. These sects were all represented in the towns, and their political future was a vital question in the 1660s.

The answer was soon delivered. The Presbyterians alone hoped for some accommodation with the Anglican Church, and that proved impossible; like the other sects they were excluded from the established Church, and so from public life. Their personal freedom was precarious, and was restricted from time to time; the Quakers in particular were persecuted during the 1660s. By contemporary European standards the settlement was generous, but it disrupted English society for a long time, and embittered conditions in Scotland. Its effects were felt immediately in the incorporate towns, where the precarious balance of factions commemorated every step in the Interregnal dance. Their parliamentary seats made the boroughs important, and their complex politics, to say nothing of their Cromwellian charters, made them natural objects of suspicion. Many towns petitioned for new charters, and got them on terms that showed the Government's intentions. Officers and members of the corporations were subject to royal veto, as they had sometimes been in the past, and a State Paper of 1661 speaks of ensuring that their Members of Parliament should be chosen only by the closed corporations. This policy was subordinated to that of purging the existing corporations, for reasons demonstrated in 1661 when the Commons decided that the franchise in Preston ought to lie not with the unregenerate and anti-royalist corporation, but with the burgesses at large, who were as well disposed toward the King as was the rest of Lancashire. Although Charles II later returned to the attack, and James II continued his policy, they were unable to impose a uniform and predictable franchise on the boroughs: the Revolution of 1688 confirmed the existing system in all its variety, and the conservatism of the eighteenth century hallowed it.

The attack upon the municipalities began in 1661, when an Act for the Well-Governing and Regulating of Corporations prescribed oaths for municipal officers, and made them take Communion by the Anglican rite. It also set up panels of commissioners, which the Crown hoped to make permanent, empowered to remove any corporate officer suspected of disaffection even if he had taken the oaths. The scheme was hindered by parliamentary and local intransigence, but it made a vigorous start; the mayor of Chard found himself a corporation of one, and sought to be relieved from the burden of his charters, and it was difficult even in a town like Reading to make up numbers after the commissioners had passed. Meanwhile the Act of Uniformity purged the Church, and the first Conventicle Act penalised those who attended other than Anglican services, whilst the Five Mile Act of 1665 forbade the neighbourhood of corporate towns to all Nonconformist ministers. This policy was modified by the Declaration of Indulgence in 1672, and still more drastically when James II tried to buy favour for the Roman Catholic Church by admitting Protestant dissenters to public offices, but even in the 1660s its rigour was spasmodic. The practice of Occasional Conformity enabled some dissenters to stay in public life, while some Anglicans took refuge in pretended Nonconformity to avoid the charge of municipal office. Despite these exceptions, the Restoration settlement perpetuated divisions that would have been better healed, and James II's attempts to make the Dissenters his allies, though unsuccessful, confirmed Anglican suspicions: the corporations remained exclusive.

Immediately upon the Restoration fashionable building began again in London, with two great courtiers, the Earls of Southampton and St. Albans, pursuing very different schemes in Bloomsbury and St. James's. Lord Southampton laid out Bloomsbury Square in front of his mansion, and leased sites to speculators as well as to private builders. This square lacked the *panache* of Covent Garden, but it had the great merit of being comprehensively planned, for the scheme embraced ancillary streets of shops and smaller houses. Lord St. Albans's device was more stately; he imagined St. James's Square as a select cloister of aristocratic palaces, a scheme that would have burned more hearts than it warmed. At first he could not raise the right tenants for his expensive short leases. In 1665 the King granted him the freehold of the land, but with London scourged by plague the moment was a poor one for developing property. Then in

September 1666 the Great Fire destroyed four-fifths of the City and the western suburbs as far as the Temple, and the Earl's new freehold was suddenly too valuable to waste upon exclusiveness.

The plague ⟨69⟩ killed nearly 100,000 people in London, and tens of thousands more in the provinces; the epidemic at Eyam in Derbyshire is famous, but Derby and the east-coast ports were also severely affected. No one could guess that it was the last outbreak, and it was the most savage for several centuries past; the country was fighting the second Dutch war, and as the epidemic dragged into the long hot summer of 1666, it seemed that London at least had plumbed its misfortunes. In a sense, too, it had, for the fire that razed the City in September ⟨70⟩ cleansed it ruthlessly, burning for more than a week, and destroying the rats and fleas that spread the disease, and the ramshackle tenements that in the past had taken more lives than had the plague. The City, unable to countenance or to pay for Wren's beautifully logical plan ⟨71⟩, might decline again into squalor, but its rebuilding could not fail to improve upon the shifts and casual accumulations of sixteen centuries. Work began under an Act of 1667 that made some changes to the street-plan, opening King Street and Queen Street from the Guildhall to the river, and prescribed new building standards. Meanwhile Moorfields disappeared, under first huts and then more elaborate buildings, and the City grew again quite rapidly as the survivors and others moved back; within ten years the pattern of streets was complete again. Moreover the new London was richer and larger than ever; Lord St. Albans's hasty creation of twenty-two plots where ten were once intended marked the boom in the West End, while the villainous entrepreneur Dr. Nicholas Barbon tore down Essex House and buried its gardens like Red Lion Fields by Gray's Inn, under orderly rows of standardised brick houses for the middlingly ambitious.

Barbon not only built, but organised fire insurance and a hundred other schemes. The City's sophistication at last kept pace with its size, as it grew on the dividends of foreign war. Banking, stock-jobbing, insurance of all kinds, including the marine insurance managed from Lloyd's coffee house, all flourished. With James II safely expelled and William III making energetic war the most hectic time was the 1690s, when London had its first real stock-market boom, and the Bank of England was founded. *Lloyd's News* began in 1696. Queen Anne's reign saw the wars continue, and though there was less building, London's cultural pre-eminence continued unchallenged. In the *Daily Courant*, which appeared in 1702, it had the world's first daily newspaper, while the literary society of the coffee-houses was regaled by an entirely new kind of journalism in the *Tatler*, from 1708 to 1711, and then the *Spectator*. Life was still violent

THE TOWN

and brutal, but there was promised here not merely a wealthier but also a more gentle society ⟨104⟩; the promise was a long time unredeemed, but it stood.

The provincial cities and towns enjoyed their measure of prosperity. At the beginning of Charles II's reign Bristol, then the country's second port, had about 15,000 inhabitants; there were perhaps twice as many by the end of the century, and more than 50,000 by 1760. Behind this increase was a rich Atlantic trade in tobacco from Virginia and sugar from the West Indies, while trade with Spain revived, especially in sherry. Bristol broke its medieval bounds after the Restoration, and houses spread into the castle precinct and on to the Marsh south of the walls, enfolding the river-quays ⟨112⟩ in the way that is so striking a feature of the modern city. Yet tradition was still strong, and in King Street, the first laid out on the Marsh, the new building was very conservative; brickwork and regular façades did not appear in Bristol until Queen Anne's reign.

Shipping grew with trade; Bristol built some warships in the seventeenth century, but naval architecture demanded special skills and, although the shipyards along the Thames were still mixed, separate naval bases were rising. Portsmouth and Chatham ⟨75⟩ had been Tudor arsenals, but they now expanded, and in the 1690s a new naval base was founded at Dock, later Devonport, by Plymouth. Plymouth was sapped by this development, but had a living still in trade and fishing, which also maintained a little port at Falmouth, chartered in 1661 and provided with one of the rare churches dedicated to King Charles-the-Martyr. On the east coast the trade in coal from the Tyne was increasingly important; and the wealth of King's Lynn at this time is still commemorated in the works of a gifted local architect, Henry Bell.

Liverpool's great career had hardly begun in 1700, although the port had grown since the Civil War ⟨83⟩. The chief towns in Lancashire were still Lancaster and Preston, but Manchester was expanding, and in 1708 Lady Ann Bland enclosed Acresfield, the site of the St. Matthew's fair, to build St. Ann's church and Square. Farther north there was much new building, with stone houses replacing wooden ones in towns like Kendal and Hexham. On the Cumberland coast Sir John Lowther developed Whitehaven in the late seventeenth century; it had a chartered market from 1660, but its future lay in the coal trade and in general shipping: Glasgow entered the Virginia trade in Whitehaven ships, and the harbour's London traffic affected Newcastle's trade west of the Pennines ⟨77⟩.

One sign of prosperity was the search for new mineral springs: more than a hundred were discovered between 1660 and 1714. Those who frequented them still went ostensibly in search of health, but the pretence was thin among those who followed the court to Epsom races or strolled at Islington at the week-end; what both old and new spas satisfied was a general desire to be entertained, to live more fully as well as more comfortably. The entertainment that they offered was still subordinate to their cures and often very simple: at Scarborough, the only spa by the sea, the sands were used as a promenade ⟨114⟩. It was not until Nash ⟨92⟩ and his colleagues took Bath in hand that the new demand called a holiday-industry into being, but meanwhile mineral wells were at a premium. London had a constellation of little spas at Hampstead, Dulwich and elsewhere, Bristol had its Hotwells, and vague hopes of gain ran high in every county.

Although Scotland's trade increased during the seventeenth century, the burghs found little pleasure in it. An enquiry moved by the Convention of Royal Burghs in 1691 provoked a universal lament; the burghs were encumbered with debt, except Dingwall to whom no one would lend money, and the poverty of the home trade was equalled only by the weakness of their foreign commerce. Glasgow had seven ships at sea, and could not believe that any would return; Perth had lost two argosies, each called the *Eagle of Perth*, the second by default of the captain, who had made off with it. It seemed unlikely, on reading the returns, that town life could survive much longer, and the Fortrose magistrates said as much, fearing that if the townsmen were charged directly with their debt, which they had "no way under heaven to pay", they would run away, as some had already. Despite these forebodings most burghs maintained public services and paid ministers, schoolmasters and even doctors, while Dundee allowed £1,200 for "maintaining the honour of the good town in waiting on noblemen and others". Those charges outran the traditional revenue which was drawn from the burghal endowment and from such incidents as tolls and mill dues. The common land had often been extravagantly leased, and the magistrates were reluctant to reveal their accounts. Faced with demands for such improvements as better policing, paving and lighting, many burghs turned in the eighteenth century to an expedient that Edinburgh adopted in 1691, and entrusted them to statutory commissioners who levied rates, a privilege that the magistrates did not enjoy.

The burghs were vexed in 1691 because they knew that trade was improving and believed that their ancient privileges entitled them to the whole gain. As it was, an Act of 1672 abrogated the royal burghs' monopoly of trade except in foreign luxuries, including dye-stuffs, and threw open trade in native commodities, while burghs of regality or barony were allowed to import materials needed for their own manufactures and to export finished goods. The Act regulated rather than innovated, but the royal burghs clung to the hope of mitigating or undoing it, and eventually they secured a new Act from William III. This restricted foreign trade, but left free the cattle trade with England and other exports by land, and

THE TOWN

it actually extended the right to buy and sell retail outside the royal burghs. In 1691 the burgesses thought to balance some further trading concessions against a reduction of their public taxes, and they probably described their plight with more art than justice. "This poor place," said the magistrates of Glasgow, "cannot subsist": an assertion belied by events. The debate was suspended by the Act of Union of 1707, which confirmed the royal burghs in their remaining privileges, and, by allotting them a number of seats in Parliament, extended to them the ossifying protection that the English and Welsh municipalities already enjoyed.

Scottish national trade made slow progress against local privilege, but it was secure by 1681, when an Act protecting certain manufacturers assured the future of the joint stock companies that promoted them. Several of these companies were established at Glasgow, which in the early eighteenth century was the Scottish town best placed to enjoy the advantages that the Act of Union offered. Glasgow absorbed the burgh of Gorbals ⟨186⟩ in 1647, and in 1668, after unsuccessful talks with Dumbarton, established Port Glasgow ⟨113⟩ for sea-going ships, eighteen miles down the Clyde and opposite the mouth of the Gareloch. The "ane little key" below the city's main bridge at the Broomielaw was joined by others, like the wharf built in 1700 for coal from the Duke of Hamilton's estates, but Port Glasgow was improved in the eighteenth century and the channel up to Glasgow was not wholly cleared until 1907. Glasgow suffered with the rest of the south-west when the Covenanters were persecuted under Charles II and James VII, and lost both men and material in the Darien scheme, but though the mob demonstrated against the Union, the merchants were quick to launch upon a trade that had long attracted them. In 1718 the first Clyde-built ship replaced those hired from England, and by 1721 Liverpool, London and Whitehaven were complaining to the Treasury about Glasgow's frauds upon the customs; a complaint inspired, as the Lords of the Treasury said, by "a spirit of envy, and not from a regard to the interests of trade or of the king's revenue". Defoe found Glasgow "one of the cleanliest, most beautiful and best built cities in Britain", and although the tobacco trade languished for a time in the 1720s and 1730s, it not only recovered but was supported by heavy traffic with the West Indies and the American plantations. St. Andrew's church ⟨187⟩ and square, built in the 1740s, the Ship banking company, and the fame of the university were the mid-century's memorials to the city's enterprise, and the university's contribution was exceptional by any standards. Adam Smith was a Glasgow graduate and professor, and the university employed James Watt as an instrument-maker when the city's gild regulations denied him a livelihood. The claims of past and future have rarely been so nicely balanced.

Adam Smith retired to Kirkcaldy to write *The Wealth of Nations* in 1767, and James Watt removed to Birmingham to become a partner at Boulton's foundry there in 1774. By that time the revolution that made Britain an industrial country had begun, but it had not made any profound impression upon the towns. The iron trade was gravitating toward the coalfields, but in the West Riding and the Cotswolds, water-power had actually drawn the textile industry into the countryside, just as it had centuries before when it was first applied to fulling. Birmingham and the Potteries drew raw materials from a distance to maintain their industries, but elsewhere the traditional pattern of urban crafts was hardly disturbed, and the mineral workings in districts like South Wales and Stirlingshire had not yet begun to breed towns. Some of the old cloth industries were in decline; the Devon weavers lost business during the eighteenth century, and the Colchester bay and say trade dwindled to a final crisis in the Napoleonic Wars, but these changes were compensated by others, notably the growing population, the quickening trade, and the improvement in communications that began with the first turnpike trusts after the Restoration. There is still much Georgian building left in British towns.

The Modern Town

THE expanding population bore heavily upon the towns, but the largest schemes of new building were to be found in places with administrative functions, or in which people spent money earned elsewhere—the two cannot be entirely distinguished—rather than in commercial towns, and in commercial towns rather than industrial ones. Just as most Britons lived in the country until the later nineteenth century, so domestic and personal service ranked high among urban occupations over the same period, and the opportunities offered by London, Edinburgh and Bath counted for more than those of the Black Country or Falkirk. London was an important manufacturing centre as well as a great market and capital city, but the West End absorbed more bricks and mortar than the City and its industrial suburbs, and cannot have employed many fewer people.

London grew to an established pattern. Although Sir William Chambers and the brothers Adam, in their treatment respectively of Somerset House ⟨124⟩ and the Adelphi ⟨123⟩, began a new treatment of the riverside, but inland the advance towards the New Road—now Marylebone Road—between Islington and Paddington was by streets and squares, an advance of a satisfactory and familiar kind. The planning was in terms of **estates, and** not of a city—that was something that London did not enjoy until John Nash undertook his great schemes for the Prince Regent, and then it showed itself singularly ungrateful for the experience. The City did give some thought to its public responsibilities, although it hampered the building of Westminster Bridge ⟨122⟩ from a fear that its own monopoly might suffer, and made belated haste to clear and refurbish London Bridge only when the rival was opened. The 1760s saw the Fleet Ditch filled, Blackfriars Bridge built, and all the gates but Newgate pulled down, after which Newgate gaol was rebuilt in an appropriately forbidding style. The gaol was, however, burnt in the Gordon Riots in 1780, and when it was completed in 1783 it became the scene of public executions, an entertainment transferred from Tyburn.

Another celebrated prison burned in 1780 and rebuilt was the Fleet, which like the Marshalsea in Southwark was used for debtors, and so continued to Dickens's day. These places were probably better conducted than they had been before the Committee on Gaols enquired into them in 1729 ⟨104⟩, but still, like Tyburn and Bedlam, they are examples of the brutality and harshness that most people took for granted: the society exposed in Hogarth's "Gin Lane", or in the Gordon Riots, when an hysterical demonstration against the Roman Catholics exploded into a week of arson and rapine. Society's disorders did not go unchallenged, and the century saw powerful philanthropic movements, like John Howard's investigations of prisons, as well as the beginning of Jeremy Bentham's profoundly influential enquiry into legal and social institutions. Howard's conclusions were published too late to influence the design of Newgate gaol, but humanitarianism made some gains, and though these were weakened by the rapid changes of industrial society the nineteenth century would have been worse without them. One striking improvement was in medical services; the medieval hospitals of St. Thomas and St. Bartholomew were rebuilt, and by the 1750s were joined by six new foundations. The first of the new hospitals was the Westminster, founded in 1719, and the last the Middlesex, which was building for twenty years from 1755. Both of these were supported by annual subscribers. Guy's was founded and endowed by a single benefactor, Thomas Guy, a bookseller who was believed to have made as much money from South Sea Company Stock as he claimed to have made from selling Bibles. Captain Thomas Coram's Foundling Hospital was helped by public concerts held in its chapel, where Handel often conducted performances of his own works.

Poverty and disease were not London's problems alone. Union workhouses appeared in the larger towns late in the seventeenth century long before they became a general expedient, and in places like Norwich or Hull they could hope to cater for all the poor, unlike the London workhouse in Bishopsgate. Infirmaries, often chartered and with qualified medical staffs, followed more slowly, but they were fairly common by the second half of the century, and a growing town like Sheffield, where the Infirmary was first discussed at a public meeting in 1793 and founded in 1797, regarded it as a natural and necessary acquisition. Such institutions imitated rather than innovated, but there was one development that was very important architecturally and socially, and that began in the provinces. This was the evolution of towns devoted chiefly to pleasure, including the pleasures of retirement.

Until Anne's reign Bath was a health resort, fashionable enough to ensure that not all its visitors were invalids, but still catering chiefly for the sick. When Anne visited the baths in 1702 and 1703, the corporation received her as it had always received royal patrons, but the entertainments were particularly lavish, and the master of ceremonies remained a permanent official when they were done. In 1705 the master of ceremonies was killed in a duel, a hazard natural in his profession, and was succeeded by Richard Nash ⟨92⟩, ex-soldier, law student, and a publicist of genius. In the next thirty years Nash made Bath's visitors into a community, binding them to a code of conduct so simple that the most boorish could understand it, and yet so coloured with apparent privilege as to make it irresistible to the English. His methods were so successful that from 1735 he was invited to preside at Tunbridge Wells during the summer, when the Bath waters were believed to be less effective than in spring and autumn, and travelled there "in a post chariot and six greys, with outriders, footmen, French horns and every other appendage of expensive parade". At this time Tunbridge was Bath's closest rival, and the general example set by these two places was widely imitated. The Epsom Wells, which might have equalled them, were then failing under John Livingstone, who had advanced views on the management of resorts, but unscrupulously overworked his resources.

The society which Nash created at Bath needed a setting quite different from the huddled town that he found, and that setting was provided by two other able promoters, Ralph Allen and John Wood. As postmaster of Bath, Allen made a fortune from cross-country posts, which he devised to save the delays of sending letters through London, and he invested his money in local improvements. He made the Avon navigable, and in 1727 he bought the Bath stone quarries on Coombe Down, just as John Wood the architect came to Bath. Wood's ambition was to create a town of Roman splendour, by moulding whole streets and squares to monumental designs, and arranging them in a manner continuously exciting to the eye. His first work, apart from some houses in Chapel Court, was Queen Square (1728–36) ⟨94⟩. In the 1740s he built the Parades, which were to have enclosed a sunken garden, Bath's Forum, but this work was never finished.

THE TOWN

Then in 1754, the year of his death, Wood began the Circus, his most imposing and successful device, with thirty-three houses united in three groups by a concave façade of three superimposed orders ⟨93⟩. The Circus is entered by three roads, so arranged that there is no dividing line across it, for a diametrical road would reduce the scheme to a mere incident upon a thoroughfare. Such subtleties were common enough in landscape gardening but not in town-planning; there had not been, even in London, a whole community leisured and discriminating enough to make the exercise worth while.

Wood was succeeded by his son John, whose Royal Crescent (1767–75) introduced an even more popular theme into urban architecture. The thirty houses of the Crescent, blinkered by a great Ionic colonnade ⟨95⟩, have more dramatic force than the Circus, and the idea was widely imitated. The first large crescent outside Bath was at Buxton, where John Carr, the architect of Harewood House, built a curved block containing an assembly room, hotel, and newsroom, with an open arcade on the street. The Buxton crescent is a heavy design, formal and durable, and it was really a public building; most crescents are terraces of private houses, and their common feature is their curve, rather than any monumentality. They were particularly popular with speculative builders at watering-places—the Royal Crescent at Brighton was one of the first at the seaside—and the curve lived on even when smartness had departed from the terrace, and still produces winding streets carelessly strung with semi-detached houses.

The circus needed more space than the crescent, and was comparatively neglected; when John Nash used it in Regent Street ⟨153, 199⟩ it was for a different purpose from Wood's. Like London's other architects, Nash had to adjust his plans to an existing city, and before he began work a new town had taken shape at Edinburgh which offered its designers opportunities that London always grudged. By the eighteenth century Edinburgh had spread southward from its spine of rock, but its site was narrow and congested, confined on the south by Telfer's Wall (1628–36), and on the north by the precipitous gully of the Nor' Loch ⟨141⟩. The loss of the Scottish Parliament after the Union diminished the city's importance, but by the later eighteenth century Edinburgh was not only wealthy, but the intellectual and social capital of Scotland, and the municipality resolved that the new town should match the city's fame. The corporation acquired lands to round off its own beyond the Nor' Loch, and spanned the valley with the North Bridge. The first plan was a grid of streets joining two squares, Charlotte on the west, designed by Robert Adam ⟨136⟩, and St. Andrew's on the east; houses were begun in George Street, the main thoroughfare, in 1767, before the North Bridge was complete, but the rest of the scheme lagged when the wars with France began in 1793.

Work began again in the last year of the Napoleonic wars, the streets spreading round Calton Hill to the east and north-east, and to the Water of Leith on the north and west. The last phase was marked in 1832 when Telford built Dean Bridge ⟨142⟩ to connect the Raeburn estate beyond the Water of Leith with the New Town. Like the West End of London the town grew by estates, but under stricter control than London knew; each area has its own centre-piece, circus or crescent, except the Moray estate at the west end of Queen Street, which besides a circus ⟨137⟩ has Ainslie Place, comprising two opposing crescents, and Randolph Crescent in the Queensferry Road. The new town contains private houses enough, but some of its special quality and scale derives from the prevalence of flats, which Roman and Scottish law, unlike English common law, endow with the privileges of freehold. Flats made tall buildings profitable, as they were in the old town ⟨64⟩, while the architects' severe neo-classical ideals imposed such order upon them that Edinburgh has even now a poise and dignity matched by very few cities.

Edinburgh's intellectual pre-eminence was enhanced by conditions in England, for although Oxford and Cambridge began to reform themselves in the early years of the nineteenth century, their narrow interests and religious exclusiveness had driven many English students to Scottish universities. In the middle of the eighteenth century Glasgow was popular with the English, but Edinburgh attracted them in the later decades. The university's medical school was the most advanced in the country; its philosophical studies were internationally famous, and the *Edinburgh Review* commanded for many years a reputation unsurpassed by any other British periodical. The university and the High School had honoured places in the city's rebuilding, although the new university ⟨139⟩, begun in 1789 to a design of Robert Adam's, was delayed by the war, and the school ⟨134⟩ is one of the last great monuments of the Greek revival in Edinburgh. The publishing trade reacted more promptly; there were twenty-seven printing-houses in Edinburgh in 1779, and families like the Murrays cut great figures in the age of Sir Walter Scott.

The Scottish ports generally found advantage in the Union, and although none had as strange a bonus as Montrose, where a salvaged cargo of bricks intended for Curaçao provided material for a distinctive rebuilding, most places have some history of improvement in the later eighteenth and early nineteenth centuries. The work was mainly private; Dundee had a Town House designed by William Adam, but peculation and the wastage of their endowments often prevented even the larger municipalities from undertaking elaborate public works. Between 1798 and 1802 the Provost of Renfrew four times proposed, authorised and supervised sales of borough property to himself. The statutory commissioners supervised lighting and paving efficiently enough, but money that came into the hands of the old corporate bodies usually stuck to them; by 1819 the corporation of Aberdeen had received £27,000 under an ill-advised act of 1810 that allowed the council to raise funds for new docks, but docks were still wanting in 1835.

Edinburgh and improvements apart, by the early nineteenth century the Scottish burgh had little new to show except wealth; there were new houses and new streets, but few new towns. In the Clyde valley industrial housing had appeared at places like Blantyre, where David Livingstone was born in 1813, while on the Leven Alexandria and Renton grew up round bleaching and dyeing works as Glasgow's textile trade expanded. Leisured communities were harder to find. Rothesay, an ancient burgh and port in Bute, which offered a mild climate and an open beach, prospered after the wars as a watering place ⟨177⟩. It had a subscription library before 1800, and "handsome mansions and pleasant villas" appeared round the bay in the next forty years, but this was a late development, and like the little spa at Strathpeffer, above Dingwall, was on a comparatively small scale.

English holiday towns were well established by the time of the Napoleonic wars, when the old spas enjoyed a respite from the challenge of the sea-side. Sea-bathing was recommended by doctors and practised before 1700, though it was hardly popular, even among the bathing classes, before the middle of the century. It had then been common for some time at Scarborough ⟨114⟩, but it was practised mainly at small fishing villages and hamlets with no harbour to spoil the beach: Blackpool, on the Fylde coast; Brighthelmstone, later Brighton, in Sussex; South End, a Thames-side hamlet of Prittlewell. Cottage rooms could be rented cheaply, and the visitors were content to provide their own amusements, although as they became more numerous they took the spas as models. Brighton borrowed the master of ceremonies from Bath to marshal its company, and Bath released him complacently. It seemed at Tunbridge Wells that the raw pleasures of Brighton would by contrast enhance the spa's urbane attractions. Yet the advantage lay with the seaside resorts, and royal patronage in the second half of the century reflected their success. At the mouth of the Thames, Margate and Ramsgate enjoyed all the popularity of the seventeenth-century London spas. The nobility came for the sea-bathing season, thousands of Londoners came on week-end trips, travelling cheaply down the river on Margate hoys, while rich townspeople built or rented houses to which they could escape from town for the summer, or even longer, a practice that Defoe had noticed at Epsom in the 1720s. Similar resorts grew on a smaller scale in districts remote from London; Exmouth drew the citizens of Exeter as early as 1750, some to bathe, and "some persons of condition" to live there.

SEA-BATHING: BRIGHTON AND SOUTHPORT

The Prince of Wales ⟨144⟩ visited Brighton for the first time in 1783, and in 1784 began to build the house that later became the Pavilion ⟨146⟩. Brighton was already the chief sea-bathing resort; the Prince's regular visits between 1788 and 1823 made it the most fashionable town in Britain, and the first outside London to attract foreign visitors as anything more than a curiosity. The court's attendant train of jockeys, prizefighters, and qualified or aspiring trollops enriched the town without entirely destroying its respectability, and although George III bathed as far from his undutiful son as he could, bringing joy to owners of property in Weymouth and Sidmouth, Brighton remained unmistakably Bath's successor. Some celebrated inland spas appeared while Brighton was at the height of its fame, but that fame implied a change of taste, and it encouraged the rise of other seaside resorts. Usually some enterprising landowner or lessee inaugurated the work, or brought the amenities of a promising village up to date. The Rolles of Bicton began to build houses on the Beacon at Exmouth in the 1790s, while Sir Richard Hotham, a Southwark hatter and M.P., descended upon Bognor to build a villa for himself and "lodging-houses which he furnished at considerable expense". On the Lancashire coast, William Sutton, an innkeeper of North Meols, first provided carts to carry visitors to a favoured bathing-beach near the mouth of the Ribble, then built a bathing-shed for them in 1792, and followed it in 1798 with the South Port Hotel, built across the end of the marshy hollow that later became Lord Street.

Southport was then a resort of the very simplest kind, although as early as 1806 some local people founded the Southport Strangers' Charity, an institution which, bringing the sick poor to the seaside for treatment, looked back to the spas ⟨91⟩ as well as forward to modern convalescent hospitals. In the 1820s, when there was a theatre as well as a church and two chapels, and "three good inns", the town consisted only of one street, casually built, with back lanes like those of medieval Appleby ⟨109⟩ or Elgin. The width of the main street, which gives it a special character today, was an accident; there were pools of water in the middle until the 1840s, and the houses were set back, leaving broad sidewalks. These and the beach served Southport as a promenade until 1838, when drifting sand and the need for a sea wall moved the proprietors to build a raised promenade along the shore. Bathing-machines ⟨114, 144⟩ appeared in William Sutton's day, and donkeys popular at Tunbridge Wells and Brighton in the eighteenth century, soon followed them. There was no pier, because although the great iron piers of the high-Victorian seaside served as promenades, they were really a product of the pleasure-steamer, an invention first used in 1812, on the Clyde ⟨177⟩. The shore served at first both for social walks of the kind practised at the spas, and also for casual landings. The steamer, with its delicate paddles and the high capacity and speed which made it so peculiarly economical, demanded a landing place with a safe depth of water and room to discharge and take on passengers in some numbers. The answer was found in the jetty ⟨147⟩, which appeared before 1830 at resorts like Walton-on-the-Naze in Essex, and later at Southport (1849) or Bournemouth, which was still in its infancy in the 1850s. Once the jetty was up, even the imposition of a toll could not deter people from walking along it, and the pleasure-pier was born.

The pier was the seaside resort's most distinctive contribution to architecture, and later, with its complement of pavilions, restaurant, theatre and railway, it was as expressive of the age and society it served as the streets and assembly rooms of Bath were of theirs. Despite its promenade, which was an aristocratic legacy, it was a popular institution, made in an age of easy travel and of pleasures that were cheap not because they were simple but because they appealed to a great many people. By contrast, the early coastal resorts were very simply equipped, and they were able to turn themselves into popular resorts because they were flexibly informal. There was no focus of interest like the spa's pump-room, and if more houses were needed than could be built within sight of the sea, they were laid out in regular streets with as much elaboration as their owners or tenants could pay for. The taste of the age assured an aesthetic competence in what was built ⟨149⟩, but early seaside-architecture has mainly an inconsequential charm; only Brighton and Hove ⟨148⟩ were intensively developed in the period dominated by the Prince Regent.

There was more building in the spas, which like their rivals were stimulated by the wars with Revolutionary and Napoleonic France. While difficulties of foreign travel drove people to British resorts, a great increase in national wealth increased their numbers and demands. There were patrons for all the pleasure resorts, and the spas' special attractions concealed the fact that they were now outmoded, and also that the sea-side's future lay rather with the popular traffic at Margate than in the state rooms of Brighton Pavilion. Queen Victoria's court, for all its virtues, was not a centre of pleasure; the Queen enjoyed seclusion at Balmoral and Osborne, and most fashionable hedonists under her rule travelled abroad, or were content with the régime of London and country-life that Bath had first modified. The likelihood of seeing several dukes swimming for pleasure in British waters vanished with George IV and his brother William IV. What saved and transformed the spas in the later eighteenth century was the appearance of people who wished not to visit them, but to live in them: people whose competence or tastes ran not to a country estate, like a medieval London merchant, but to a house in Bath or a villa in Cheltenham, there to draw a pension, annuity or dividend, and live comfortably in congenial company. The practice grew with the colonial empire and its wars, and retired officers ⟨151⟩, colonial merchants and administrators descended upon both old and new spas.

Bath grew all through the eighteenth century. The new streets were matched by new public buildings ⟨97⟩, including the Guildhall (1766–75) and the Pump Room in 1789–99, but most of the new work was housing. The last decade of the century saw the Bathwick estate developed, while the town also expanded beyond the Royal Crescent ⟨96⟩ and along the London road. Meanwhile Cheltenham, which was only a market town before the first chalybeate spring was discovered in 1716, came to rival Bath. The first pump room was built in 1748, but it was not until the 1780s that royalty patronised the place and the value of land began to rise. A suburb called Montpellier ⟨129⟩ was laid out south of the town, followed at the beginning of the nineteenth century by Pittville to the north, built on land acquired by Joseph Pitt, an M.P. and political manager, when the common fields of the town were enclosed in 1806. In its terraces and crescents, as in its assembly rooms and public buildings, Cheltenham followed the pattern established at Bath, but contemporary taste gave it a special character. Generous planting softened its streets, making the park an element of, rather than a background to, the town. Its architectural style is Regency ⟨150⟩, derived from Georgian through the work of the brothers Adam; elegant still but less formal; sometimes meagre in detail; content with stucco where a more severe age demanded stone. It reflects the taste of a wealthy, fluid society, in which new demands have to be satisfied quickly, but to old and familiar patterns—or apparently old and familiar, for the cast-iron that multiplied balcony rails so conveniently was used also for verandahs, where retired officers might dream themselves back in India, or equally important, where those to whom the army and India were only names might enjoy the dividends, without the hazards, of empire. There were other changes too, for the cult of the Picturesque brought the villa, the country house, into the town, and two conjoined houses could be made to look like one imposing house just as a terrace of houses could be made to look like a palace. Villas and semi-detached villas appeared beside the terraced houses, unwitting but ominous assailants of the urbanity so lately established at Bath.

Cheltenham remained popular through George IV's reign; it was rivalled in the 1820s by Leamington, and then by Harrogate and Droitwich, but like Bath maintained its own following. There was still a demand for spas as health resorts or for such dignified recreation as Mr. Dombey was induced to take at Leamington in the 1840s, but their chief characteristic in the nineteenth century was that people retired to live in them as readily as they visited them. The retired were also a feature of the seaside towns, but not their principal feature: after the Napoleonic wars Douglas in the Isle of Man was favoured by half-pay officers because the living was cheap, but the steamer traffic from the Mersey eventually swamped the veterans ⟨181⟩, just as Cockneys swamped the Margate stockbrokers. Significant as these places were economically and socially, however, they saw no architectural innovation; for that we have to turn again to London, where John Nash, on the eve of the chaotic changes of the Victorian age, produced one of the most brilliant schemes in the history of British towns.

Nash was already a practised exponent of the Picturesque when in 1811 he was chosen to lay out Marylebone Park for the Crown as an aristocratic housing estate ⟨155⟩. His appointment was apparently engineered by his patron the Prince Regent, who lent his title to the park and to the new street cut through the West End to connect the estate with Westminster. Nash's first plan envisaged some fifty villas and a monumental circus in the park, with great terraces of houses on three sides, and a second circus to carry Regent Street across the Marylebone Road. The Regent's Canal was intended both to beautify the park and to supply a market set in a grid of subsidiary streets to the east, where there was also a large barracks. Time and the Treasury eroded the plan and when the first terrace—Cornwall Terrace—was begun in 1820, the central circus had been abandoned, and only one half of the other built, the street now called Park Crescent ⟨153⟩. The canal ⟨156⟩ was made to skirt the park instead of wandering through it, but when a branch ran south to the basin behind Chester and Cumberland Terraces Nash set up a little garden suburb on its banks— Park Village West and Park Village East—in modest compensation for the villas lost to the park. Meanwhile the plan for Regent Street had also been modified in a very happy manner. Nash was too intelligent to force his street across London in a straight line, and accepted an indirect course from the beginning. In this way demolitions were mainly confined to cheap property on the edge of Soho, without carrying the street too far from the fashionable streets and squares to the west. By the time that the New Street Bill went before Parliament the course of Regent Street was determined, but Nash probably still hoped to impose a regular style upon its buildings. If so, he soon accepted commercial necessity as sensibly as he had in planning the course, and by brilliant improvisations satisfied individual owners in a style that was homogeneous because it was his own. In one place where uniformity was essential he took up the leases himself, and built the Quadrant, carrying the street west and north from Piccadilly Circus in an elegant curve ⟨152⟩.

London has treated Nash's work shabbily ⟨199⟩, but his schemes are still full of interest. His real genius lay in town-planning rather than in design: shrewdness was enriched by an almost theatrical sense of fitness. The great plan was impaired by two accidents: Regent's Park was deprived of all but a handful of its villas, giving their carefully engineered setting a meagre, unfinished look, and the Prince Regent's final rejection of Carlton House, which was demolished, not only weakened the southern end of Regent Street, but presented Nash with a commission to make a palace of Buckingham House, which was beyond his real powers. Yet while George IV's palace ⟨158⟩ rose and fell about his ears, Nash laid out Trafalgar Square, and planned a new arterial road to Bloomsbury that was much later recognised as a necessity. His architectural detail was criticised by his contemporaries and reprobated by the Victorians, but until its devastation in the 1920s Regent Street was recognised as the most handsome street in London, and it is still, as Nash intended it to be, one of the most heavily used.

The comprehensive planning round the park also deserves respect. The graded houses east of Albany Street, which decline so blatantly from the grandiose standards of the terraces, were designed for a whole society, a feature often regarded as a lively innovation in twentieth-century planning. The estate was not just a grid of streets, but a little town with houses for workmen and shopkeepers, and its own garden suburb—the Park Villages. Cumberland Market, to which the Hay Market was removed from Piccadilly in 1830, was joined by its canal-wharf to what was then the most up-to-date system of transport in the world. The park itself ingeniously developed the commonplaces of the day, offering the villa-owner the illusion of living in landscaped private grounds, and the terrace-dweller, at least as he approached his front door, the joys of an emparked mansion. It combined the functions of the urban square and the open suburb on a site that was economical of land, in view of open country, and yet had ready access to St. James's, an amenity that would not appeal least to those who had no occasion to go there.

Nash's work stands alone; there had not been many opportunities for planning on this scale before his day, and in the later nineteenth century neither patrons nor architects seized their chances as effectively as the Prince Regent and his master-builder. The New Town at Edinburgh was occupied largely by people of substantial means, who abandoned their tenements in the old town to the less fortunate, and until Victoria's reign it remained something between an aristocratic suburb and a town specialised in the way that eighteenth-century Bath was specialised. In London the market and the streets of cheaper houses that the Earl of Southampton had attached to Bloomsbury Square had been widely imitated as the great estates were built up. Modern Bloomsbury was growing while Nash developed Regent's Park; the Russells' chief architect was James Burton,

THE TOWN

Decimus Burton's father, who developed St. Leonard's-on-Sea. His work has fared better than Nash's, but it is more conventional and includes nothing to compare with Regent Street. After Blackfriars Bridge was built in 1756 George Dance junior laid out a skeleton of roads round St. George's Circus, which governed the development of south London into the early nineteenth century. The plan, which owed something to French models, was sponsored by the City, but the roads were built up only slowly.

Outside London almost everything was left to the speculator, often with quite happy results, as at Clifton, where serious building began in the middle of the eighteenth century in an attempt to expand Hotwells, Bristol's own spa. The spa was only moderately successful, but in the 1790s there was a brisk demand for good suburban housing. A slump during the wars ruined many of the speculators, but work began again in the early nineteenth century and terraces and crescents were still rising in the 1840s. The result is one of the most handsome suburbs in the country, but its plan has an improvised air ⟨143⟩.

Before building in brick and stone was general the fires that periodically scoured both large and small towns ⟨84⟩ offered some opportunities to improve streets, markets and the like, although the ordinary demands of trade prevented very elaborate innovations. All Saints' church in Northampton is a handsome memorial of the great fire there in 1675, and Holt in Norfolk is still living on the aesthetic capital raised after a disastrous fire in 1708. Perhaps the best-known rebuilding of this kind was at Blandford Forum, Dorset ⟨86⟩, where in 1731 a "dreadful fire" consumed most of what had not been burned in an earlier conflagration in 1713. The poor were housed in a temporary barracks, like that on Moorfields in 1666, and money raised on a "brief" under the Great Seal, which authorised a national collection in churches, a common way of recruiting funds after a disaster. There was plenty of work for builders, including some from outside the town, but one family, the brothers Bastard, dominated the rebuilding, and left their mark, still happily to be seen, on church, town hall, and "several other public & private edifices". Such emergencies apart, homogeneous building was possible only when towns were deliberately created. Stourport grew where the Staffordshire and Worcestershire Canal joined the Stour and the Severn, but individual promoters usually worked to a smaller scale. Mistley Thorn in Essex was fashioned by its squires, the Rigbys, first as a little port and then, in the 1770s, as a spa. Robert Adam's design for a salt-water bath came to nothing, but the towers that he added to the church are still standing, and the port's amenities include a green and a fountain. Tremadoc ⟨132⟩ on Cardigan Bay had even more solicitous attention. It was founded on land reclaimed at the mouth of the Glaslyn in 1800 and given a broad town-square, a market-hall and a theatre.

Tremadoc theatre now does mild penance as a chapel, but even if it be regarded as a whim of its founder, its presence in so modest a settlement is interesting. The gap between town and country life widened in the eighteenth century, even before mechanical industry tore them apart, and the theatre was only one of the excitements that spread from London into the provincial towns ⟨99, 100⟩. A building did not always imply a resident company. Great Yarmouth had occasional plays in hired rooms until a theatre was built in 1778, but the theatre was used only in the summer by a company of Norwich players, winter performances "having been found by former experience not to answer". Coffee-houses, reading and assembly rooms also spread widely during the eighteenth century, not only in the spas, but also in county and market towns. The Thames-side pleasure-gardens at Vauxhall ⟨103⟩ and Ranelagh, where for a shilling one might hear "the sweet song of numbers of nightingales, in concert with the best band of musick in England", were imitated or invoked in provincial arbours and bowling greens, while the capital's intellectual pleasures were often more evenly matched in local societies where clergymen, lawyers and merchants talked as learnedly and well as their more famous contemporaries did in London. The Quarter Sessions brought the gentry to the county towns, just as Parliament brought them to Westminster, so that a provincial society that was still self-sufficient and strong was constantly informed of metropolitan tastes and interests. Local newspapers, which began in the eighteenth century with weeklies like the *Exeter Flying Post* and the *Worcester Journal*, long depended on London for their news.

In England the provincial towns were wealthier in the eighteenth century than they had ever been, and some, like Norwich, enjoyed a standing that they could not maintain in the face of later changes. When the great French wars began they were better built, and often better places to live in, than ever before. Municipalities had always tried to keep their streets seemly, but the most effective work was done by local commissioners appointed under an Act of Parliament, and by the eighteenth century many corporate towns, and some places like Manchester that were not incorporated, had bodies able to levy rates for what the age called Improvements. Streets were paved—that is, metalled, although there might also be sidewalks for pedestrians—cleared, widened and lighted. Until gas-lighting spread in the early nineteenth century—the first London company was licensed in 1808—the lamps burned whale oil, but they were generally an improvement upon casual enterprise by individuals. Mechanical industry still played little part in these changes; it made some mark on the Tyne coal-field, and in the West Midlands, but Shropshire, where the first great advances in ironworking were made and where iron was first applied to buildings on a large scale—at Ironbridge and Shrewsbury—is not primarily an industrial county today. Except in Scotland and London the poorest living-conditions in the towns were probably no worse than in the countryside. The old streets of Edinburgh were so filthy that even Londoners commented upon them; but it was the flats, which concentrated the population, rather than a special indifference to squalor, that made the walled town so fearful.

Meanwhile, conditions were bad enough, and though there was more polite society up and down the country, the impolite still outweighed it. Poverty and disease were entrenched, and often the only bond that joined the privileged and the destitute was a taste for vicious and degrading pleasures. Cock-fighting ⟨116, 117⟩ was a national sport, and so was bull-baiting, which was fostered for centuries by municipal regulations, ostensibly to improve the meat. The London journeymen took their holidays on the eight hanging-days at Tyburn, affirming the capital's pride and interest in its most popular institution. There were some humanitarian gains during the eighteenth century, but the strongest reforming impulse came late, when the national temper was particularly averse to change. The flood of cheap gin was stayed by legislation in the 1750s, but heavy drinking persisted, and the Gordon Riots showed what the London mob could do with a little encouragement. The really poor were beyond the consciousness of the rest of society, while their numbers defeated the efforts of individual philanthropists. The meetings conducted by John Wesley and other Methodist preachers ⟨87⟩ went some way toward solving the problem, but the Methodists were likely to be heeded only by those who were free from evils more immediately pressing than that of damnation. On the other hand the new sect was an active one, and the frenzied energy that Wesley's critics found so distasteful gave it great force. The Quaker John Howard, the prison reformer, worked to relieve misery by administrative improvements of a simple but effective kind. This approach was matched by Jeremy Bentham, from whose enquiries into the principles of jurisprudence Utilitarianism sprang, and whose philosophy underlay the great social reforms of the nineteenth century, while the Church of England's social conscience was stimulated by the Evangelical movement, of which the earliest fruit was the agitation against the slave-trade and slavery, led by William Wilberforce.

These movements were opposed by a strong conservatism that dealt evenly with them all, and that is particularly well illustrated by the state of the towns. The revolution that dispossessed James II in 1688 was secured by a parliamentary settlement that manifestly worked, and that served the interests of the great landowners and their Church in a thoroughly satisfactory way. The ruling political principle was therefore to preserve all existing institutions unchanged, and to ignore anything that the original settlement had not envisaged. The towns fell into both categories: those that were incorporate were inviolable; those that were not had to remain unprivileged. It was unfortunate that the second class contained many vigorous and wealthy communities, with Manchester and Birmingham at their head, while the first included places that it would be flattery to call moribund—such as Dunwich ⟨159⟩ and Old Sarum—but to meddle with either would have set a precedent for change that might imperil the whole constitution.

What was particularly at issue was the right to return Members of Parliament, a privilege that by the eighteenth century seemed to be as arbitrarily distributed among the towns as were votes among their inhabitants. No towns had been enfranchised since 1667, and those with seats represented the casual accumulation of four centuries, in which places like Liverpool, that had come to justify their old privileges, were outnumbered by those like Newtown, Isle of Wight, that had not. The franchise varied widely from town to town, sometimes confined to the council, and sometimes, as at Preston, spread more liberally among the householders than it was after the Reform Act of 1832. The Scottish burghs had a particularly small electorate as groups of them shared Members, and even Edinburgh's Member was returned by some thirty votes. Besides boroughs like Gatton, where custom had made the nomination part of the landlord's estate, there were many where the return was comfortably predictable. Harwich had a self-appointing corporation of thirty-three, which elected the borough's two Members. As the naval dockyard gave the Crown a useful patronage, the M.P.s were returned to support the government of the day, and the complaisant townsmen were rewarded with profitable offices. Where the free burgesses had the vote, the same result might be achieved by simple bribery, as it was at Sudbury, but with a large electorate bribery was commonly a last resort. Hereditary freemen were brought to Colchester elections from Yorkshire, and at Ipswich there was understood to be a scale of payments which even covered the expenses of burgesses coming home from abroad. By these means the outcome of the election could be kept in doubt, and the larger boroughs probably maintained a better record of independence than they had in the sixteenth century. Even when their great men were much of a mind, there was usually some local issue that a resolute candidate could play on. The merchants of Liverpool generally supported Sir Robert Walpole's administration, but Sir Thomas Bootle managed to hold one of the borough's two seats from 1727 to 1734, by championing the cause of the free burgesses at large against the town council.

One of the council's actions that Bootle challenged was the admission of new free burgesses to sway elections, a practice easier to deplore than to stop. In the first half of the eighteenth century Carlisle was divided by the rivalry between the gilds—long-lived, as in the Scottish burghs—and the corporation, both parties claiming the right to admit burgesses, and both trying to please the neighbouring families which provided candidates and funds. In 1759 the weakened corporation was constrained to admit Sir James Lowther, later first Earl of Lonsdale, who improved the town's finances and administration, but packed the corporation at the same time. In 1784 he ordered the admission of nearly 1,200 freemen, 500 of whom were colliers from his own estates. The scheme was spoiled by the House of Commons, where Members were always surprised and indignant to discover how elections were conducted; the Lowther candidate was debarred, and after the next election freedom was limited to gildsmen again. Lord Lonsdale therefore had to share the borough with a rival family, the Howards, and pay for his votes like other men. A more secure compromise was reached at Appleby between the Tuftons and the Lowthers, but there the votes attached not to the burgesses but to burgage tenements, some of which had long reverted to grass. After a particularly bitter contest in 1754 the election was annulled, and as the two families had bought every tenement with a vacant title they agreed in future to nominate a candidate each ⟨109⟩.

As William Pitt and Earl Grey were among the distinguished Members returned under this arrangement, Appleby fared better than some towns with a freer choice, and in all but the most decayed boroughs the forms of election had to be maintained, so the candidates at least learned something of public opinion ⟨108, 110⟩. The mob might be voteless, but it could voice opinions and influence votes, and in the hands of competent managers in the 1820s it took an important part in the agitation for parliamentary reform. That reform might have come much sooner if it had not been for the wars with France. The violence of the French Revolution discredited the British reformers who had sympathised with its early stages, and still more those who professed democratic and republican beliefs, while the revolutionary and Napoleonic wars identified political reaction with patriotism. At the same time the war stimulated the country's economy, increasing the size and wealth of the unrepresented industrial towns, and posing social problems of an entirely new kind.

The unreformed municipal corporations were richly disgraceful, and on the whole worked less well than the Parliament that sheltered them. They were open only to professed Anglicans, and so excluded substantial sections of the population—such as the Bristol Quakers, or the Baptist and Congregational descendants of the East Anglican Puritans. Beyond this, power usually lay with the self-appointing town councils, while the free burgesses at large contented themselves with common-grazing and doles. In Scotland burgesses still had the remnants of their trading monopoly, but

SOCIAL AND POLITICAL ABUSES

used them rather to vex or blackmail than to exclude unfree traders, and in the larger towns, as generally in England, the old restrictions were forgotten. The freeman's residual privileges were not very striking, but they mattered disproportionately to poor men, and the councils could usually make the small effort needed to keep their burgesses quiet. There were not many towns like Liverpool, where the general assembly of burgesses appointed the mayor and so to some extent controlled the council, nor were there many councils that could claim, as Liverpool's could, that they spent the corporate funds honestly. Some Scottish reformers tried to force councils to publish accounts, but their opponents sheltered behind English law if Scottish law failed them, which was not very often. By the 1830s the cause of municipal reform was obviously subordinate to that of parliamentary reform, although as late as 1832 the burgesses of Newcastle-under-Lyme regained, by judgment in King's Bench, the right to elect their mayor, long usurped by the closed council.

Before this victory those burgesses had taken to electing a mock-mayor each year in ribald defiance of the council ⟨163⟩, and the habit survived after the town's government was reformed. There were also mock-corporations; some of them harmless sodalities, like the mock-corporation of Sefton, where Liverpool businessmen dined and attended church in state, but others political. One at Walton-le-Dale, near Preston, began as a Jacobite society, and so apparently did the "Ancient Corporation of Cheadle", which, before it petered out, inspired the more innocent Venison Feast at Hanley. Whatever their objects, all these clubs informed public eating and drinking with a sense of purpose, and in that they were no more frivolous than the bodies that they satirised. A large proportion of all town funds was spent on food and drink: wine—"good wine, and plenty of it", as a Cambridge alderman complacently remarked—when the corporators were few and the politics cosy, beer where the freemen were many and ravening. Even today the ancient plate of the municipal corporations abounds in drinking-vessels, despite the reformers' virtuous purges. It may well be that the income in many boroughs would not have sufficed for any more useful works, though it might have been more tactfully spent. Extravagance in building was certainly not a municipal vice; Liverpool's Town Hall ⟨121⟩ and Doncaster's Mansion House were as exceptional as Liverpool's honest corporation, although some of the smaller boroughs found means to house their corporations decently.

The corporations moved the unprivileged towns to contempt rather than envy. By the late eighteenth century Birmingham was one of the largest and wealthiest provincial towns and in the first census, in 1801, ranked third, after Manchester and Liverpool, with more than 70,000 inhabitants; but in law it was only a manor, while East and West Looe were incorporate boroughs. There was an attempt to secure a charter for Birmingham in 1716, but this arose from a local struggle for power in the manorial court, and failed; later in the century no one could entertain so revolutionary a proposal. An Improvement Act of 1769 established a commission to maintain and light the streets, and another four years later empowered the commissioners to buy property to make improvements, and to police the streets at night. Their authority was further extended by later Acts, but it was not until 1824 that they obtained the right to the market tolls or until 1828 that they were empowered to build a market house and a town hall for their meetings. Meanwhile Birmingham was as well governed as any other town, and much better than most, while its society was less artificially constrained than it would have been by a chartered constitution. The Nonconformists who were so important commercially were also prominent in the town's public life. The celebrated Lunar Society, which was founded before the improvement commissioners lit the streets, and so met on nights of the full moon for convenience and safety, brought Dissenters and Anglicans together in the most distinguished assembly of its kind in the country: a philosophical society where enquiry ranged as widely over human knowledge as did Birmingham's industries over human achievements. Boulton and Watt's great Soho foundry beside the Birmingham canal was as portentous as Joseph Priestley's scientific experiments, for the engineers were fashioning a new society, just as the Unitarian minister was extending not only knowledge but also the technique of empirical enquiry.

Priestley's researches were ruined when a mob sacked his house in 1791, in one massive demonstration against natural science, philosophy and liberal politics. The Soho works escaped reprobation, though by implication they were no less revolutionary than Dr. Priestley's thought. It was ironical that a town in which mechanical industry and speculative enquiry were so advanced could not protect its inhabitants against mob violence, but the magistrates and the watch were helpless, and what began as a demonstration against an unpopular political dinner turned into a three-day riot, in which chapels and houses, belonging principally to the Unitarians, were sacked and burned. The pillage put democratic philosophy to a severe test, but the town's helplessness only emphasised the absurdity of condemning a prosperous and elaborate community to the legal status of a village. That anomaly had been mitigated a little when a Court of Requests was established in 1752 for minor civil cases, and by the Improvement Commission and the existence of a Board of Guardians for the parish of Birmingham; but these were only palliatives, and less than the Birmingham of the Lunar Society or of the splendid productions of John Baskerville's printing house could be said to deserve. There were similar absurdities elsewhere: Manchester had an active manorial court beside its improvement commissioners; the commissioners maintained a night watch, but by day the merchant-princes and their counting-houses lay under the eye of a manorial constable. Among the holiday resorts, anciently incorporated towns like Bath and Scarborough were exceptional; their government could be altered by revising their charters and within the limitation of public policy could keep pace with economic change. Brighton and Cheltenham had to wait for the reform of Parliament before they could be recognised as towns in the sense that Winchelsea was a town, and they remained until then under the general supervision of county magistrates.

The revolutionary and Napoleonic wars prolonged this state of affairs. When the wars' wasteful demands gave way to the uncertainties of peace, the government thought more of maintaining order than of redressing public grievances, and the demands for reform lately stigmatised as treasonable were now denounced as subversive. Industries were depressed and their workers unemployed, while farmers demanded protection against the foreign foodstuffs that threatened to lower the prices which the war had kept so comfortably high. The problem of governing the new towns was therefore reinforced by the problem of feeding them, and the solutions looked very ominous. The manufacturing towns showed an alarming interest in cheap food as early as 1791, when the Corn Laws were under discussion. When Parliament was reformed it might be very difficult for it to resist even the most extravagant demands of the industrialists and their men; or so it seemed to those who made the common mistake of supposing that all who called for reform had the same reform in mind. The apprehensive Tories turned to a policy of repression, provoked partly by a reform meeting in 1816 at Spa Fields in Clerkenwell which became riotous. The crisis passed, as trade mended a little, and then was renewed in 1819, when a peaceful meeting at St. Peter's Fields, Manchester, was dispersed by a troop of yeomanry, upon an unnecessary panic by the local magistrates ⟨161⟩. Eleven people were killed and several hundreds injured in the interests of domestic concord. The Government congratulated the magistrates upon their resolution and manly bearing, but public opinion condemned the action, under the ignominious name of Peterloo. Popular protests were answered by the Six Acts, designed to curb public meetings and restrict the Press.

This alarm was followed by another period of quiet; the agitation for reform was freed from its overtones of violence, and more enlightened governments passed a series of liberal measures. Peel at the Home Office transformed the criminal code, abolishing the death penalty for hundreds of offences, and in 1829 created the Metropolitan Police Force, one of the most far-reaching innovations of the century. The Corporation and Test Acts were repealed in 1828, removing the formal restrictions upon Dissenters in public life, which had been mitigated for some time by annual Acts of indemnity; the Combination Acts, which forbade the association of workmen and—less rigidly—of employers, were abandoned, although new restraints were put upon trade unions. The Corn Laws were also modified by a sliding scale of duties, and the Tory reforms closed in 1829 with the passage of the Catholic Emancipation Bill, which strained loyalties even more severely than did questions of protection and free trade, and split the cabinet and party. When in 1830 the question of parliamentary reform was re-opened, the Tories were in no state to adjust themselves to the idea. A Whig government came in, and submitted the first Reform Bill to the Commons in March 1831.

The Reform Act was not passed by the Lords until May 1832. When the first Bill was rejected a general election gave the government an effective majority, to the accompaniment of illuminations and thank-offerings in the great industrial towns. The Lords' rejection of the second Bill in October provoked much stronger demonstrations, and while muffled bells tolled in Birmingham, there were riots in Derby and Nottingham ⟨162⟩. At Bristol the arrival of the Recorder, who was known to have opposed both Bills, provoked a riot that went on for three days, wrecking the Mansion House and burning the chapter-house of the cathedral. The danger was appreciated by conservatives and radicals alike. Those peers who were unconvinced were borne down by the King's undertaking to pack the House of Lords, and the third Bill passed, with separate acts for Scotland and Ireland.

The Act disfranchised 56 boroughs in England; Weymouth lost two of its four seats, and another 30 boroughs lost one of two. Cornwall's 44 members dwindled to 13, while 22 new boroughs, including Manchester and Birmingham, were given two members each, and another 20, including Cheltenham and Merthyr Tydfil, received one. Five of the new boroughs were in greater London, although even so the population of Middlesex was still under-represented. The old franchises were swept away and a vote given to the resident owners or occupiers of property worth £10 a year. The same franchise obtained in the Scottish burghs, which had their total representation increased from 15 to 23. The new votes went mainly to the middle classes, although where rents were high, as they were in London, many more working men came on to the register than in towns like Leeds, where the average working-class rent was well below £10. In some boroughs, and notably in Preston and Westminster ⟨110⟩, the electorate was actually reduced.

The more astute reformers were neither surprised nor disappointed by this result. It was enough that the franchise was widened, and the new towns represented; any change was better than none, and an earnest that more would follow. The middle classes who predominated in the new electorate had broken very few windows and were unlikely to break any now that they had the vote, but they were critical of the old order and confident that they could improve upon it. The municipal corporations could not hope to escape, and commissioners were appointed at once to enquire into their affairs. The commission sat from 1833 to 1835, and in that year the Municipal Reform Act dissolved the corporations of nearly two hundred boroughs and replaced them by councils elected by the ratepayers. The Act did not affect some small boroughs, like Wootton Bassett, and did nothing for the towns that were still not incorporated; it rationalised the government of the places that were now recognisably urban but archaically managed, and brought their property and revenue under some degree of popular control. There were still some anomalies, and nine Scottish boroughs which had fewer £10 ratepayers than councillors were allowed to keep their old corporations, but the commissioners, with all their eagerness to condemn the old system, did not have to exert themselves to find evidence against it. The unregenerate corporations gave willing battle; they raised a common fund, to which Liverpool declined to contribute, and obstructed the commissioners' enquiries to the limit of the law. In a strong field, the town clerk of Leicester ⟨165⟩ was probably the least amenable of the English municipal officers, and he rounded off a very able resistance by securing compensation for loss of his employment and expectations.

The new corporations made no sensational use of their powers. In general they felt bound to dissociate themselves from their scandalous predecessors, and this could best be done by austere and unobtrusive living. A good deal of plate and regalia was sold ⟨164⟩ or locked away, and municipal ceremony was eyed with suspicion. The Great Exhibition of 1851 reawakened some interest in mayoral robes and regalia, but many towns were reluctant to spend money on them until quite late in the century. Large issues excited the same caution; the few towns that had been well governed in the past could spend their money more confidently than those where honesty was a new and inhibiting intruder in public affairs. The unincorporated towns shared this problem. The Government was willing to consider applications for charters, but shrank from framing a general Act to incorporate. The issue was therefore debated separately in each town and excited various local objections. The Tories in Manchester and Birmingham suspected that the new governing bodies would not be even Whig, but Radical or worse, and argued that the existing commissioners managed affairs well enough, and that a borough council would cost more. The Manchester Radicals criticised the improvement commissioners on the grounds that they were not subject to popular control, but knew well enough that the municipal franchise would be no more widely distributed than the parliamentary vote. Both Birmingham and Manchester received charters in 1838, after a

THE TOWN

bitter struggle inside the towns; both places elected councils which were immediately hamstrung by a dispute over powers, and were unable to act effectively until their charters were tested at law in the 1840s.

One reason for this was a new threat of public violence, which unnerved the Government and embarrassed the moderate reformers. The popular enthusiasm stirred by the great agitation before 1832 was not satisfied by the Reform Act, and a new and uncompromisingly democratic movement arose, strengthened and embittered by the middle-class triumph. In 1838 this movement produced the People's Charter, which gave it the name Chartist, and demanded a number of outrageous reforms including manhood suffrage and a secret ballot. All its demands have since been met, except those for annual Parliaments and equal electoral districts, but the programme excited many different hopes of fulfilment in its champions' minds. Some Chartists were committed to socialism of the kind practised by Robert Owen, the Scottish philanthropist, who spent his manufacturing fortune on model communities in Britain and America; some saw parliamentary democracy as an end in itself; some thought of educating and persuading their opponents; others thought of revolution. Support for the movement varied from year to year: a depression in the later 1830s that brought the full rigour of the 1834 Poor Law into the manufacturing districts made many converts to Chartism; so did a financial crisis in the 1840s. It was unlucky that the Birmingham Political Union first suggested a national petition in support of the charter as the depression deepened, and so touched off an agitation far beyond its control. There were serious riots in Birmingham and a dismal little rising in Monmouthshire in 1839 ⟨171⟩, which raised a quite unjustifiable fear that the radical sympathies of the manufacturing towns would prevent them from maintaining an effective police force if they were given the power to do so ⟨170⟩.

When the charter was agitated again in 1848, the new municipalities had proved themselves, and so had their police. The government took military precautions, but Chartism was a spent force, and the prosperity of the mid-century finally swamped it. The movement was also weakened in the 1840s by the agitation against the Corn Laws of 1815. This united many interests in the manufacturing districts by presenting a simple issue in forceful terms: were the old claims of the countryside to outweigh the new towns' demands for cheap and abundant food? Well-conducted meetings publicised the advantages of free trade, and the Anti-Corn Law League benefited greatly by exploiting the Penny Post, the invention of Rowland Hill, a Birmingham man. The repeal of the Corn Laws in 1846 was only the symbolic climax of the movement toward free trade which had begun with Peel's ministry in 1841, but it marked the supremacy of Britain's industrial economy, and of the towns that could no longer be fed from the country's won resources. The real benefits of free trade were not felt until after the crisis of 1848, like the effects of some other changes in this decade. The Mines and Factory Acts of 1842 and 1844 improved on legislation of the 1830s, but took time to ameliorate working conditions. The new Poor Law, with its avowed object of making the workhouse a man's last and least acceptable resort in distress, bore harshly on the poor, causing particular misery in the north, where it was applied to the unemployed in manufacturing districts. It also, however, set up a centralised administration that pre-figured all the successful reforms of later decades, and, under Edwin Chadwick's tireless urging, the Poor Law Commission began some very necessary enquiries into the causes of poverty and sickness. Jeremy Bentham died in 1832, but Chadwick was his enthusiastic disciple, and if the Poor Law exemplified the shortcomings of Utilitarianism in its harshly impersonal rigour, it also showed its strength in deploying the State's new resources to solve new problems.

It would have been better if the Poor Law Commissioners had begun their enquiries before their Act was enforced. Knowledge was needed very urgently if society was to face its responsibilities, and the towns in particular were changing in an astonishing way. The decennial census, begun in 1801, revealed an extraordinary growth. The population of some towns, notably Manchester, Salford and Liverpool, increased by more than 40 per cent in successive decades. Glasgow expanded by more than 30 per cent every ten years from 1801 to 1841, when the city had more than a quarter of a million inhabitants. In the same period London's population grew from 864,845 to 1,873,676, and five towns in England and two in Scotland —Glasgow and Edinburgh—passed the 100,000 mark, previously exceeded only by London. Ten others acquired a population of more than 50,000; in 1801 only the five largest English towns had come into this category—by 1881 it included nearly fifty. In all this amazing change there was one new factor, the railway, and that was in its infancy in 1841; for the rest there was only an unparalleled concentration of human beings, in towns that were still towns as the eighteenth century knew them.

The railways began as industrial equipment, tubs on tracks, pushed by men or pulled by horses. They developed in the coal-mining districts, particularly on Tyneside, as the canals spread through the countryside, and by the end of the eighteenth century were often mechanised by stationary winding-engines. The Liverpool & Manchester Railway, which was the first to use locomotives for all its trains, goods and passenger, was opened in 1830. The Great Western, largely a Bristol project, launched appropriately by the Merchant Venturers of Bristol and other interests in that city, was authorised by Act of Parliament in 1835, and the first section of the line was opened in 1838. The London & Birmingham Railway, later the London & North Western, opened its line from Euston to Boxmoor, Herts., in 1837, and by then there was also a suburban line, the London & Greenwich. This railway introduced the long viaduct with arches designed to be occupied by houses or workshops, an idea quite Benthamite in its disregard for sensibility, and popular with railway architects for many decades.

The Greenwich line, which was opened in 1836, issued what were probably the first railway season tickets, and carried some 30,000 passengers a week; but like the other early lines it was chiefly important for what it implied. There was still a good deal of open country on the south bank of the River Thames, and the inhabitable viaduct was an ingenious experiment rather than a necessity. The Euston line destroyed some streets of houses, but not on the scale of the North London Railway's works in the 1860s, or other lines threaded round and through the City itself ⟨196⟩.

Gratifying as the passenger traffic was, the railways' chief function was still industrial: they enabled goods to be brought into the towns cheaply and plentifully. They also enabled those who could afford to do so to move quickly between towns, but hardly as yet inside towns, and they held out little immediate hope of cheap travel. That followed in the 1840s, with parliamentary trains, formidable stoppers with a statutory low fare. Meanwhile those townsmen who had no carriage of their own and disdained to walk had to turn to hackneys, which were improved in the 1830s in competition with the Hansom Patent Safety cab, or to George Shillibeer's omnibuses, introduced in 1829, and travel expensively through the streets at pre-railway speeds, though not much more slowly than modern motor cars ⟨227⟩. The urban tramway did not appear until the late 1850s, when an American brought it first to Birkenhead and then to London (1861), but it was strongly opposed in London where the trams were a nuisance to heavy traffic, and by 1868 when the tramways began to spread again the revolutionary underground railway had begun.

In the 1830s the railways with their promise of cheaper supplies only intensified the towns' problems. There had always been slums, and they were usually the oldest quarters of the town, where rents were low and properties neglected, or suburban fringes occupied by squatters. The growth of industry modified this rule in places; the docks east of London attracted many thousands of people from 1800 onward, turning villages like West Ham into working-class towns, and the Glamorgan ironworks swamped Merthyr Tydfil with houses. Life in these places was rough, but not intolerably so by contemporary standards, and while there was work at least their inhabitants could and did look after themselves. The initiative that turned places like Merthyr Tydfil into towns, fashioning clubs and societies, was almost entirely spontaneous and local. The most desperate

THE RAILWAYS; SLUMS

conditions were still found in the older towns, where larger populations had greatly increased the demand for labour, but where there was no room for new, cheap housing. The very poor had to live near their work, but could not afford to pay high rents; the more precarious and wretched their employment, the more likely it was to lie near the heart of the town, where the value of land was usually rising and the increase in commercial property was diminishing the space available for housing. The result was overcrowding in old property ⟨189⟩, particularly along railway lines and around stations, where houses spoiled by noise and smoke were divided into tenements: great areas of north London rotted in this way.

Local conditions sometimes sharpened the misery. At Nottingham the freemen were unwilling to allow the borough fields to be enclosed, and so increased the competition for land inside the old town. Their own poverty made them the more anxious to keep their grazing rights, and the slum-landlords prospered. By the time that the fields were enclosed and laid out for building under an Act of 1845, Nottingham's slums were among the worst in the country, and the town had to spend nearly a century in destroying them ⟨212⟩. Other towns like Manchester and Liverpool had no special reserves of land to look to; when local landlords did lease their estates for building, the houses were usually cheap and insanitary, and became slums within a generation. Meanwhile cholera, which first came to England from Russia in 1831, killed thousands of people in the towns in successive outbreaks ⟨167, 168⟩. It was a water-borne disease, which spread irresistibly where the pumps on which streets and sometimes whole parishes depended were infected by sewage. Nottingham had piped water in the 1840s, thanks to Thomas Hawksley, the Nottingham engineer who later supplied Liverpool and Sheffield, but other places depended on water-carriers, or on pumps that rose from undrained courts. Until the principle of infection was understood there was not much that could be done about cholera, but the uncertainty resulted in some general reforms and precautions. The successive epidemics, which attracted more attention than equally destructive enteric diseases present all the time, provoked a series of important sanitary measures: temporary Boards of Health in 1832-3, later revived by Chadwick; a Public Health Act in 1848, appointing a central Board of Health; reform of the Board in 1854, and Sanitary Inspectors as municipal officers in 1866.

In 1875 Disraeli's Public Health Act offered to all muncipalities the powers that in the past only the most enterprising had sought, and a Housing Act enabled them to clear and rebuild insanitary areas. Everything still depended upon local energy, but there was a new spirit in municipal politics at the time, and some of the larger towns welcomed their opportunities. Even so, the government might have encouraged and even directed local effort to greater advantage. As late as 1889 it was left to local authorities to enforce notification of certain infectious diseases, and the Act empowering them to do so was not made compulsory until 1900.

The Public Health Act of 1875 was improved by the Housing of the Working Classes Act of 1890, under which the London County Council (established in 1888) did some valuable work ⟨202⟩, but outside London the new powers were only fitfully used, and conditions improved very slowly. The last quarter of the century saw a great extension of municipal water ⟨194, 195⟩ and sewage-works, but there were still many bad houses, and even where enterprising authorities prescribed minimum standards a large gap remained between informed opinion and current practice. In many towns houses were drained—as some still are—into cess-pits that had to be emptied by carts, and where water-closets were installed they were not always properly trapped, and might open directly on to the sewer. Houses were still built too close together; necessary improvements made them more expensive, and builders and their clients had to economise to keep prices down; which commonly meant no bathroom and no garden: only a zinc bath and a yard to hang it in. That was an improvement, but there is more to public health than drainage and sanitation: and as the towns grew larger it became more difficult to escape from their pinched and dismal streets by any route but the public-house door. Parks, recreation grounds and swimming baths ⟨203⟩ were one answer; allotments, which local authorities were first empowered to lease in 1887, were another and the bicycle's popularity later meant that men could rent allotments at a distance, where satisfactory land was cheaper. But these were palliatives, and they had not achieved very much by 1914: indeed, they acknowledged the fact that large towns were disagreeable places to live in, and so pointed to flight, rather than amelioration, as the way to solve the problem. The result was a healthier suburb, rather than a healthier town.

The last British town substantially remodelled on an ancient plan was Newcastle-upon-Tyne, where a very opportune partnership between a local architect, John Dobson, and a discriminating speculator, Richard Grainger, carried the ordinary course of eighteenth-century rebuilding into Victoria's reign ⟨172–175⟩. Supported and encouraged by the Town Clerk, John Clayton, these men transformed the centre of the city, equipping it with houses, shops, and public buildings, all harmoniously combined in one sensitive and intelligent plan. Grainger lost money on some of his later schemes, but the rebuilding was completed after 1854, when a destructive fire in Gateshead spread across the river and burned many of the remaining old houses in lower Newcastle. The high-level bridge over the Tyne, built by Robert Stephenson, brought the railway to Dobson's fine station in a dramatic fashion ⟨175⟩ and Newcastle emerged very enviably from a period that ravaged less fortunate towns. The spread of heavy industry and poor housing on Tyneside has not detracted from Dobson and Grainger's achievements.

No other industrial town enjoyed these advantages, and by the time that Manchester and Birmingham turned to major improvements the debasement of architectural taste and the retrenchment of local interests prevented them from rivalling Newcastle. The best opportunities lay with the new towns, which were not encumbered by an intractable mass of old building, and where an enlightened individual or corporation might control a whole community. This control never matched the ideal plans that were discussed from the 1840s onward, under the influence of Robert Owen's socialism and in reaction to the fearful shortcomings of most of the existing towns. Schemes like James Silk Buckingham's Victoria, a model city with an elaborately balanced economy and an equally elaborate code of morals, failed to recommend themselves to the all-powerful owners of capital; the reality was always less tidy.

The railway companies created several new towns, beside stimulating the growth of old ones. New Swindon was entirely a product of the Great Western, and Wolverton of the London & North Western Railway. Crewe was begun by the Grand Junction Railway, and completed by the London & North Western. At all these places the companies took reasonable care with housing and ordinary amenities, but all fell short of utopian plans. Wolverton was the smallest and simplest, with a church, school and library, the houses neat but plain and raw. Swindon's houses were fairly well built, but meanly laid out, and lost value very quickly. Crewe had a church, town hall and schools by 1861, and was large enough to attract people other than railway workers; but although it had public baths there was no general water supply as late as 1879. That deficiency was shared by towns like Torquay and Tunbridge Wells, as well as Rawtenstall and Stoke-on-Trent, and could be remedied when the science of public health matured. The drab uniformity that marks an unmixed and comparatively poor society was a more serious matter. Sir Titus Salt ⟨193⟩, the Bradford manufacturer who founded Saltaire, was aware of this danger, as well as realising some years in advance of general opinion that a town ought to be drained as well as attractively laid out. He rebuilt his mills on a new site in Airedale, and housed his employees around them in a compact and carefully designed little town ⟨192⟩ containing everything for which they might wish, except public houses. The houses were built in several kinds, including endowed almshouses, and besides Nonconformist churches there was a hospital and dispensary, a well equipped club and institute with a library, and a public park. Salt was probably the most practical idealist of his kind and age, and his conception of the town as a community, united in more than its work, was the best part of his achievement.

THE TOWN

Saltaire was not widely imitated, and its closest parallels appeared later in the century. In 1879 George Cadbury rebuilt his chocolate factory outside Birmingham, and gradually created the model town of Bournville, but he did so not to govern his workers paternally, but to show that attractive and healthy new towns were profitable. As soon as the factory was manned, houses were provided for people not employed there, and Cadbury resigned his personal interest to the Bournville Village Trust, although his firm and family remained benefactors to the town. W. H. Lever's Port Sunlight in Cheshire reverted to the idea of the company town; soap this time instead of cloth, and named after the product. Port Sunlight was more elaborately planned and equipped than Saltaire, and conceived less as a philanthropic venture than as a profit-sharing scheme in which the employer's and the employees' interests are hardly to be distinguished. Like Salt, Lever—later Lord Leverhulme—denied his town a public house, though in time he allowed his employees to over-persuade him, but he supplied this deprivation by schools, baths, theatres and clubs on a scale unmatched by earlier philanthropists. The open streets and gardens of Port Sunlight and Bournville encouraged the Garden City movement, which developed from earlier and vaguer schemes when Ebenezer Howard's *Tomorrow*, later called *Garden Cities of Tomorrow*, was published in 1898.

Saltaire, Bournville and Port Sunlight were small places, well within the control of a determined individual. They also housed seemly industries or were sheltered from noxious ones. The larger towns came to grief for want of similar care, although occasionally there were happy accidents. Birkenhead developed early in the nineteenth century as a detached and wealthy suburb of Liverpool, and when Laird's shipyard appeared there in 1824 the inhabitants exerted themselves to maintain the town's character. They were not overborne until 1844 when the docks were begun, and meanwhile the town was well planned and drained, and had one of the first municipal parks in the country. Londoners had enjoyed the royal parks at least since the seventeenth century, but most towns had open country within easy reach until the early nineteenth century, when many discovered suddenly and too late that they had not. The Aboretum at Derby was presented to the town in 1840, three years before Birkenhead secured an Act of Parliament to buy a park, but both the good fortune and the enterprise were rare. Middlesbrough was less fortunate, for it began as a port for the Stockton & Darlington railway, and was then overwhelmed in the 1850s by the Cleveland iron trade, which almost obliterated the modest pretensions of the company town.

The other northern iron-town, Barrow-in-Furness, had a remarkably similar history, but escaped more lightly. The Furness Railway began a harbour at Barrow in the 1840s, which was greatly stimulated by the haematite workings. The population reached 3,135 in 1861, and 8,176 in 1864, and then after a brief depression leapt to 18,911 in 1871 and to 47,259 in the next decade. Until 1867, when it received a charter, the town had no government beyond the manorial court of Dalton-in-Furness ⟨12⟩ and the railway company, but its growth was foreseen, and under Sir James Ramsden, the company's general manager, its plan at least was drawn on generous lines. Although the houses were mostly left to private speculators, the wide streets ⟨197⟩ and squares gave Barrow a dignified coherence, and provided a better setting for its public and private buildings than most industrial towns enjoyed.

The most favoured communities were the holiday resorts, which reveal as much about Victorian society as do the spas about its predecessors. The taste for sea-bathing had spread so widely by the 1830s that almost all modern resorts have a Regency if not an eighteenth-century history, but the railways favoured some at the expense of others. Beaumaris ⟨149⟩ and Caernarvon were eclipsed by the resorts nearer Liverpool that were opened in the 1850s—Rhyl, Colwyn Bay and Llandudno. Freeston Shore on the Wash gave place to Skegness, which rose at the end of the century under the Great Northern Railway's determined patronage. When the railways began the only resorts with a popular trade were those served by steamers. The spas were apparently holding their own, but the seaside was already competing with them as a place for the retired to live in, and as pensioned officers from the great wars were reinforced by business and professional men the seaside's greater potential won it more and more of the trade. The architectural consequence of this movement was that the new resorts apotheosised the suburb, just as Bath had reflected a very English idea of the town.

As ordinary towns became more disagreeable to live in, more people could afford to live on the outskirts, and the villas and semi-detached villas spawned by the Picturesque movement suited their tastes and needs there very well. So did the current muddle of architectural styles, which expressed the confusions of a society suddenly and even violently enriched. Taste usually comprises both what people like and what they feel they owe themselves, and the Victorian suburb, with its varying patterns of gables and evergreen, its nice balance of privacy and display, spoke faithfully of the assurance and uncertainties of middle-class life. It also reflected an interesting change in working habits, for when they joined their families its householders were removed from their daily work as very few other people were, or ever had been. The residential suburb was itself half-way to a holiday resort, and needed little adaptation to make it one.

The resorts that still illustrate this period best are Torquay and Bournemouth. Torquay was a hamlet transformed by the wars, when Tor Bay was

THE TOWN

a naval anchorage. After the wars the place found itself a resort, and its chief proprietors, the Palks and the Carys, began to develop it. The visitors, who included invalids attracted by the mild winter climate, had to take some pains to get there before the railway was opened in 1848. It was hoped that they would represent "families of the first distinction": a definition that perhaps implies that they were not quite that. The early planning was general: Sir Lawrence Palk laid out roads and provided some public buildings, besides enlarging the Royal Hotel, but he left the housing to speculators, and some of it was poor. At first terraces were preferred, but by the 1860s, when the Mallocks began to lease their estates in Cockington for building, the villa was well established and the town was agreeably open, with winding cliff roads ⟨178⟩ enhanced by private gardens. Torquay was one of the first towns to be mapped by the Ordnance Survey at the local authority's request, so that its services and street improvements could be extended on a regular plan.

Bournemouth began later than Torquay. A Dorset squire, Lewis Tregonwell, built a house at the mouth of the Bourne in 1810, and amused himself by creating a tiny bathing-resort there, but the town really developed in 1835, when Sir George Tapps-Gervis inherited the neighbouring property, and decided to found a full-scale watering-place composed entirely of detached houses. After Tapps-Gervis died in 1842 his trustees called in Decimus Burton, who planned the heart of the town, bridging the Bourne stream at the place now called the Square, and recommending the creation of the Lower Gardens, which are so important a feature of modern Bournemouth. In the 1840s Commercial Road and the roads round it were built as a service area, but the rest of the town continued to grow in a leisurely alternation of tree-lined roads and gardens. An Improvement Commission was appointed in 1856, and the town incorporated by charter in 1890, so the landowners' enterprise gradually gave way to municipal works. As the town prospered the corporation's schemes became more elaborate, extending beyond piers, promenades and gardens to a concert hall and the first permanent municipal orchestra in the country. With the Continent open again to the wealthy, holiday-making remained a middle-class affair for most of the century, although it was constantly modified as both holidays—in the sense of days free from work—and better wages spread among the working class. The better-paid workmen, such as some Lancashire cotton-operatives, were able to travel far and even abroad by the 1850s, but the Chartists called their projected national strike a "National Holiday" quite unselfconsciously, and "holidays with pay" formed no part of the trade unions' programme until average wages met ordinary needs. Cheaper railway travel, however, made holidays away from home increasingly popular, and the resorts took in both new visitors and new kinds of visitor. The most important change came when servants disappeared from the family caravan; those who shot grouse in Scotland kept their personal attendants about them, but the average holiday ménage probably did not include even a governess. The hired villa therefore gave way to the boarding house, where a landlady with or without servants of her own catered for her clients as simply or elaborately as they were entitled to expect. As the number of holiday-makers increased, so did the boarding houses, although individually they often grew simpler and smaller at the same time, as the popular holiday returned for good economic reasons to the gregarious traditions of the aristocratic spas.

The resorts grew unevenly. Brighton contrived to become popular without losing all its fashionable appeal, and increased its residential as well as its holiday population. Margate, though smaller, was chiefly a popular resort, its 10,000 inhabitants in 1851 regularly swamped by visitors. Bournemouth and Torquay maintained exclusiveness as long and as far as they could, and their position in the remoter South saved them from heavy invasion. Southend-on-Sea was still a village in the 1860s. The North supported a similar variety of resorts; Scarborough was the largest (12,915) in 1851; much larger than Southport (4,243), which was nearly twice as big as Blackpool. In the 1830s it was feared that "persons of distinction and fashion" were turning from Blackpool to the Lake District or the Continent, but the crowds that, by implication, they shunned were neither very great nor resident crowds until much later. The Lancashire wakes commonly passed in day-trips at first: trips to Derbyshire or the Lakes as well as to the seaside. The week by the sea, with its more elaborate demands on the holiday town and its services, did not begin to inflate Blackpool until the end of the century, when the population rose to 47,346 in 1901, and on to 101,000 in the next thirty years. By that time Blackpool was also a residential town, filling with season-ticket holders from Preston and Manchester, while Southend, which started even later and reached 120,000 in 1931, shows the same process at work around London: the holiday resorts drawing off the surplus population of industrial and commercial towns. Until this movement began none of the northern resorts grew very large, but there were a great many of them; some neat and small like Grange-over-Sands and Arnside, others like Morecambe on the same bay bidding for the popular trade. In Wales, besides the north-coast resorts, Aberystwyth and Tenby ⟨179⟩, both old boroughs, became seaside towns. Queen Victoria helped to make Scotland holiday-ground, but the difficulties of travel kept the tourists to the Highlands comparatively few. The Scottish holiday trade was smaller than England's, but St. Andrews and Aberdeen added sea-bathing to their other amenities, and Aberdeen today is probably unique as an ancient burgh that is simultaneously a sea-port, manufacturing city and seaside town.

THE TOWN

The popular holiday resort, ubiquitous and various, was only one feature of the extraordinary urban society that Britain had created in less than a century. By the 1850s more than half the country's population lived in towns, and although the rural population did not decline for some decades the town's preponderance increased steadily thereafter. Yet it was not until the second half of the century that the crowded towns began to use the technical skills that they commanded in their own service, and to take shape as communities again. Some of the ground was long preparing. The great changes in commerce and industry demanded a literate population, and the response in England was slow: Scotland made much more ingenious use of its resources. In the eighteenth century the Dissenting Academies, in one of which Priestley had taught, supplied some of the deficiencies of the English universities, though on a small scale. The first university outside Oxford and Cambridge with power to grant degrees was founded at Durham in 1832. In 1836 the University of London was established to blanket the animosity between the non-sectarian University College, founded in 1828 with the name of London University, and its Anglican imitator and rival, King's College. The new institution was a scheme rather than a university, and its examinations were open to all, without religious tests or other artificial restrictions. Not only could individual candidates read for degrees wherever they might be, but aspirant colleges could prove themselves by submitting their students for the London examinations. This process, which was immensely important to the future of university education not only in England but in the whole of the British Commonwealth, did not begin until 1851, when the Owens College in Manchester was founded under the will of John Owens, a Manchester merchant, and accepted by the University of London as an affiliated college.

Owens College expressed an idea very characteristic of the nineteenth century: that a great industrial city ought to house a university, not because its own wealth depended on learning, but because it deserved that honour and adornment. The College had some anxious years before it was metamorphosed, through the Victoria University (1880), into the University of Manchester in 1903, but it was widely imitated. By 1880 there were colleges in Leeds, Bristol, Birmingham and Sheffield, and by 1914 the old British universities were supplemented by fourteen new universities and university colleges, including St. David's College at Lampeter, which like Durham was an ecclesiastical foundation, opened in 1827 and empowered to grant bachelors' degrees in 1852.

If none of these was a civic university in the sense in which Edinburgh had once been, there were not many men willing and able, like Josiah Mason of Birmingham and Mark Firth of Sheffield, to bear the cost of making a college, and most new foundations were very glad of municipal support.

EDUCATION: NEW UNIVERSITIES

The institutions from which the Universities of Southampton and Reading grew had to fulfil several functions, housing libraries and museums, in order to command public funds. Nottingham University College began with an anonymous benefaction, offered in 1876, that was conditional upon the Corporation providing a building, and the Corporation paid the college's teachers until 1938. Of the two colleges, now universities, founded between 1914 and 1945, that at Leicester was launched as a war memorial, and so aroused in that town a local interest that earlier schemes had failed to excite. Even since 1945, with new universities an urgent national preoccupation, the University Grants Committee has sanctioned only projects where, as at Brighton, individual efforts have assured a pertinacious local support.

The nineteenth-century colleges were small and grew slowly, because their supply of students was limited until the State provided universal schooling. Even then, secondary education was not made a public charge until 1902, and meanwhile the new universities represented only a national determination to have higher learning in its traditional form. Working Men's Colleges, derived from the People's College in Sheffield founded in 1842, and the older Mechanics' Institutes, so alarming to those who thought of Tom Paine whenever they saw a literate working man, helped, with other technical and professional institutions, to create an informed society. Municipal public libraries, authorised by an Act of 1850, appeared more fitfully, and were sometimes a subject of bitter local debate at the very end of the century: they performed a service that many people wished to leave to private endeavour or philanthropy. Educational policy aroused similar controversy, but existing institutions were quite rapidly adapted, and the old grammar schools generally reduced their classical instruction to make room for modern and even commercial subjects. That was not a concession which everyone welcomed, but one that had to be made. A university, by contrast, implied no concession at all; by transcending merely practical needs it became the test of a city's worth.

The recovery of civic pride after the old corporations were safely buried showed in more than academic competition and a revived interest in plate. Town halls became in England, as they had long been in Scotland ⟨63⟩, buildings designed to command respect by their size and opulence; something true of few places in the eighteenth century ⟨121⟩ and of hardly any before that time. Unlike most other peoples, and especially the Flemings and Italians, the English saw no need for specialised public buildings until the Victorians thrust their strong sense of propriety into architecture as into everything else ⟨182⟩. The new town halls often wasted money and space on display, but they had to be larger than ever before, to house an increasingly busy administration.

The scale of civic works grew as the municipalities tried, belatedly, to match the century's engineering skills against the century's problems. Liverpool led the way with its own Sanitary Act in 1847, under which 5,000 cellars occupied in defiance of the city's by-laws were cleared and demolished in the first year's operations. The corporation went on to pipe water from Rivington Moors in 1857, and in 1880 began the great reservoir at Lake Vyrnwy ⟨195⟩. Glasgow tapped Loch Katrine in 1859, when the supply was turned on by Queen Victoria herself, and under a Street Improvement Act of 1866 built thirty new streets on the site of old properties ⟨189⟩ and widened another twenty-six. The city also built model lodging-houses. Manchester laid out Deansgate under an Act of 1869, but the most famous clearance of this kind was that carried out in Birmingham in 1875-6 under Joseph Chamberlain's mayoralty, when Corporation Street was cut through some of Birmingham's worst slums and into the heart of the city. Birmingham's improvements fell at an unhappy time architecturally, but showed impressively what energetic men could do with a great city's resources.

The demonstration came none too soon, for the whole civic exertion of the 1870s could usefully have been employed thirty years earlier. There had been private efforts as well, but they were ill matched to the problem for reasons easier to understand now than then. The age placed great emphasis on church building, which was felt to be the most useful of all social services. So much so, for example, that in 1865, when Barrow-in-Furness had no hospital and such industrial accidents as might be expected, the Barrow Haematite Steel Company voted £4,000 for a new church and £500 for education and medical services, and in 1878 when the cottage hospital had twenty-five beds and the town 37,000 inhabitants, four churches were consecrated on one day, an event unmatched then in any other town. The century might well choose to be judged on its churches.

Church building posed two problems: the comparatively straightforward one of paying for new churches, and the imperfectly apprehended one of meeting the peculiar needs of large towns. During the Napoleonic War simple arithmetic showed that the population had outgrown its churches. In 1818 the Church Building Society was founded, to make grants both for new buildings and enlargements, while the commissioners appointed under a parliamentary Act of the same year built more than two hundred churches, many of them in London and industrial towns, at a cost of £1,500,000. Even this programme proved inadequate; in 1834 Bishop Blomfield pointed out that ten parishes in east and north-east London had on average one church or chapel for every 19,000 people, and Birmingham two years later was reckoned to have churches for little more than a third of its population. Still more churches were built without closing the gap; Blomfield himself consecrated nearly two hundred, and yet his successor Archibald Tait set out in 1857 to raise £1,000,000 for new foundations.

The energies expended on building were not very well co-ordinated, and many of the new churches were awkwardly imposed upon an antiquated system. Reform of the Anglican dioceses, which like most other reforms then followed the need at a respectful distance, did not begin until the 1830s, when the Ecclesiastical Commissioners recommended a number of boundary changes, and the foundation of new sees at Manchester and Ripon. Until 1843 new parishes could only be established by Act of Parliament, an expensive and elaborate procedure replaced in that year by the simpler device of an Order in Council. But just as the ruling architectural taste produced churches that imitated medieval designs, often without regard to aesthetic or practical fitness, so the force of tradition perpetuated the parish, which had developed in a predominantly rural society, in the inappropriate setting of an industrial city. Records of decayed and abandoned churches suggest that even medieval towns found the parish an inflexible unit; it would have been remarkable if it had proved more adaptable in Victorian Birmingham or Manchester.

The successful town churches ⟨184⟩, with a vigorous social life and popular services, usually run from a collegiate clergy-house, were outnumbered by those that were never full. Congregations were more difficult to raise and keep than churches, and most large towns today have a crop of decaying Gothic monuments to the nineteenth century's brave hopes. When money was available it could not always be spent where it might be thought to do most good. The problem was not peculiar to the Church of England, but affected all denominations in some measure: the districts that needed churches most were not those best able to pay for them; if the money was raised to build a church in a poor neighbourhood the clergy might soon overcome local hostility, but they would always have to struggle with their congregation's poverty. Help from outside was spasmodic at the best; people are more readily moved by what they see than by what they are told, and most people with money were, and are, ill acquainted with want.

The churches' work might be compared with that of some secular charitable organisations. Bodies like the Peabody Trust and the Improved Industrial Dwellings Company did valuable work in building model dwellings for the London poor, but the accommodation that they provided, though ungrateful by later standards, often proved to be too expensive for those who needed it. The trusts had to make a profit, because the temper of the age demanded it, but the effect of that restriction was not very different from a bishop's dilemma, if he were offered money for a suburban church, when one on a disgusting site in some central district would have suited his purposes better. The difficulty was, as always, that the undeserving poor —those wretches whose problems are for any reason incomprehensible— need help more than the deserving, whose problems are by definition soluble and to hand. It was not until William Booth's Christian Mission ⟨190⟩, renamed the Salvation Army in 1878, applied its brash and cheerful pertinacity to work in the slums, that there was a real hope of attracting national attention to them. Even then there were still discoveries to be made, as Charles Booth's *Life and Labour of the People in London* (1891-1903), or Seebohm Rowntree's enquiries in York showed, but efforts of this kind were an essential condition of the governmental action which, however reluctantly it was contemplated, was desperately needed.

Social work at the end of the century, thoroughly publicised and widely discussed, provoked a revulsion from the whole idea of the industrial city, which to some people seemed irredeemably tainted by its price in human misery. The notion was not a new one; Robert Owen and William Morris had each in his time passed the same judgement, and the Garden City movement was stimulated equally by old and new dissatisfactions. Letchworth was established by Ebenezer Howard in 1903, and Welwyn Garden City followed in 1920; they were successful after a slow start, but they failed to inspire the mass movement for which their supporters had hoped. Hampstead Garden Suburb (1909), designed by Raymond Unwin and Edwin Lutyens, embodied the Garden City's architectural principles, which were anticipated by Norman Shaw at Bedford Park in 1876, but these places had no industry, and offered only a more agreeable place to live in than older and less carefully designed suburbs.

It was inevitable that the Garden City should first appeal to a comparatively small group of people, intelligent and prosperous, but without any industrial influence, and then that its superficialities rather than its fundamental principles should gradually become popular. Practically, its chance of succeeding had always been slight, for a radical change of the country's economy would involve an unthinkable waste of capital. A thousand Letchworths could not replace the industrial power of the cities that they renounced, nor could they feed the population that the cities supported. Although interest had to be paid on the errors of the past, there was still a chance of improving the towns. The great works of civic engineering, new means of transport ⟨197⟩, a new interest in town planning, such as showed itself in Cardiff's civic centre at Cathays Park or produced the first Town Planning Act in 1909, all held out the hope of making cities worthy of their name, even if the obstacles were still enormous.

There were signs long before 1914 of profound social changes worked by technical innovations. The revolution in transport standardised the building trade, making Welsh slate and Midland bricks universally available; the results were unhappy while architectural taste was in flux, but might be turned to advantage in the future. When Gordon Selfridge came to London in 1906, fresh from transforming Marshall Field's great store in Chicago,

British retail trade was still based on the personal contract between craftsman and customer, and offered satisfaction in almost direct proportion to the customer's means. The departmental store began to rationalise marketing in the same way that machines had rationalised manufacture, and offered the same benefits: lower prices for higher sales. Entertainment developed in the same way, as football became a spectacle quite different from any game that the watchers might play for themselves. The stadium was not a substitute for the playing field—the street was that, if anything was, and the sooner it was superseded the better—but football and other public shows gave people an exciting sense of community.

These changes pointed the futility of rejecting the new order, but others promised further disruption. The trade unions seemed to threaten revolution in the years immediately before 1914, under the influence of syndicalism, while the political acerbities that beset the Liberal Government of 1906-14, over reform of the House of Lords and the future of Ireland, suggested that the State was seriously weak. There was also the threat of European war. Those who prophesied the imminent dissolution of society, though wrong in detail, were close to the truth, and no one could be certain that they were wrong at all. For the moment what mattered was that society should not fall apart.

The first world war solved that problem; at an unspeakable cost in human life it united the nation again, and directed its economy as never before. Materially it wasted rather than destroyed: German warships shelled Scarborough and Hartlepool in 1914, and there were air raids on London and other towns, but there was nothing to compare with the devastation in Flanders. Inside the country the main impact of the war was felt in the casualty lists; the rest was inconvenient novelty until 1917, when submarine warfare threatened famine. The threat was met by convoys, rationing ⟨207⟩, and a new attention to the land that had almost been forgotten as a source of food; but the generals' demands could be met only with human lives, and that price was paid for another year. The towns endured the blackout and petty restrictions. Carlisle, a great railway junction because it was once a border town, gathered in such numbers of soldiers and munition-workers that its public houses and inns were taken over by the State, which holds them still. Elsewhere the changes worked by the war seemed to be temporary, except for the presence of women in factories, offices and polling-booths, where in 1914 there had been none.

The war imposed such strains on the country that some at least of the public promises made to encourage the national effort had to be honoured, but the peace was as inopportune a time as any for change. The economy, run-down, was slow to gather momentum again, just when public funds were urgently needed, and people were impatient of further controls. One great innovation was the Housing Act of 1919, that both empowered and compelled local authorities to build houses, and offered subsidies for the new council houses and for those raised by private builders. The subsidies were reduced when prices began to rise, but more houses were built than could have been built privately, at a price that tenants could afford, and whatever their aesthetic shortcomings they usually improved on the buildings that they replaced ⟨209⟩. By 1923 more than 205,000 new houses had been built, but large arrears remained. London's East End was swollen by the influx of Jewish refugees from the Continent since the late nineteenth century; Glasgow had slums among which the Gorbals were distinguished only by fame and by rather better-built houses than other districts could show: houses large enough to be fearfully overcrowded, and too well built to fall down. These areas needed urgent attention, and their condition was aggravated by the slump that began at the end of the decade. Slum clearance had hardly begun again in the late 1930s when the war stopped new building.

The depression ⟨211⟩ bore most heavily on the areas least well equipped to withstand it. When mining and iron-working failed in South Wales, or ship-building on the north-east coast, there was no other employment to hand; what seemed to be a complex national economy was suddenly shown to be a simple and local one. Towns like Jarrow and Maryport rotted, and the blight remained on them when the rest of the country began to recover. The government's efforts to help the unemployed were on a smaller scale than the catastrophe, and offered clumsy palliatives more readily than cures. The towns that had grown round a single heavy industry provided employment and very little more; when employment vanished they stood exposed as shams. Residential educational centres, camps and settlements did valuable work, but could not infuse life into moribund communities. What saved the industrial areas was not the country's conscience, but rearmament, which gave the rest of the nation an unearned chance to think about what the depression had revealed.

While the distressed towns decayed, others underwent more subtle changes. Real income rose in the later 1930s, and it was spent on a wider range of things than ever before—less beer (a momentous change in itself) but more clothes, more household goods, a greater variety of pleasures. Cinemas ⟨215⟩, dance halls and milk bars multiplied in the towns, and rural omnibus services ⟨216⟩ expanded to feed them; the motor transport stimulated by the General Strike ⟨210⟩ brought life to small country towns and to districts that the railways had missed. The spread of holidays with pay not only meant new business for the established resorts—Blackpool had 7,000,000 visitors a year by 1939—but called holiday-camps and their individualist rivals, caravan parks, into being. Except in the depressed areas, the building trade flourished, in response to an uneven but plain rise in standards of living.

Two great marks of the new prosperity were the semi-detached house ⟨213⟩ and the motor car, which together carried the towns farther and farther into the countryside, helped by such agencies as the flourishing Building Societies, and London Transport and the omnibus companies. With electrical power also spreading, the highly concentrated industrial town had become something of an anachronism; distances that were worth saving when the railway was the only reliable means of transport often no longer mattered, and there was no need for factories to crowd upon a railhead. The danger was that the space inside the town would fall derelict; slums had to be cleared, but their removal implied to uncritical minds that it was the site and not the property that was at fault. That might be true in a coal-burning economy, but it need not be true in the future.

The approaching war overshadowed these and other considerations. Under the threat of aerial bombardment the towns were dangerously congested, and as it seemed certain that the war would begin with devastating air-raids the only sensible measure was to empty them. In practice this proved even more difficult than it was expected to be, and the number of women and children removed from the chief towns in September 1939 —about 1,250,000—fell far short of the figure proposed in plans discussed since 1938. There was a secondary exodus from the south-eastern coast in September 1940, when a German invasion was expected, but by that time it was known that towns could withstand greater damage than contemporary weapons could inflict upon them, and that civilian morale was more resilient than anyone had supposed in the 1930s. The point was proved, with much human suffering and material damage in the next few years, in London, at Coventry and Hull, on Clydeside, and in many other towns. Once again the country's economy was shaped to a single effort, under greater difficulties and with much more assurance than in the First World War, and once again the neglected land was called upon to help to feed the towns.

In 1945 the material problems of reconstruction were much more acute than those of 1918; life was more thoroughly disrupted than in the first world war, and the air-raids, intensified in the last year of the war by flying-bombs and rockets, inflicted incomparably greater damage. This was true not only in London or Glasgow, but in coastal resorts like Clacton and Bournemouth, which suffered scores of minor raids in addition to serious neglect and dilapidation, while Dover and neighbouring towns were shelled from Cap Gris Nez. The most urgent problem was the rebuilding of cities like Plymouth ⟨220, 221⟩ and Hull, which had suffered such damage that their whole future was in doubt, but every town in the country had some scheme which the war had delayed and soured, and which the general shortage of materials and labour now threatened to postpone again. The government's answer was to plan recovery as the war effort had been planned, a decision which produced happier results than the 1920s had seen.

Among the first measures of reconstruction were the New Towns Act of 1946, and the Town and Country Planning Act of 1947; the first aimed at controlling the growth of towns by making new ones under careful supervision, and the second at controlling the use of land, now the most limited and valuable of the country's resources, The New Towns ⟨222–225⟩, twelve of them in England and Wales, including Welwyn Garden City, which was brought under the Act, and three in Scotland, were planned as whole communities. Eight were placed round London and two by Glasgow, but far enough away to save them from the fate of the dormitory suburbs that sprang up in the 1930s and lived parasitically upon their cities. Their planning represented half a century of study, and its most important feature was probably its emphasis upon the town as a compact as well as a self-sufficient community. This point did not emerge at once, for in some respects it contradicted the values of the Garden Cities, which had a large claim to have inspired the New Towns, but experience suggests that urban sprawl is a greater problem, and in the long run a greater evil, than congestion.

The number of motor cars in Britain increased from 1,500,000 in 1939 to 8,500,000 in 1960, and the population also increased by some seven millions. During that time the war and its aftermath increased the danger that the centre of the towns would ossify while their perimeters spread, and the remoter but real chance that their perimeters would eventually meet. The so-called conurbations of London, Birmingham and the North attracted apprehensive study before 1939. They have shown no sign of shrinking since then, and a country of Britain's size can ill afford them. One aggravating feature was remedied in the 1950s when increasing prosperity made the repair of old property possible and profitable. Some parts of London formerly condemned to decay already enjoyed a quiet renaissance, and a variety of interests extended the process to other towns. Edinburgh restored parts of its old High Street and the Canongate during and after the Festival of Britain in 1951; Thurso and Great Yarmouth both reclaimed houses that twenty years earlier might have been marked for clearance. This welcome movement was followed in 1959 by the House Purchase and Housing Act, under which the government can support Building Society loans on houses built before 1919, a policy that might rescue much more old property from undeserved neglect.

These measures promise to restore the centres of the towns again, and indeed the scale of building in the late 1950s suggests that decay was caused as much by the depression and its aftermath as by any deep change in the towns themselves. The spread of suburban building is less easy to check, for in England at least the semi-detached and detached house and its garden plot are still much loved. That taste was nurtured in the nineteenth century by the electoral laws, which made small freehold plots particularly valuable, and encouraged the growth of building societies devised to multiply enfranchised householders. In the twentieth century the semi-detached house has spread by emulation, with assistance still from the building societies, and from municipal councils which have found houses less expensive and troublesome than flats. Since 1945 the terrace house has regained some favour on aesthetic grounds ⟨222⟩, although cheapness often dictated its use in municipal schemes in the 1920s and '30s, but the semi-detached tradition, wasteful of ground and tedious to the eye, is still strong.

Besides the semi-detached house there are some other suburban trappings, municipal rock-gardens, grass plots with kerbs and the like, which share its ancestry of aesthetic and sanitary revolt against classicism on the one hand, and industrial squalor on the other, and which have also outlived their usefulness. These, joined with heavy motor-traffic and its apparatus of signs and such amenities as lamps on concrete poles, have confounded town and countryside to the advantage of neither. The ensuing muddle expresses a real uncertainty about the town's future. The railway's success in the nineteenth century meant that British roads were first neglected and have since lagged fifty years behind the traffic that runs on them, but while roads can be remodelled the towns that they join are less tractable ⟨227⟩. The town's whole tradition depends upon people congregating: living and working together, and sharing services and pleasures that attract and hold them. The twentieth century's technical innovations have weakened that tradition; the motor car, electrical power, the telephone and television have made propinquity less important in human affairs, though not yet to the extent supposed by their most energetic champions and detractors, and so have sapped some of the advantages of living in towns. Moreover the motor car, moving or stationary, makes such demands on space that its use can hardly be reconciled with towns planned on the scale customary in Britain.

There are other forces, however, that may work in the town's favour. Not all services can be dispersed, and some are more concentrated than they were: shops are larger, and the supermarket belongs as entirely to the town as does the department store. Television emphasises isolation as readily as it mitigates it, and although cinemas have lost part of their audiences, theatres, dance halls, restaurants and public libraries are not notably poorer for television's success. The town therefore has some new strength, and the advantages of an assured tradition. Most of its present perplexities arise because it is still attractive, and while that is so, its greatest advantage is unchecked, for what the town really offers is sociable living. There is still no substitute for human company, and people will find human company in towns as long as they seek it there: that has always been the town's greatest attraction.

1. Caernarvon in 1750, a fortified town still contained by its walls: the growth of the modern town has now masked them on this side. Caernarvon was not only a strong-point, but also the administrative centre of North Wales after Edward I's campaigns in Snowdonia (p. 14). Notice the ships drawn up under the castle on the left; the castle's defences were once meant to protect the dock with an elaborate water gate.

2. Like Caernarvon, Stirling has outgrown its medieval site, but there is still open country at the foot of the castle rock. The original burgh clung to the safety of the high ridge, outside the castle gates.

3. The walls of York still enclose some open ground; the bank inside the wall here falls to Tanners' Moat, a plot of common ground leased to the Tanners' Gild in 1476. Lendal Bridge (in the middle distance) is modern; in the Middle Ages the river was closed by a chain strung from the North Postern, seen at the end of the wall-walk, to Lendal Tower on the opposite bank.

4. The north face of the Bargate, the landward entrance to Southampton. By 1853, the date of this drawing, the drawbridge and ditch had disappeared, and a more elaborate street grown up (Above-Bar Street) than in the little foregate suburb at Caernarvon ⟨1⟩, but the gate still blocks the roadway.

5. New Winchelsea was the most ambitious of Edward I's ventures in town-planning, and is now a rare example of a medieval town very little disturbed by later building. It was laid out in 39 rectangular lots (about 150 acres) between 1280 and 1288, while Old Winchelsea was finally overwhelmed by the sea. Like its predecessor, New Winchelsea was the chief port on the Channel coast, but in the fifteenth century the sea withdrew from the new town, leaving the marshland that stretches towards Rye, now also stranded, beyond the top of the picture. By 1575 fewer than 60 of its houses were occupied—there were more than 600 in 1292—and in the early eighteenth century Defoe found it "a town, which is rather the skeleton of an ancient city than a real town ... where the ruins are so buried, that they have made good cornfields of the streets".

This aerial view, looking north-east, shows most of the 12 blocks that are occupied today. In the middle is the chancel of St. Thomas's, the only survivor of three churches in the town. The area round St. Thomas's seems to have been the best residential quarter, the market and commercial streets were at the south end, well to the lower right of this view. The Strand Gate, at the edge of the town east of the church, overlooked the harbour; the original town hall can be seen facing the cross in the north-west corner of the churchyard. Many of the houses have stone-vaulted cellars of late-thirteenth- and early-fourteenth-century date, and the pattern of buildings and open spaces is very characteristic of a medieval town: Winchelsea's misfortunes have preserved rather than eroded its plan.

6. The Vicars' Close, Wells, was built *c.* 1350 to house the college of the Vicars Choral of Wells Cathedral, with a common hall to the south and chapel to the north (top of picture), but its great interest is that it was planned not as a quadrangle but as a street. Although individual houses have been altered, the very unusual effect of a uniform terrace of medieval houses survives. Even the front gardens were laid out before 1402.

7. *Right.* Two pictures from the fourteenth-century register of benefactors of St. Alban's Abbey. They show William Langleye and Agnes Langeford, with the houses in Dagnale Street and Soppewelle Street, St. Albans, which they gave to the abbey. William's is a two-storeyed wooden-framed house with the upper-floor jettied, and a flag on the gable. Agnes's house is also half-timbered, but single-storeyed, with a louvre protecting the smoke-hole over a central hearth. The louvre appears to be crowned with a bird's nest, perhaps a stork's. Town houses of this kind were common all through the Middle Ages, but the multi-storey house was spreading, and so were flues and chimneys—a luxury in the one-storeyed house, but a necessity where there were upper floors.

8. *Below.* Christ serving his parents—drawing water, tending the fire, and laying the table—from the Holkham Picture Bible. The manuscript tells the story of Man's Fall and Redemption, and was apparently produced by a Dominican friar for a wealthy, middle-class audience, almost certainly in London. This scene shows the simplest kind of chimney—a hood projecting from the wall—carrying the smoke to an aedicular pot like Agnes Langeford's louvre. The absence of an upper storey is not significant in a drawing of this kind, but in London the use of coal—common from the thirteenth century at the latest—must have discouraged the open hearth. The cooking pot and bellows were common to town and country, but the table-cloth is a touch appreciated only by a reader used to such refinements.

9. *Above.* The heart of a town is usually its market-place, and its market the chief feature that distinguishes a town from a village. In the Middle Ages most retail trade was specialised, in the sense that the craftsman commonly sold from his own house. The market, bringing all manner of producers and their customers together, was the counterpart of the modern general shop. This drawing of Norwich market-place, by John Sell Cotman (*c.* 1807) shows the great square below the castle crowded with tented stalls, and town- and country-people, as it still is today. Norwich was an important centre of trade long before the Norman Conquest, but the Old English borough lay east of the castle hill. The castle and cathedral were planted in it late in the eleventh century, and the city then spread westwards, with this market place as its new centre. The civic church, St. Peter Mancroft, stands to the south; the west side of the square is now occupied by the modern City Hall. (*By courtesy of the Tate Gallery.*)

10. *Right.* Shepton Mallet, Somerset, in 1882: the compact market-place of a small country town, undisturbed by modern refurbishing and motor-traffic. On the left is part of the market cross, with the shambles—a range of open sheds—opposite; these were fifteenth-century. Beyond the shambles is the wool-hall—seventeenth-century, but housing a trade that paid for the splendid church, and sustained the town from its earliest days: Shepton originally meant Sheep Farm.

11. *Above.* Selby, West Riding, a market and town at the gate of a great abbey, like Peterborough, or Bury St. Edmunds ⟨78⟩.

12. *Below.* Dalton-in-Furness, *c.* 1810; an unadorned market-place, poorer and starker than Shepton Mallet, with an unpaved roadway and, at this date, the stocks and whipping-post still part of the official furniture. The tower behind the market-hall originally housed the Abbot of Furness's manorial court.

13.

Right. Chichester Market Cross, built by Bishop Edward Story and given by him to the city in 1501. A handsome covered cross (the cross-head has been rebuilt) raised for "the succour and comfort of the poor people", who could sell their goods there under cover, unvexed by "toll nor other duties". The cross served this purpose until a Market House was built in 1808, after which it was railed in until 1872; it is now open again, but is isolated by motor traffic. There has been a clock on it since 1724.

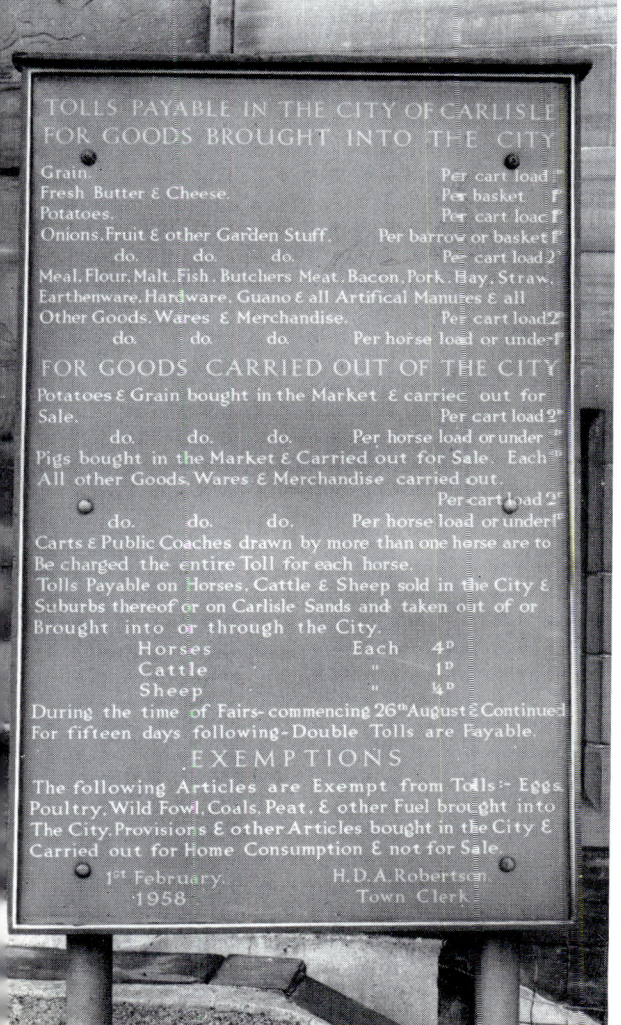

14.

The right to levy toll was one of the marks of a self-governing town, but in England the privilege was curtailed, even in the Middle Ages, by royal grants in borough charters of freedom of toll throughout the king's dominions. In later centuries the remaining charges were usually waived, but Carlisle, charged with the special burdens of a border town, maintained its tolls into modern times. In the nineteenth century the railway companies commuted their debts, which otherwise would have been impossibly intricate and heavy. The city therefore cannot abandon the tolls without incurring an equally complicated obligation; they therefore remain technically in force, but are not collected. They are displayed here by the site of the English Gate, the southern entrance to the walled city.

15. *Above*. The Toll House, Great Yarmouth, one of the oldest municipal buildings in the country. Built in the thirteenth century, it was in private hands in the fourteenth, but later returned to the town, and was used for corporation assemblies from 1622 to 1882. The ground floor was used, apparently from the thirteenth century, as the borough gaol.

16. *Below*. The Gildhall, York, built 1448–59; the low gable of the hall is set back from the river, left of the roof of St. Martin's Church. At York as at London the river was an important thoroughfare, and the Gildhall opened on to the old common-landing, seen here, to which a public right of way was preserved under the building.

7. York Gildhall interior. Splendid as the hall is, it is a municipal building only by use; even a city of York's consequence needed only a great hall and some ancillary chambers, not a specialised building. The hall was badly damaged by bombs in 1942, and re-opened in 1960.

18.
King John's Cup, King's Lynn. Although feasting was an essential part of municipal government from the earliest times, very little medieval town plate has survived in Britain. This cup from Lynn, English silver-work of *c.* 1320, is the earliest and one of the finest pieces known. It has no connection with John, but it may have been used by Edward III when he was entertained by the town.

19.
Below. A town's charters were the source and guarantee of its authority, and were often, though not always, elaborately and appropriately decorated. This unusual initial-letter from a royal charter to Bristol (1347) shows malefactors punished in the way that the charter authorises. Above disturbers of the peace are being imprisoned in a wooden hutch, while below a baker is drawn through the streets with his short-weight loaf displayed above his head. The drawing is probably local work.

20.
Left. The mace was a much-prized badge of authority, and many medieval examples have survived. All are quite small, being directly derived from the war mace, a practical weapon very different from the unwieldy ceremonial clubs of later times ⟨79⟩. This early sixteenth-century mace from Aberavon, now owned by the corporation of Port Talbot, is of particular interest, because it bears the arms of a private subject, a member of the Granville family, instead of the royal arms. No comparable example is known.

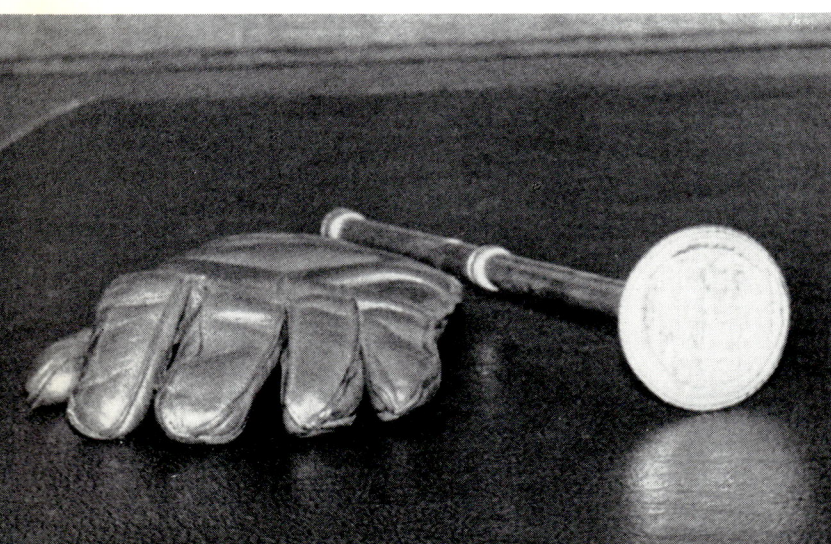

21. Swearing in the mayor of Bristol; a page from the *Kalendar* of Robert Ricart, town clerk of Bristol 1479–c. 1506. The retiring mayor holds the Bible for his successor, while the clerk reads the oath. Former mayors stand at the back of the dais, serjeants and officials to the left and before the table, aldermen to the right, while the lower hall is filled with citizens. Notice the sword-bearer, with the mayor's hat, the mace-bearers ⟨20⟩, and the blazons in the window (St. George, England, Bristol); the object at the right end of the table is probably the casket containing the city seals. The faces in the drawing suggest an attempt at portraiture.

22. *Above*. The Cutlers' Gild Hall, Thaxted, Essex. Thaxted was a wealthy manor that became a town in the later Middle Ages, and from 1554 to 1684 was a chartered borough. The change was promoted by the cutlery trade that flourished there until the sixteenth century, and the cutlers' gild hall (*c.* 1490) also served as a market-house and town-hall.

23. *Below*. Misericord from St. Lawrence's Church, Ludlow. The social and craft gilds of Ludlow contributed handsomely to the fabric and fittings of the parish church. It has been plausibly suggested that this burgess-like figure from one of the choir seats (installed in 1447) represents the warden of the gilds, surrounded by tools of the constituent trades, and flanked by a school-master and a macabre group of sexton's tools, a tomb and a censer, representing two important ancillary functions of the gilds.

Right. Visiting the Sick, a glass panel from a merchant's house in Leicester. By the end of the Middle Ages, stained glass was probably fairly common in the houses of rich townsmen. This panel is one of twenty-eight, depicting the Seven Sacraments, the Corporal Works of Mercy (of which this is the sixth), and a combination of two popular series known as the Life of Mary and the Joys of Mary. They were installed in a house in Leicester about 1500, and remained there until 1860, no doubt spared from the ordinary hazards of changing fashion by the economic depression that enfolded that town from the middle of the sixteenth to the eighteenth century. The furnishings of the sick-room shown here—bedclothes, chair and chamber-pot—are less elaborate than those shown in the panel depicting Extreme Unction, where the room is presumably more appropriate to the house for which the windows were made. Here the glazier's patron is the benefactor, bestowing money on the sick man, whose wife expresses gratitude and perhaps astonishment; the same munificent figure performs the other works of mercy. The picture's details and the glass itself, which is probably local work, are interesting reminders of the rising standards of comfort in the towns.

Right. The memorial brass of John Taylour, wool merchant of Northleach, Gloucestershire, and his wife. Northleach church was raised on the profit of the Cotswold cloth industry, and has kept a fine collection of brasses, which were a popular kind of memorial among merchants and professional men in the later Middle Ages—less expensive than stone effigies ⟨30⟩, but impressive and enduring.

26. *Above.* Bishop Bekington's conduit in the market-place at Wells, Somerset. Towns have always needed and found a constant supply of water, but until the nineteenth century ⟨194⟩ it was more often provided by philanthropists or private contractors than by public bodies. The simplest method was to build a central conduit or fountain, fed from a convenient spring, but Exeter has a system of underground channels cut in the early thirteenth century to supply several parts of the city, while at Northampton the corporation maintained two conduit houses by 1480. This conduit at Wells crowned Bishop Thomas Bekington's work there in 1451. Wells was always the smallest English cathedral city, and largely dependent on the cathedral close and the palace; Bekington emphasised its dependence by making three gatehouses in the close-wall, which commanded the streets, and building uniform ranges of houses in the market-place, flanking the gateway known as Penniless Porch. He then built the conduit by the town's former High Cross, supplying it from the spring which rises by the bishop's palace, and after which the town is named. The conduit, seen here in picturesque decay, has been rebuilt, but the water still flows from it through the streets.

27. *Above right.* Merton College, Oxford; the Front Quadrangle. The colleges which are the special characteristic of Oxford and Cambridge Universities did not appear until the later thirteenth century, more than 100 years after Oxford emerged as a centre of learning. Until then the students lived in halls or ordinary lodgings; they were unpopular with the townsmen, but were a source of profit of a then unusual kind: a "residential population". The colleges were well-endowed corporate bodies, aloof from town and university alike, but gradually dominating both. Merton College, established in Oxford in 1274, was the first properly endowed and regulated, and a model for all its successors, but its physical shape was at first accidental, some existing houses and a derelict church becoming, with the addition of a dining hall and a chapel, a pair of quadrangles. The building above marks one of the sites that Walter de Merton acquired; it was apparently rebuilt for the Warden's use in 1299–1300.

28. *Above*. Misericord from New College chapel. New College, founded by William of Wykeham in 1379, was the richest and most influential of the fourteenth-century foundations in Oxford. This carving from the warder's stall seems to depict the college, a city to itself inside a city wall, with the founder welcoming scholars (!) who emerge again as cardinals and bishops; an exact expression of Wykeham's intent.

29. *Right.* St. Mary Redcliffe. Redcliffe was only a suburb of medieval Bristol, and St. Mary's only a chapel-of-ease to Bedminster church, but the suburb grew rich with the city, and built one of the largest and finest churches in parochial use in England. The spire was not finally capped until the nineteenth century, but the rest of the fabric was completed by William Canynges the younger, who also paid for the whole range of clerestory windows which shows so impressively in this picture.

30. *Below.* The effigies of William Canynges the younger, and his wife Joan, in St. Mary Redcliffe, Bristol. Canynges was one of Bristol's leading merchants and ship-owners, and a great benefactor of St. Mary Redcliffe. His career has an unusual interest, for after his wife died in 1467, and he raised this handsome memorial, he took Holy Orders and died in 1474, Dean of Westbury-on-Trym. St. Mary Redcliffe also contains his memorial as Dean, which is sufficiently like the earlier effigy to show that both are portraits. The panelled sides of the tomb bear Canynges's personal mark. Merchants' marks were originally used to identify property, but were soon elaborated in imitation of heraldic devices and used proudly on seals and monuments; Canynges's appears throughout his work at St. Mary Redcliffe. The marks were not recognised by the heralds, who were probably irritated by their jejune reflection of heraldic forms, but they owe more to heraldry than to the symmetrical patterns of public notaries' marks, which at first sight they resemble.

31.

Left. The George Hotel, Glastonbury; built by Glastonbury Abbey *c.* 1500 as a hostel for pilgrims and visitors, one of several ancillary buildings of the abbey surviving in the town. Pilgrimages offer the closest medieval parallel to modern holidays, for they not only afforded companionable and exciting travel, abroad to shrines like Santiago de Compostella as well as at home, but also maintained a number of subsidiary industries ⟨32, 33⟩.

32.
Above. Pewter cap-badge from the Thames, depicting St. Thomas of Canterbury, and advertising a pilgrimage to his shrine. Himself a Londoner, St. Thomas was particularly venerated in the capital.

33.
Above. Pewter badge depicting the Annunciation, from the shrine of St. Mary at Walsingham, Norfolk.

34.

Left. Invalids and cripples seeking cures at the shrine of St. Fremund at Dunstable; a drawing from a fifteenth-century Life of Saint Edmund.

35. *Right.* Initial letter from Edward II's charter to Carlisle, 1316. Until the twentieth century British towns were comparatively little affected by war, except in the Anglo-Scottish borders and parts of Wales, which had a long history of periodic battle. Carlisle was strongly fortified, and usually held out behind Scottish incursions; this drawing commemorates, in a very unusual way, Sir Andrew Harclay's defence of the city against Robert the Bruce in 1315. Harclay, identifiable by his coat of arms, stands on the tower beside an arbalister, having transfixed a Scot by the siege-engine below. The lower half of the letter contains a Scottish archer and a sapper. The drawing depicts the ninth day's assault, and is almost certainly local work.

36. *Above.* Melrose Abbey, Roxburghshire. Unlike the English Cistercian abbeys Melrose sponsored a small town at its gates, which was eventually (1609) chartered as a burgh of barony. Both abbey and town suffered severely from English raids, particularly in 1385 and 1545. The abbey's picturesque decay dates from that last expedition, although local lords also pillaged the damaged buildings, stones from which were soon worked into houses in the town.
37. *Left.* Civil War siege coins from Scarborough and Newark, 1645–1646; tokens roughly stamped from silver plate, to pay garrisons and maintain orderly trade in the towns.

38. The New Inn, Gloucester. The courtyard-house appeared in the later medieval town and survived for several centuries. It fitted and lighted a large building behind a comparatively narrow street-frontage, in which a wide gate gave access to the yard or yards behind, and its plan was as convenient for inns as for large private houses, which in medieval towns were large because they sheltered large households, often including journeymen, rather than because space and privacy were prized for their own sake. As the towns became more congested, as they noticeably did in the Tudor period, the height of buildings increased, three and four storeys becoming commonplace in the principal streets ⟨44, 58⟩. Open galleries and staircases gave the inn-yards a life of their own, and one which, quite apart from their architectural influence upon the theatre ⟨99⟩ took a tenacious hold on the popular imagination. One powerful ingredient of later nostalgia, however, the regular stage-coach, did not appear until the seventeenth century.

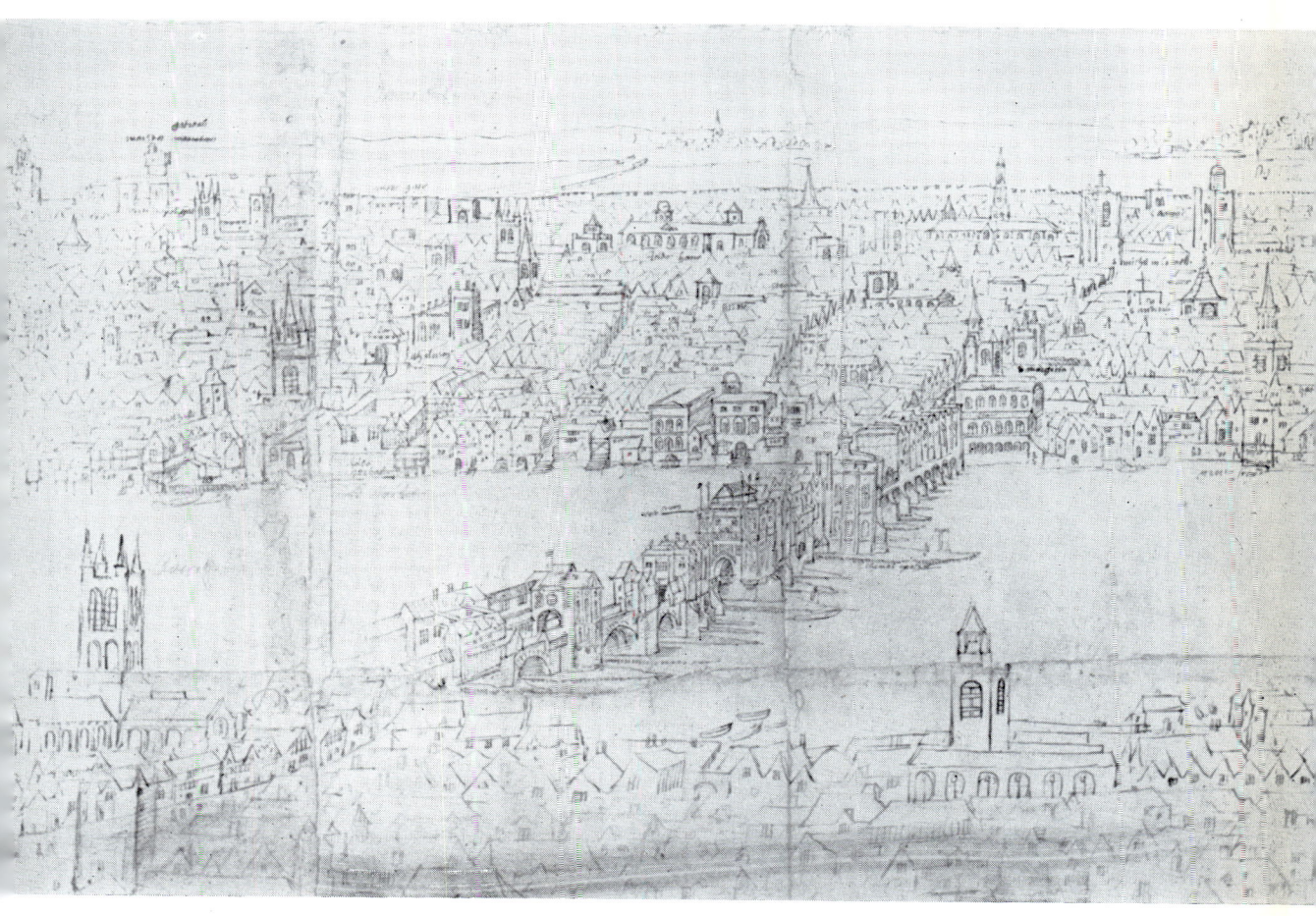

9. London Bridge, Southwark, and the City, c. 1560, part of a panoramic view of London and Westminster by Anthonis van der Wyngaerde. The city is still contained by its northern wall, with Shoreditch and Finsbury detached suburbs, separated by the open ground of Moorfields; inside the wall the building is congested, the streets being marked by unbroken ranges of gables. The riverside buildings include the Steelyard, the great depot of the German Hanseatic merchants, on the north bank, across from St. Mary Overy's (Southwark Cathedral) tower; this was still the chief centre for the Baltic and Rhenish trade in England, although the Hansards' privileges were finally abrogated at the end of Elizabeth's reign. The central feature of this view is London Bridge, at this time "upon both sides by houses built, so that it seemeth rather a continuous street than a bridge" and the houses "large, fair and beautiful buildings, inhabitants for the most part rich merchants and other wealthy citizens" (Stow). The oldest building on it is St. Thomas's chapel, projecting downstream, which was finished c. 1205. A little to the south is the tower controlling the drawbridge, which was raised to close the bridge—as during Sir Thomas Wyatt's rebellion in 1554—or to allow ships to pass up river. In the later sixteenth century large ships began to unload in the Pool of London, leaving the upper river to light craft. Stow comments on the decline of the quays at Queenhithe, above the Steelyard, and the consequent rise of Billingsgate down-river, and the closing of the Steelyard in 1598 was another symptom of change. The corresponding gradual movement of fashionable residents westwards ⟨61⟩ is exemplified by the fate of the great house called Cold Harbour, or Pountney's Inn, next downstream from the Steelyard Wharf. Once owned by a succession of rich merchants and noblemen, it was demolished by the Earl of Shrewsbury before 1590 and replaced by small tenements "letten for great rents to people of all sorts".

40.
Left. St. Andrew's Hall, Norwich. This was the church of the Dominican Friary, granted to the city after the Dissolution, and used for civic assemblies and banquets. As the friars' churches were designed chiefly as preaching-halls, they were readily adaptable to secular use.

41.
Below left. Boston, Lincs.: the Schoolhouse. Boston had a medieval grammar school, re-endowed like many others in the sixteenth century. This hall, which originally housed the whole school, was built by the town in 1567.

42.
Below. Cardinal's College Gate, Ipswich; the only remnant of the college founded by Wolsey to serve Cardinal College (now Christ Church), Oxford, as a grammar school. Although endowed with confiscated monastic lands, this short-lived foundation was really the last medieval grammar school tied, as St. Mary's College, Winchester was to New College, to an Oxford college designed to outshine all others.

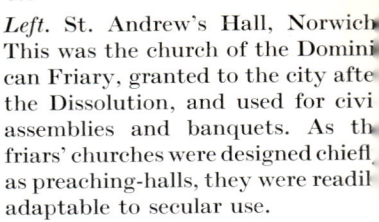

43. *Above*. Trinity College, Cambridge; the Great Court and fountain (see p. 15). Trinity was founded in 1546 by the amalgamation and sumptuous re-endowment of King's Hall and Michaelhouse. Its buildings were a casual accumulation until the 1590s, when Thomas Nevile (Master, 1593–1615) began to impose splendid order on the site, demolishing, rearranging and augmenting the buildings to make the Great Court. Although the architectural detail and features like the Gatehouse are still Tudor—sub-medieval—the regularity and scale of the court look forward to the revival of Classical taste in style and planning ⟨61⟩.

44. *Below*. Butcher Row, Coventry, the Great Court's prosaic context. A mid-nineteenth-century view of a sixteenth-century street; houses and shops undifferentiated and irregularly built; the roadway un-paved. The butcher's shop, with its open shutters, trestled counters, and fugitive livestock is a simple medieval survival.

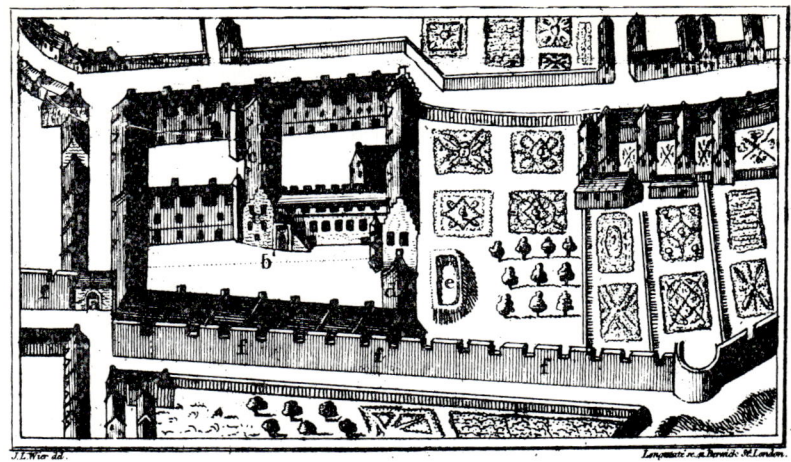

a. *Potterrow Port, formerly the Kirk of Field Port.*

b. *Upper Area of the College, where the Kirk of Field formerly stood.*

c. *Hamilton House.*

d. *The Provost's House where the Principal afterwards (1646) had his Chambers.*

e. *Ruins of the Prebendaries Chamber in which Darnley was blown up: on a line with the Town wall at the Potterrow Port.*

ff. *The late Town wall extends beyond the line of the wall at the Potterrow Port.*

46.
Left. Robert Rollock (*c.* 1555–1599), first principal of Edinburgh College. A graduate of St. Salvator's College, St. Andrew's, and an able teacher, Rollock was appointed first professor in the College in 1583, and in 1586 Principal, a post which he held, with benefices in the burgh, until his death. This portrait is a seventeenth-century copy, but apparently an authentic likeness.

45. *Left.* The old College of Edinburgh. Edinburgh University was the only one founded in Britain between the Reformation and the early nineteenth century, and the first civic university in the country, one created wholly on the initiative of a municipal corporation. Edinburgh and Glasgow received a gift of all monastic lands within their boundaries from Queen Mary in 1567, and the re-endowment and reformation of Glasgow University between 1563 and 1577 confirmed Edinburgh's desire to strengthen the reformed Kirk and win lustre by setting up a university on the Genevan model. The council chose the site of Kirk o'Field, just inside the southern city wall, and classes opened there in 1583. The institution was at first called a college, but it taught the liberal arts and granted degrees. Its benefactors included the Faculty of Advocates and the Writers to the Signet, but for many years the university was under the direct supervision of the Town Council and the ministers of Edinburgh. Its real fame began in the eighteenth century, when its medical school first acquired a European reputation.

47. *Below.* Leycester Hospital, Warwick. The hall of a medieval gild re-endowed in the sixteenth century as an almshouse. The medieval gilds of Holy Trinity and St. George, associated with St. James's chapel on the west gate of Warwick, were suppressed in 1547 (pp. 23-4), and their hall passed through private hands to the Corporation. After using the hall for a time as a grammar school house the burgesses granted the hall to Robert Dudley, earl of Leicester, who in 1571 founded the hospital for twelve poor men, veteran soldiers, and especially his own tenants and servants resident in Warwick. By surrendering the hall the town gained a valuable charity, at a time when the care of the poor was a special anxiety (p. 25). The brethren of the hospital were bound to attend a daily service in St. James's chapel, from which this picture is taken, and always to wear in public the livery of hat and gown seen here, with the Earl of Warwick's badge, the bear and ragged staff.

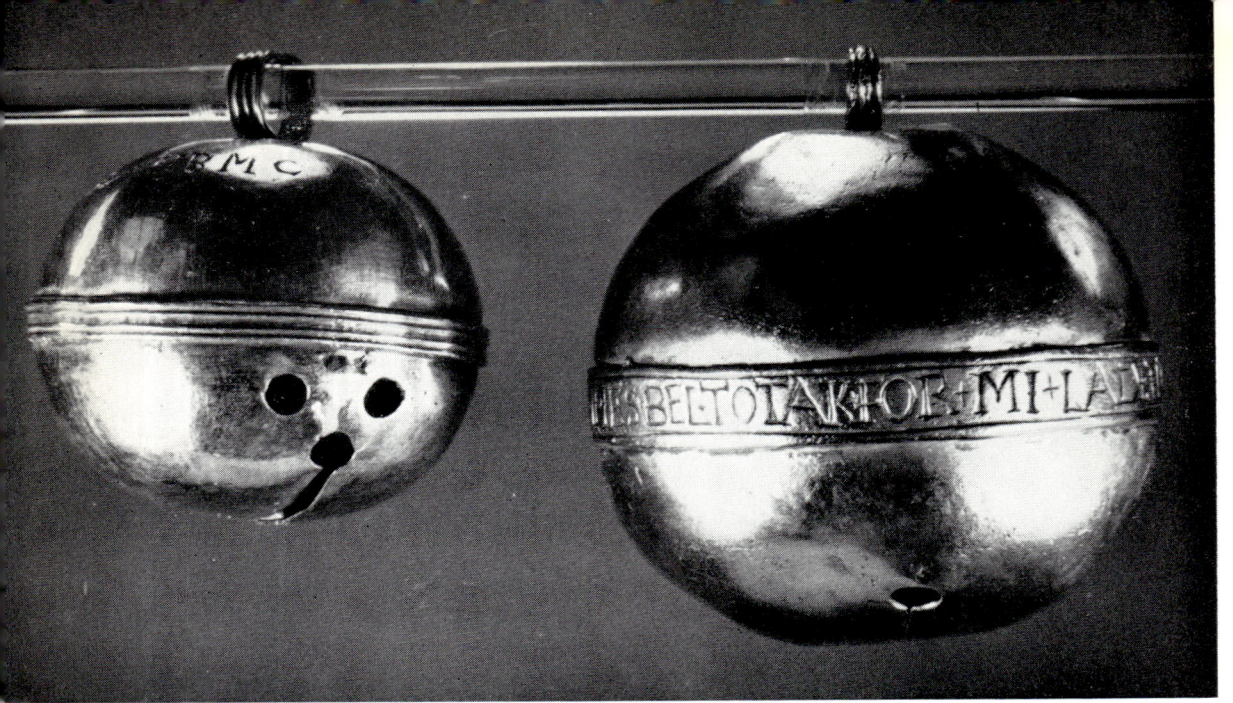

48. *Above.* Racing bells, Carlisle. Two silver harness bells, awarded as prizes for horse-racing. The smaller bell (1¾ in. diameter) is dated 1599, and marked H.B.M.C., for "Henry Baines, Mayor of Carlisle". The larger (2 in. diameter) is inscribed "The Sweftes horse thes bel to tak for mi Lade Daker Sake". Lady Dacre may have been Elizabeth, widow of William Lord Dacre of Gilsland, governor of Carlisle in 1550. The races, like those at Chester in the sixteenth century, were anciently part of the Shrovetide celebrations, and at this time were becoming a more formal social occasion, despite Puritan disapproval. These bells are the earliest known racing plate in Britain.

49. *Left.* Standing Salt (1589), Richmond, Yorks. Municipal plate became more common as the country prospered in the later sixteenth century, and most corporations regarded it as a necessary mark of dignity. This silver-gilt drum-salt was presented to Richmond for the Alderman's use in 1595, by John Cotterell, who coupled it with an endowment for a town-preacher, "Godly, grave and sufficient".

50. *Right.* The Charterhouse, Finsbury; Thomas Sutton's tomb. The medieval Carthusian priory outside the City, by Smithfield, was founded in 1371 and became a private house after the Dissolution, and then in 1611 was bought by Thomas Sutton, who endowed it as the Hospital of King James and the boys' school still known as Charterhouse. Sutton was believed to be the richest commoner in England when he died; the sources of his wealth included lands in the Durham coalfields. The panel at the top of his elaborate tomb, which was made by Nicholas Stone and Nicholas Janssen and finished in 1615, portrays a sermon in the Hospital chapel.

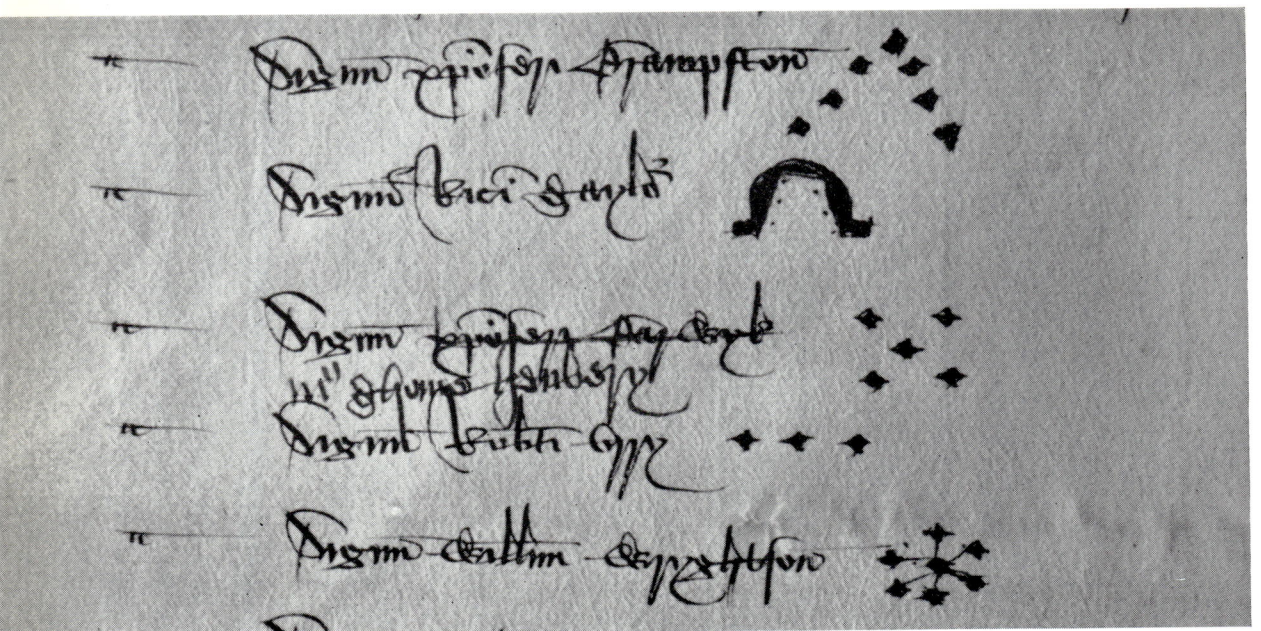

51.

Above. Baker's marks, Lincoln Common Council minutes, 1522. Part of a register of marks officially allocated to bakers in the city and its suburbs, to help to control the quality and price of bread. The marks are those of Christopher Brampston, Richard Taylour, Christopher Barwyk (re-assigned to Thomas Henbury), Robert Urry and William Wryghtson.

52.

Left. Newcastle Town Hutch. Down to the seventeenth century, at least, most towns kept their records and treasure in a chest rather than a strongroom. This iron-bound safe at Newcastle, called the Hutch, was last strengthened in the eighteenth century, but must then have been some centuries old. Despite its solidity, most of Newcastle's records were lost, in the Scottish attack of 1644, and less dramatically at other times.

53.

Right. John Stow's monument, St. Andrew Undershaft, London. John Stow (c. 1525–1605), antiquary and chronicler, wrote the *Survey of London*, an elaborate topographical and historical survey of the city. He followed his father into the Merchant Taylors' Company, but devoted most of his life to historical studies. Stow belonged to an older generation than William Camden (1551–1623) and his fellow-scholars, but like theirs his work belongs to the modern world of learning.

54.

Below. The Four Prentises of London; the title page of Thomas Heywood's play, written c. 1600 and published in 1615. The play described the adventures of four nobly-born apprentices who quit London to follow their father on Crusade, a story calculated to appeal to a city audience. The Red Bull theatre stood in St. John's Street, Clerkenwell, and was probably a converted inn-yard ⟨38⟩.

55.

Left. Wymondham, Norfolk; the market-house (1619). A combination of market-hall and cross, although since the Reformation the cross has become a vestigial feature. There are similar buildings, rectangular in plan, but more closely allied to Wymondham than to, e.g. Thaxted ⟨22⟩, at Witney, Oxon., and Market Harborough, Leics., where the room above the market shelter was the grammar school house.

56.

Below left. Chester: the Rows. A photograph of the first-floor walk in Bridge Street, c. 1900; notice the display windows on the outer side of the gallery.

57.

Below. A Bristol Nail (? c. 1580). One of four brass pillars now outside the Corn Exchange; this is one of two which are probably Elizabethan, the other two were given by city merchants in 1625 and 1631. They were used as accounting- and writing tables outside the Tolzey, or Counting House: street-furniture from the days of the pedestrian's supremacy

Bishop Lloyd's House, Watergate Street, Chester. The Rows at Chester (p. 28), which are confined to the four main streets, are now mainly seventeenth- and eighteenth-century structures over medieval cellars. This house, traditionally associated with George Lloyd, Bishop of Chester (1605–1615) shows their chief features: steps to a first floor entrance, shops and cellars between the steps, just below pavement-level; and an arcaded walk above, with the upper floors projecting to the street-line.

59.
Great Yarmouth; entrance to a Row (pp. 28–29). The Yarmouth Rows probably grew up in the same way as the Lands of Scottish burghs ⟨64, 65⟩. The long narrow plot is characteristic of town properties, and at Yarmouth the side passages and lanes were preserved and emphasized instead of being diverted and obliterated. The houses between them grew haphazardly, but as many of them were built in the seventeenth century they have a common plan and style. The Rows were damaged by bombing, but their atmosphere survives in places. Some entrances are arched over; this one is comparatively wide, and shows the fronts of houses facing on to the Row.

60.
Denbigh, arcades in the High Street. The town at Denbigh moved down from the Castle Hill at the end of the Middle Ages, but the suburb, as the new settlement was called, was deserted for a time and damaged during the Civil War. The arcades, which face the market-place, date from a general rebuilding of the town *c.* 1700.

Above. Covent Garden in the seventeenth century, looking north, up James Street. This view, which may be an eighteenth-century copy of an early painting, shows the square with its arcaded houses complete on the north and east, and Inigo Jones's church, which was rebuilt in 1795. The general effect is urbane and dignified, quite Italian, in spite of such solecisms as the dormer windows, and in the strongest contrast to all else that London had to show in 1636. Although raised on a nobleman's estate this is a product of royal patronage—the only effective expression of Charles I's autocratic intentions.

Below. Lincoln's Inn Fields: an eighteenth-century view. The houses in Lincoln's Inn Fields and Great Queen Street were not arranged as formally as those in Covent Garden: Inigo Jones's responsibility for them was more sketchily official and supervisory than in Covent Garden, and their details were correspondingly coarser. They were nevertheless markedly different from traditional work, and their regularity stood out, as in this picture, beyond all their other features.

63 and 64. *Above left and right.* Glasgow, the Tolbooth Steeple; 64, Gladstone's Land, Lawnmarket, Edinburgh. Just as the town's legal status and privileges were better defined in Scotland than in England, so the burgh had a distinctive architecture, especially for its public buildings. This was partly because building in stone spread late and fairly rapidly, and partly because Scotland was more responsive to fashions in the Low Countries and France than to English tastes. The Glasgow Steeple is now the only remnant of the Tolbooth built there in 1626, but the rest of the building is of the same height and outline as the original, which served as Town Hall and common gaol until 1814. The only unusual feature of the tower—a dignified accessory which was widely adopted in Victorian England ⟨182⟩—is the crown, a medieval device with no known parallel on a Scottish civic building.

Gladstone's Land is a good example of an Edinburgh town house. The arcade is now the only original example left in the city, but derives from the wooden galleries that fronted most of the medieval houses there ⟨133⟩. The whole front of the Land, indeed, was built in 1631–6 in place of the timber forebuilding of an earlier house, which survives behind it; together they make a single block of five five-roomed flats. The building takes its name from Thomas Gladstanes, an ancestor of W. E. Gladstone.

65. Aberdeen, Provost Skene's House in the Guestrow. The Scottish burghs were mainly timber-built in the Middle Ages, but after 1500 stone houses became more common. The oldest parts of this house were probably built *c.* 1580. Like Gladstone's Land ⟨64⟩ it rose piece-meal, with one house on the street and an "inland" behind, but when Sir George Skene acquired it in 1669 it was a single block. Skene inserted new windows, and built the staircase turrets. The celebrated painted ceilings inside are probably early seventeenth-century in date, and the whole is a good example of the solid comfort which the richer Scottish burgesses enjoyed at this time. The house is now isolated, as the decayed mansions around it were razed as slums before it was restored.

66. Denbigh: Sir Hugh Middleton's cup. In 1616 Hugh Middleton, citizen and goldsmith of London, and promoter of the New River ⟨68⟩ presented three identical silver cups to his native town of Denbigh, to Ruthin and to Oswestry. Middleton's father, Sir Richard Middleton, was a governor of Denbigh Castle, while Hugh, who was made baronet in 1622 for his work on the New River, represented the borough in six parliaments between 1603 and 1628. Besides his City interests and trading ventures, Middleton prospected for coal round Denbigh, and owned the silver mines in Cardiganshire from which the metal for his cups came.

67. *Right*. The water tower on Chester Bridge Gate. This tower was built by John Tyrer, between 1601 and 1611, to improve the city's water supply. Tyrer installed wheels to raise water from the Dee in the mills by the bridge.

68. *Below*. The source of the New River, Amwell, Herts. By the sixteenth century London had outgrown its water supplies. A scheme for tapping springs in Middlesex or Hertfordshire was discussed in Elizabeth's reign, but no contractor could be found until Sir Hugh Middleton formed the New River Company and started work in 1609. The cost outran his own substantial means, but the Crown joined the venture, and the New River opened on 29 September 1613. It runs to Finsbury, where the head offices of the Metropolitan Water Board still stand, and originally followed a course of 38 miles, of which 16 were taken up in detours to allow a continuous flow without tunnelling or other elaborate engineering work.

Buried in thes 8 Parishes and at the Pesthouse in the Year 1665, 17174, whereof of the Plague 12218.
Collected by [illegible] Sellers.

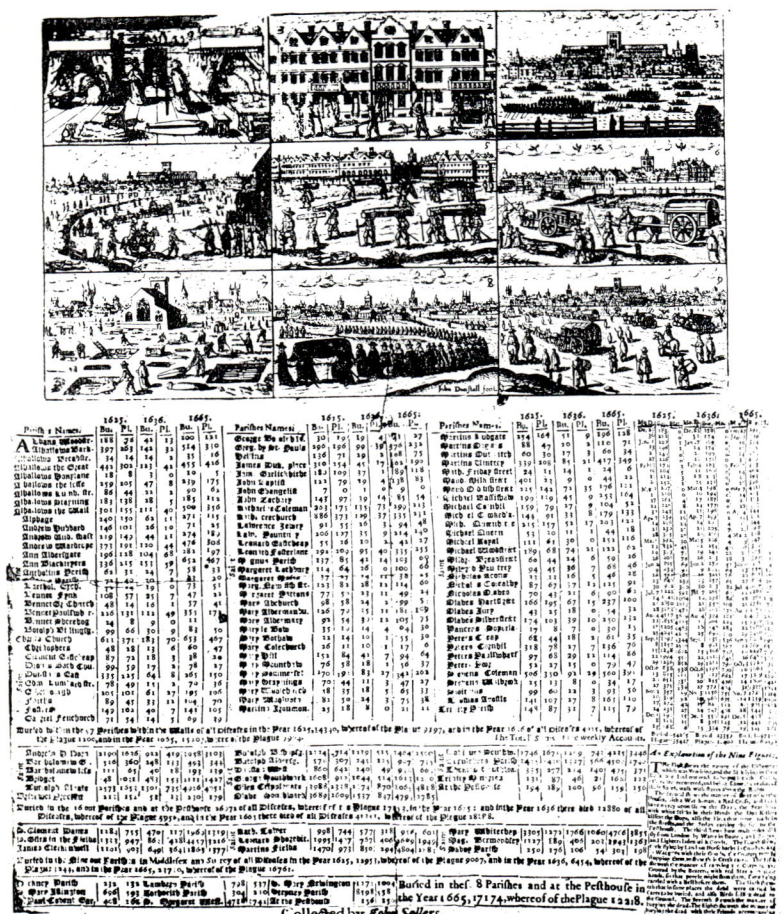

69.

Left. Part of a contemporary broadsheet, depicting the Great Plague of London, 1665–6. The scenes include a pest house, quarantine patrols, the flight from the city by land and water, and public and private burials; the text gives the reported death-roll in each parish. Broadsheets served both as newspapers and mementoes, and enterprising publicists welcomed disasters like the Great Plague and the Fire.

70.

Below. The Great Fire of London, September 1666. A painting by an unknown contemporary, showing the western city in flames, in the later stages of the fire. The Tower (right) masks the unburned north-eastern fringe ⟨71⟩, and the whole area to the west, together with much of London Bridge, has been razed. The ruined church in the foreground is St. Botolph's by Billingsgate.

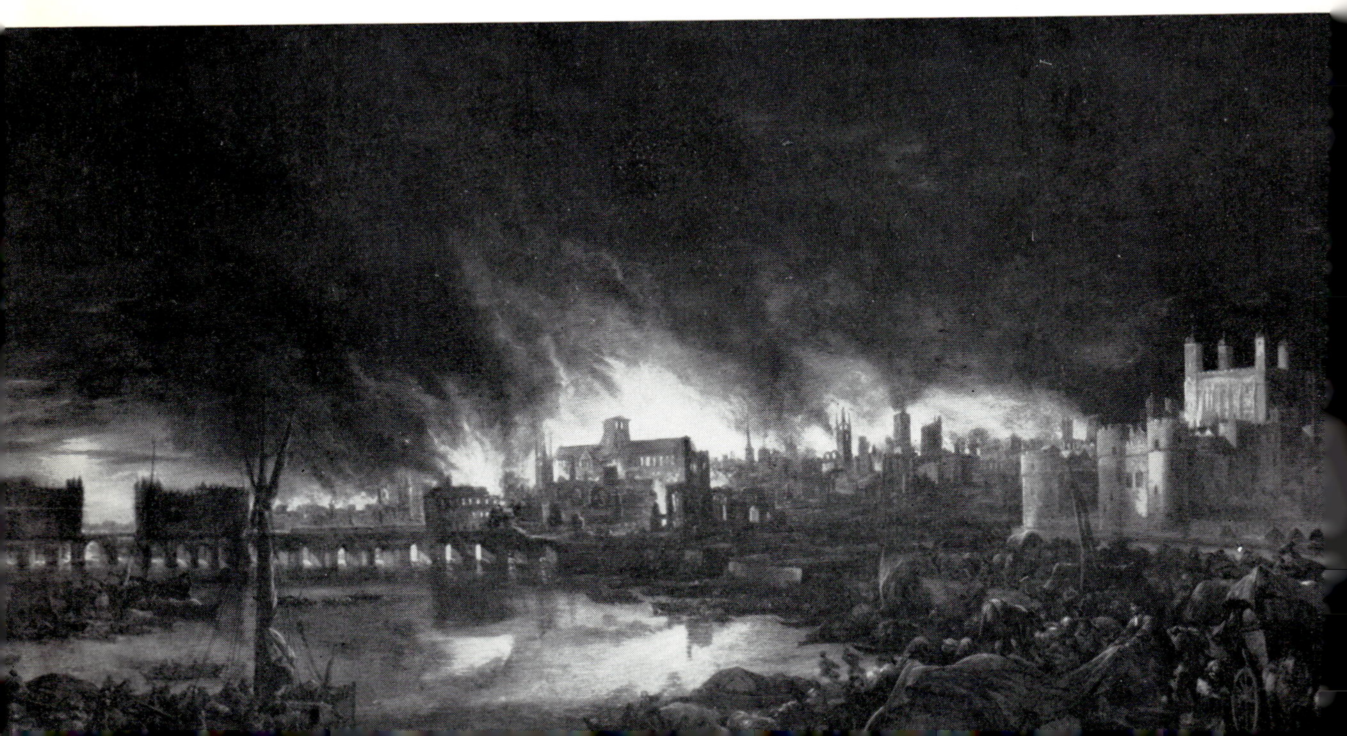

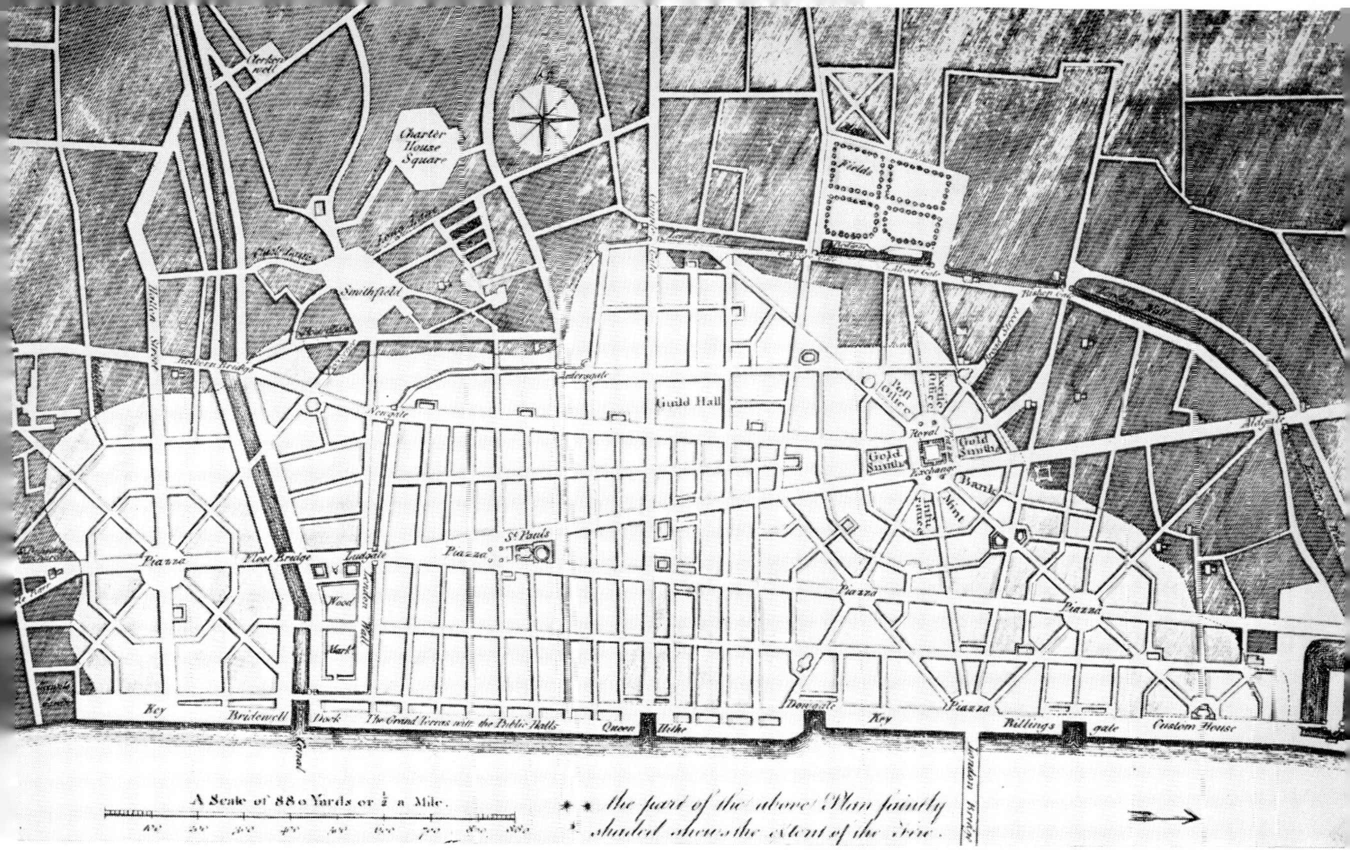

71. *Above.* Wren's plan for rebuilding London: September 1666. Wren completed this plan within a few days of the end of the fire. It is an interesting attempt to rationalise the city's street-plan, with St. Paul's and the Royal Exchange as the chief centres of interest, commanding a bold pattern of radiating streets. The area unaffected by the fire is shown by dark hatching. The urgency of the City's rebuilding made the plan only an academic exercise.

72. *Below.* Wren's London, from the River. Although Wren's plan was not executed, his work on St. Paul's and the City churches gave London as distinctive a character as the most thorough replanning could have achieved. The new city's special quality has since been destroyed by insensitive building and by war, but it emerges happily in this eighteenth-century painting.

73. Bath, the King's Bath, 1662, by Willem Schellinks. Bath was still only a health resort and a natural curiosity in the 1660s, and its appearance had not changed greatly since the Middle Ages, when the baths were managed by the abbey. The King's Bath was a reservoir of the Roman baths (which were not discovered until the eighteenth century) and has always been open to the sky; the surrounding balustrade shown here was built in 1624 by Sir Francis Stonor, whose arms appear under the statue of King Bladud, the mythical discoverer of the hot springs. The date of the statue is uncertain, but it seems to be older than Stonor's work; it might have been set up in the sixteenth century, when the town first acquired the baths. The King's Bath is used here, as it was in the eighteenth century, by both men and women, who swim freely or rest in the niches round the sides; there are brass hand-rings, of which the earliest surviving today is dated 1612, set in the walls. In the middle there is a spired turret, since rebuilt, recessed for bathers in the water, and hung about with crutches that testify to past cures. The fashionably-dressed company watching the bathers is being entertained by musicians (left), and plied with food and drink by serving-girls. Musicians performed at the baths in the sixteenth century; and by the 1660s there were plays during the season, but it is clear from this drawing that the amusements were quite informal, and their setting, even if we make allowance for the artist's fancy, a scene of almost rustic simplicity. Even so, Bath had a well-established tradition of royal patronage, and was much better equipped than its upstart rivals to exploit the new enthusiasm for spas that grew with the national wealth after the Restoration.

74. Tunbridge Wells in 1718; an engraving by Johannes Kip. Tunbridge Wells (p. 33) is unusual, not because it owes its existence to a special cause—a common enough matter ⟨77, 192⟩—but because it is well documented, and has preserved its character during three centuries without ossifying. The mineral springs were discovered in 1606 on open ground near an elaborate junction of civil boundaries, so that the town originally lay in two counties, while its first church straddled the boundaries of three parishes. Until the Restoration visitors either found accommodation five miles away at Tonbridge, which so gave its name to the spa, or stayed in tents or huts on the heath. In 1676 the lord of the manor, encouraged by the wells' popularity, and especially by a series of royal visits, hired the tenants' rights in the waste land for fifty years and began to build houses and shops around the promenade—the Pantiles—and the market place, where a kind of fair had grown up in the spa's season. In 1684 a chapel was endowed by public subscription, and dedicated to King Charles the Martyr in accordance with the strong Tory sympathies of the nascent town. In Queen Anne's reign the springs were capped with stone basins, one of them presented by Anne herself.

This view shows the wells in a triangular enclosure, screened by trees, beyond the Pantiles and the market. The Pantiles have their celebrated arcade on one side, and a fence and a row of trees dividing the roadway from another walk above the Market place. King Charles's Chapel, a plain building with a small turret, stands on the other side of the road behind the wells; beyond it, on the edge of the town, are inns with signs across the roadway. In 1726 the lease of the waste expired, and the manorial tenants were awarded a share of the buildings by lot; they had the good fortune to draw the central area, including the walks and the Assembly Rooms. A later agreement had the curious effect of making the twelve attendants (called Dippers) at the wells manorial officers, so that they were elected by a jury of tenants and presented to the lord of the manor for confirmation. The town was long supervised by the county justices, and was not incorporated until 1899. The inlaid boxes and toys called Tunbridge Ware, and wooden cups for drinking the waters, were made and sold locally from the later seventeenth century, supplying the shops in the Pantiles with a rich trade in souvenirs.

75.
Left. Chatham, Kent, c. 1665, by Jacob Esselens. Chatham became a naval base in the sixteenth century; the original arsenal was by the quays where the crane ⟨76⟩ stands, but in 1622 the yards were extended eastward, down-river. The church tower was built in 1635 at the Admiralty's expense, and the body of the church enlarged. The ships anchored in the river are laid up unrigged; if the Dutch had attacked Chatham, which was imperfectly defended, during their raid on the Medway in 1667, they would have inflicted even heavier damage on the English fleet than they did.

76.
Below left. Crane from Harwich dockyard, c. 1670. The crane at Chatham ⟨75⟩ was probably of this kind, which was widely used for heavy loads from the Middle Ages onward. It is powered by two 16-foot wheels in the shed which were worked as treadmills. The crane was removed from the old naval yard at Harwich and rebuilt on the Town Green in 1933.

77.
Above right. Whitehaven in 1738, after a painting by Matthias Reed (1669–1747). Whitehaven was developed in the seventeenth century by the Lowthers (pp. 40, 58), who obtained a market charter for it in 1660, built a pier, and promoted ship-building and a trade in coal from their estates. By the 1730s the hamlet had grown into this town of 6,000 inhabitants, well built on a regular plan, with a fleet of more than 100 ships. Sir James Lowther's house stands inland (left) on the Egremont Road, and his collieries appear in the hills behind. Matthias Reed was a ship's painter who was encouraged by local patrons; he painted altar-pieces for two Whitehaven churches, and a large number of decorated panels and chimney-pieces for private houses in the town.

78.
Right. Bury St. Edmunds, The Corn Hill, c. 1700. An anonymous picture, probably local work; an early and interesting view of a provincial town. The house-fronts are irregular, but solid and comfortable; the streets are neat and clean, despite the open market. Notice the pigs, rangy beasts that would be at home in a medieval painting; the local farming is good, but the agricultural revolution has not yet begun. Bury survived the dissolution of its abbey, was incorporated in 1606, and prospered; by the 1720s it was the centre of a strong, self-contented provincial society, a place for assemblies as well as for fairs and markets, like Exeter or Carlisle in their own districts.

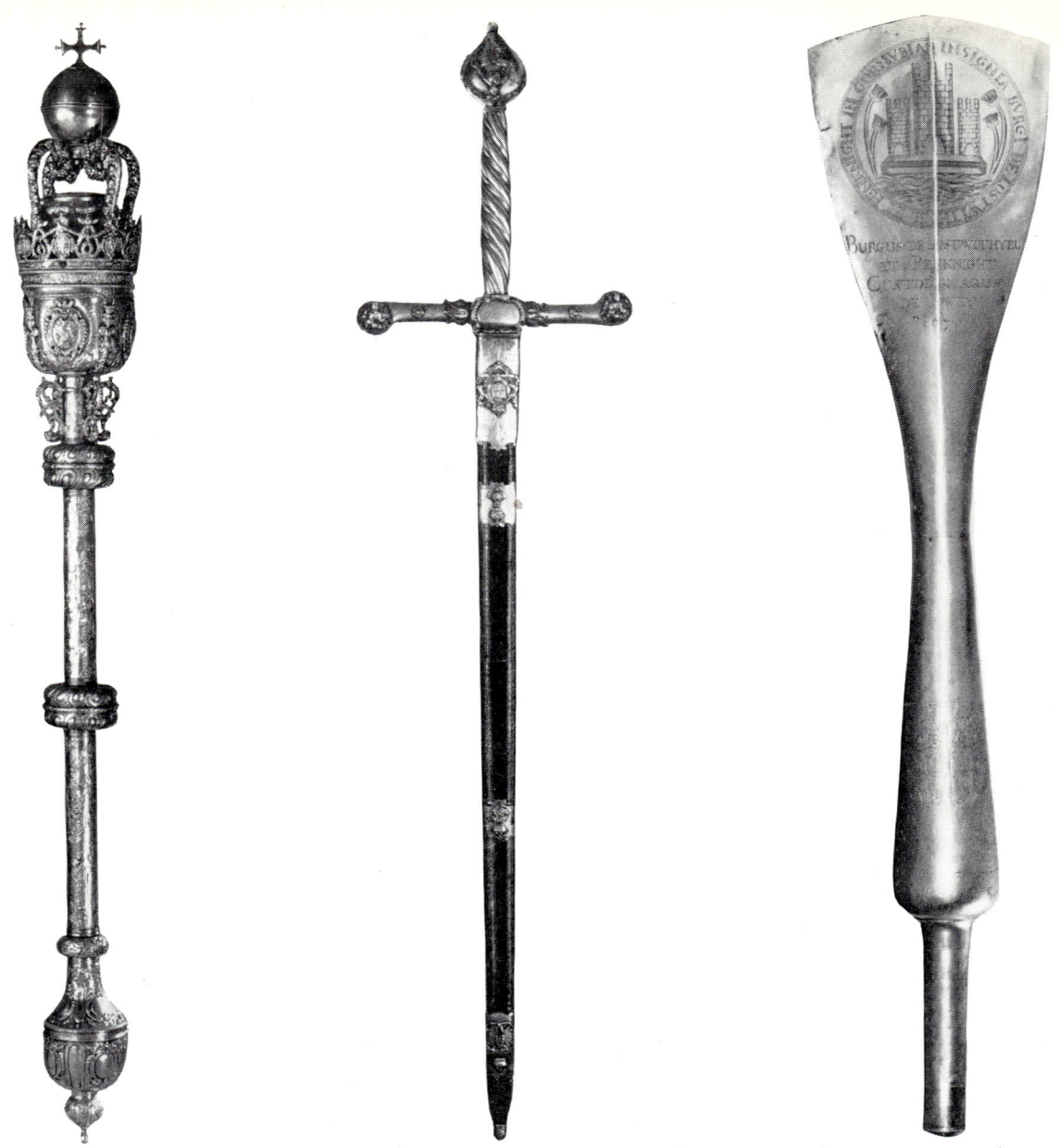

79. Marlborough, Gilt-Mace, 1652–1660. **80.** Thetford, Sword of State, *c.* 1675. **81.** Lostwithiel, Silver Oar-mace, 1670. In the later seventeenth century borough maces began to conform to a general pattern, which has only recently been interrupted. Marlborough bought a new mace in 1652, which celebrated the end of monarchy with the inscription "The Fredom of England by God's blessing restored". On Charles II's restoration the sentiment was embarrassing; the royal arms were added, and the inscription was made both up-to-date and loyal by substituting 1660 for 1652. At Congleton the burgesses resolved the same difficulty by adding "to C.R." (for Carolus Rex), to their mace, and left the Commonwealth emblem above it, but at Marlborough this was removed, and an orb and cross perched on the crown. A sword of state was a mark of dignity that was sparingly granted; only 13 towns enjoyed the privilege by 1500 and fewer than 30 by 1700. Thetford received it on incorporation in 1581. The sword shown here was presented to the borough in 1678 by Sir Joseph Williamson, who represented Thetford in parliament between 1669 and 1685. Oars and oar-maces are even rarer than swords, being a mark of Admiralty jurisdiction ⟨164⟩. Lostwithiel claimed suit of court and service from all owners of boats on the Fowey, and its jurisdiction extended as far upstream as a pair of oxen might be driven on the river-bed. Its oar, which is dated 1670, was presented by Silas Titus of Bushey, Herts., who was then M.P. for Lostwithiel.

82. *Above*. Bruton, Somerset, Sexey's Hospital. Hugh Sexey, auditor of the household under Elizabeth I and James I, founded an almshouse and boys' school in his native town. The building was completed in 1638 and looks like a medieval college: hall and chapel making one range of a quadrangle, dormers and mullioned windows; only the founder's bust over the hall doorway dates the work.

83. *Below*. Liverpool, the old Blue Coat School. This school and hospital was built and endowed 1714–1717 by Bryan Blundell, ship-owner and merchant, to house a school for destitute orphans. It is one of the first substantial signs of Liverpool's Atlantic trade and, although its style is posthumous Queen Anne rather than early Georgian, it belongs to a different world from Sexey's Hospital.

84. *Above*. Southwold, Suffolk, South Green. Southwold was one of the neighbouring ports that prospered as Dunwich declined ⟨159⟩, but in 1659 it suffered severely from a fire. The most striking feature of the rebuilt town, which recovered only slowly, is the series of open spaces called Greens, which give it a special character, rather like the effect of the Stray and its outliers in Harrogate. The Greens may have been introduced as fire-breaks, but by the early nineteenth century, when Southwold was developing as a sea-side resort, they were preserved as a valuable part of its resources, which they are yet.

85. *Left*. Fire-mark of the Sun Insurance Office. The practice of issuing fire-marks began in the late seventeenth century, when the insurance business was growing rapidly in London. No. 838 was issued in 1711 for a house in Church Row, Fulham, and is the oldest survivor of the Sun Office's marks. These badges were used until the nineteenth century; their original purpose was to authenticate the policy and to guide the company's own fire brigade, but strong competition among the companies soon led them to accept a general responsibility for extinguishing fires, and the fire-marks, which were brightly painted and gilded, served chiefly as advertisements. An unintended consequence of the company brigades' efficiency was that the parish fire engines were neglected, and the incentive to create a public fire service was weakened until the second half of the nineteenth century.

6. Blandford Forum, Dorset, Church of SS. Peter and Paul. The church, with a number of other buildings, was designed and built by the brothers John and William Bastard after the fire that destroyed Blandford in 1731. The monument in front of the church was built by John Bastard in 1760 to commemorate the fire, and originally contained a pump "to prevent by a timely supply of water, with God's Blessing, the fatal Consequences of Fire hereafter".

87. *Above*. George Whitfield (1714–1770) preaching in St. Luke's Fields, London. The unorthodoxy of the Methodists' activities excited their opponents, but their tactics were only those every new sect uses when it first competes with its established rivals. Whitfield had longer experience than John Wesley as a missionary in America, and he used it effectively, but the movement ended in solid chapels and sober congregations. This print is commemorative, and the size and nature of the audience are only notional.

88.

Left. Carmarthen, St. Peter's Church; arch over the mayoral pew. The furnishings of the civic church, sword rests, mayoral pews and the like, belong particularly to the eighteenth century, when only professed Anglicans could hold civic office and when Church and State had a strong conservative interest in the settlement of 1688. In Wales this connection, like its connections with the gentry, was a source of weakness to the Church, and helped the spread of Methodism as a protest against the established order.

89.

Right. Poole, Skinner Street Congregational Church. Like the Baptists, the Quakers, and other disturbers of the Stuarts' peace, by the end of the eighteenth century the Congregationalists had settled to an orderly prosperity. When disputes occurred they were private and not public matters. The first regular meeting-house in Poole was licensed for Presbyterian worship in 1706 in Hill Street, but in 1760 part of the congregation seceded with the minister and established an Independent meeting in Skinner Street. This large church, accommodating a congregation of 1,000, was built in 1777. Poole's radical aggressiveness in one century makes for larger meeting-houses than usual in the next.

90.

Great Yarmouth, St. George's Chapel. St. George's was a chapel of ease to the great church of St. Nicholas, Great Yarmouth, and it was built by the corporation in 1714, partly to provide a church for the southern part of the town, and partly because the burgesses were in continual dispute with the bishop of Norwich over the affairs of the parish church. The new chapel's associations helped to preserve it from discordant restoration and refurnishing until it was closed in 1959. Its handsome interior shares the great traditions of a Nonconformist meeting-house; it is a simple auditorium, and not a complex of hall and chapels like a medieval church. At the same time it is enriched with a self-assured yet delicate taste, as evident in the mayor's pew as in the desks and pulpit shown here, that reflects the privileged position of the Anglican church.

91.
Above. Bath, the General Hospital: "Dr. Oliver and Mr. Peirce examining patients." Bath's promoters did not make the mistake of neglecting the spa's best resources, and both Nash and Ralph Allen were trustees of the hospital, now the Royal National Hospital for Rheumatic Diseases, begun in 1738. William Oliver, who gave his name to the Bath Oliver biscuit, was one of the first three physicians at the hospital, and Jeremy Peirce the first surgeon.

92.
Left. Richard Nash (1674–1762). Although Nash had shown talent in organising entertainments while he was at the Inner Temple, he first went to Bath as an adventurer and gambler. The post of Master of Ceremonies, in which he succeeded Captain Webster in 1705, suited his temperament and abilities exactly, and the whole effort of the Woods and Ralph Allen in equipping Bath (p. 45) would have lost its force without his contribution. This portrait corrects some of the overtones of his nickname, Beau Nash, which was really a tribute to an unusual personal authority. Even Goldsmith, his biographer, could say of Nash only that he had "a genteel address, much vivacity, some humour and some wit", but few men have used those qualities to happier advantage.

93. *Above*. Bath, The Circus (1754–58). John Wood's most original composition. Bath's later growth and the advent of motor traffic have obscured the Circus's special qualities; the figures in this print are an appropriate reminder that Wood's buildings were designed as the setting of a very small and privileged society.

94. *Below*. Bath, Queen Square, designed by John Wood I (1727). Wood's first major work at Bath (p. 45).

95. Bath, The Royal Crescent (1767–74), by John Wood II. The Royal Crescent was one of the most influential innovations in the history of British town planning, its design is even more monumental than that of the Circus, and its individual houses correspondingly subdued. Notice the basement areas, marked by their railings, which also appear in the Circus ⟨93⟩; they are a natural consequence of the rising value of building sites, and one open to long abuse.

96.

Left. Bath, The Royal Crescent in 1801, still on the edge of the town, and seen here as its architect set it down. The abrupt edge of the paving in the roadway is a reminder that Bath is an oasis, a place where roads are metalled, at a time when most roads are not. The feature may still be found in modern suburbs.

97. Bath, The Upper Assembly Rooms, *c.* 1790. The Assembly Rooms, which included a Tea-Room and a Ball-Room, were designed by John Wood II and built in 1769–71. They were badly damaged by bombing in 1942.

98.

Left. The Comforts of Bath, by Thomas Rowlandson; 3, The Pump Room. The pump-room was the heart of a spa, and the natural centre of its social life in the late morning. The waters were more palatable than sea-water, which was drunk in extraordinary quantities at the sea-side resorts, but the occasion was often lacking in spontaneous gaiety.

99. *Above.* Bristol, The Theatre Royal, designed by James Paty, 1764–6. The Theatre Royal is the oldest theatre in continuous use in Britain, and has the best Georgian auditorium that survives; the third tier of boxes was added in 1800.

100. *Right.* Colchester, The Mayor's Theatre Ticket (silver). The first theatre in Colchester was built in 1764, in the Moot Hall yard, and the proprietor was bound by the lease to provide a mayoral box. The ticket was used by the mayor at the second theatre, on another site, until 1910.

101. *Below.* Covent Garden Theatre, 1763. Popular enthusiasm for the theatre in the eighteenth century turned very readily into violence. This print shows a riot at Covent Garden in February 1763, caused by the management's attempt to charge full prices for late admission during a performance of Thomas Arne's *Artaxerxes*.

Above. Newmarket, Suffolk, from a drawing probably by Peter Tillemans (1684–1734). As at Epsom, the racing at Newmarket probably began with royal hunting parties on the Heath in James I's reign. Charles II rebuilt the royal lodge in the town, and entered his own horses for the races, which flourished under his patronage; since that time the town has been as dependent on a single industry as any mining or manufacturing centre. The strings of horses in the drawing are still a familiar sight on the Heath, in and out of season.

Below. Vauxhall, New Spring Gardens; the Grand Walk and the Orchestra, 1766. The New Spring Gardens were opened about 1661, on the south side of the Thames opposite Millbank, and were a fashionable pleasure ground for more than a century. Besides the walks and the band-stand, this print shows the private booths for dining.

104. *Above.* The inquiry into the conduct of the Fleet Prison, 1729; a painting from William Hogarth's studio. This investigation by a committee of the House of Commons produced the first reform of prisons in the eighteenth century, although many abuses persisted. The committee is shown in session at the Fleet; a prisoner is demonstrating the use of iron fetters, and Thomas Bambridge, the warden, is standing on the left. Bambridge, who was twice acquitted on a charge of murdering prisoners, was removed from office and imprisoned in Newgate after the inquiry.

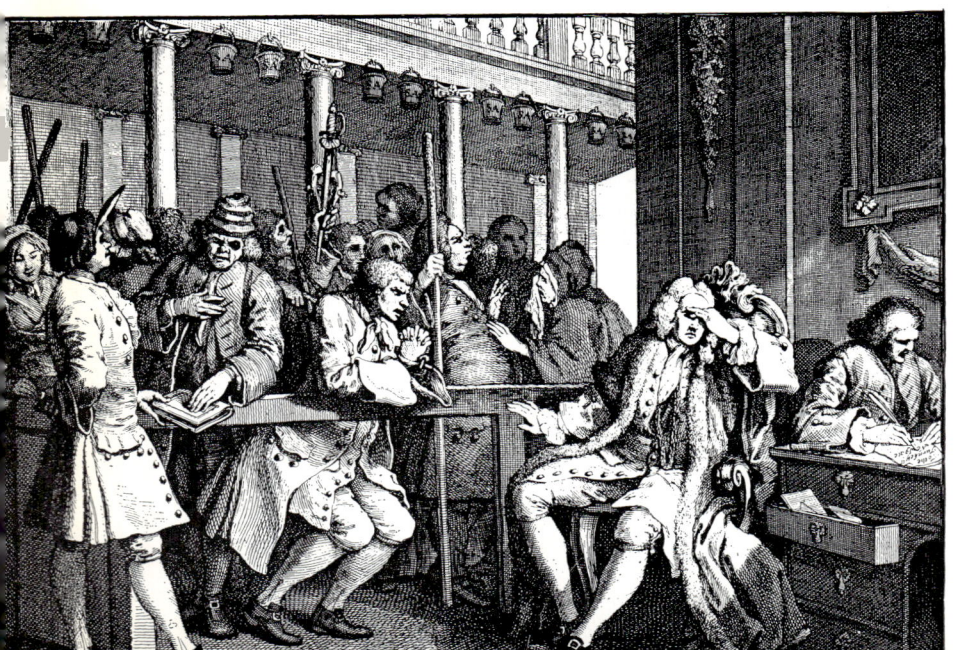

105.

Left. Industry and Idleness, 10, by William Hogarth, 1747. A magistrate's court at the Guildhall, London, at which the Idle Apprentice is brought before his industrious fellow, now an alderman, and impeached by his accomplice, who is taking the oath. The weapons taken from the prisoner are held above his head.

106. *Above*. The Harlot's Progress, 4, by William Hogarth. Nell in Bridewell, set by the master to beating hemp. Bridewell was originally a royal palace, converted in 1555 to a House of Correction. It was used for prisoners with short sentences; its regimen was particularly harsh, and as ineffective as that of any other prison of the time. Hogarth's engravings, in this and other series ⟨108⟩ are intended for an urban audience: the many people in London and elsewhere who wanted pictures, but could not afford paintings.

107. *Below*. The execution of Laurence, 4th Earl Ferrers, at Tyburn, 5 May 1760. Ferrers, who was insane, shot his steward, and was hanged after trial by his peers. Tyburn never lacked an audience, but the execution of an earl raised as much enthusiasm as those of the clergymen, Dodd and Hackman, for forgery and murder, in 1777 and 1779.

108. *Above.* An Election Entertainment, 1, by William Hogarth, 1755. Dinner at an inn, with a hostile demonstration outside; the agent in front of the table at the right has been knocked senseless with a brick while reckoning the votes; a wounded champion in the foreground is salved with gin while others leave to fight in the streets. The candidate is being embraced on the left. The series from which this is the first plate is believed to be based on the Oxfordshire election in 1754.

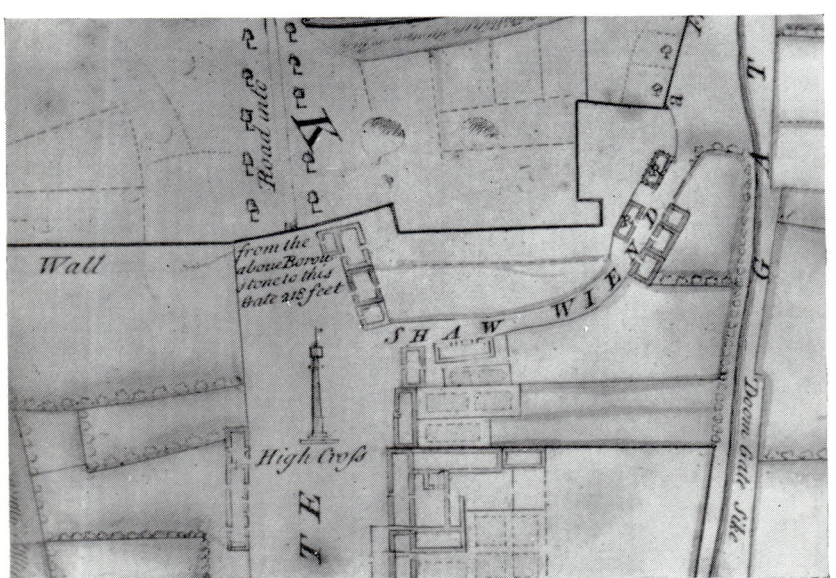

109. *Left.* Appleby, Westmorland; part of the burgage map drawn up after the great contest of 1754 (p. 58). The burgage plots, which include some open ground, are outlined in colour to mark their distribution between the Lowthers and the Tuftons, who after this time agreed to nominate members in turn. The tenements marked *R.* were challenged and rejected.

110. *Above.* The Westminster Election of 1796, water-colour by Robert Dighton. Westminster had a wider franchise than most boroughs, as the vote was given to male householders; as it was also the seat of government its elections attracted particular notice, and in the later years of the eighteenth century, when its Member was Charles James Fox, it was the scene of some sensational campaigns.

111. *Below.* Queenborough, Kent, The Poll Book, 1754. "A town memorable for nothing, but for that which is rather a dishonour to our country than otherwise . . . a miserable, dirty, decay'd, poor, pitiful fishing town; yet vested with corporation privileges" (Defoe). And, until 1832, with two Members.

112. *Above*. Bristol, Clare Street and the Drawbridge, *c.* 1770. Bristol drew great wealth from the Atlantic trade in the eighteenth century, but the waterways that had served the city since the Middle Ages for inland as well as ocean traffic, like this stretch of the Frome, were no longer able to take the largest ships. The Floating Harbour on the Avon was not started until 1804; meanwhile the quays and streets were intermingled as they always had been. The sledges shown here were used until the early nineteenth century, supposedly from a fear of breaking the sewers under the streets, two outlets of which can be seen by the bridge.

113. *Below*. Port Glasgow, 1768. Port Glasgow was founded in 1666, and was the terminus for much of Glasgow's shipping until the nineteenth century. The long building in the foreground of this picture is a rope-walk; four rope-makers are working in the open doorway.

114. *Above*. Scarborough in 1735, by John Settrington. Scarborough was the only sea-side spa, and it began to exploit the seashore at an early date, because the well-house was actually on the sands. The Spaw, as the Pump Room itself was known, is under the cliff at the left; the sands in front are used as a promenade, and the bathers in the sea are served by the earliest-known bathing-machines.

115. *Below*. Portsmouth Point, by Thomas Rowlandson. The water-front of the country's chief naval base, at the departure of the fleet.

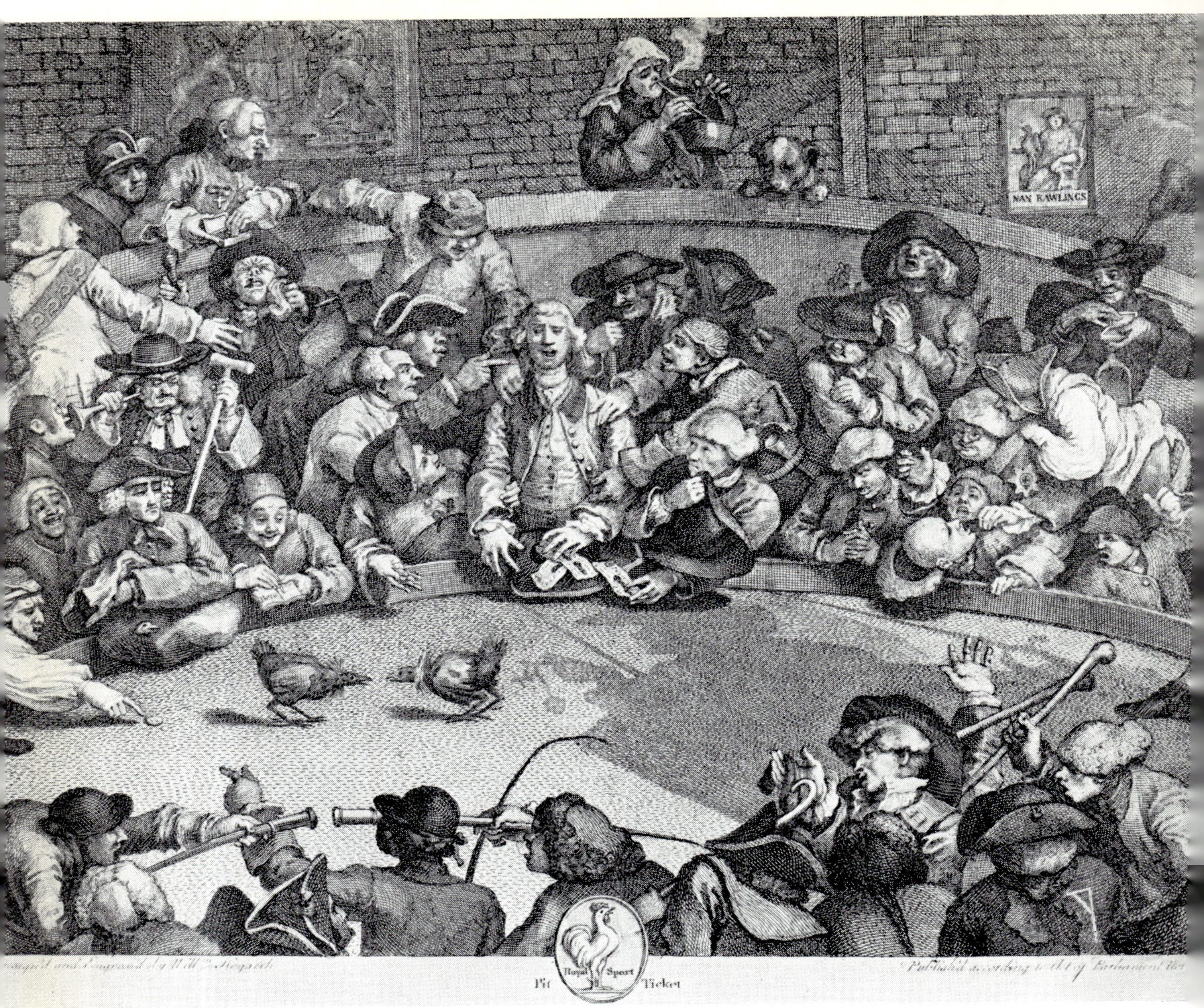
NAN RAWLINGS
Royal Sport
Pit Ticket

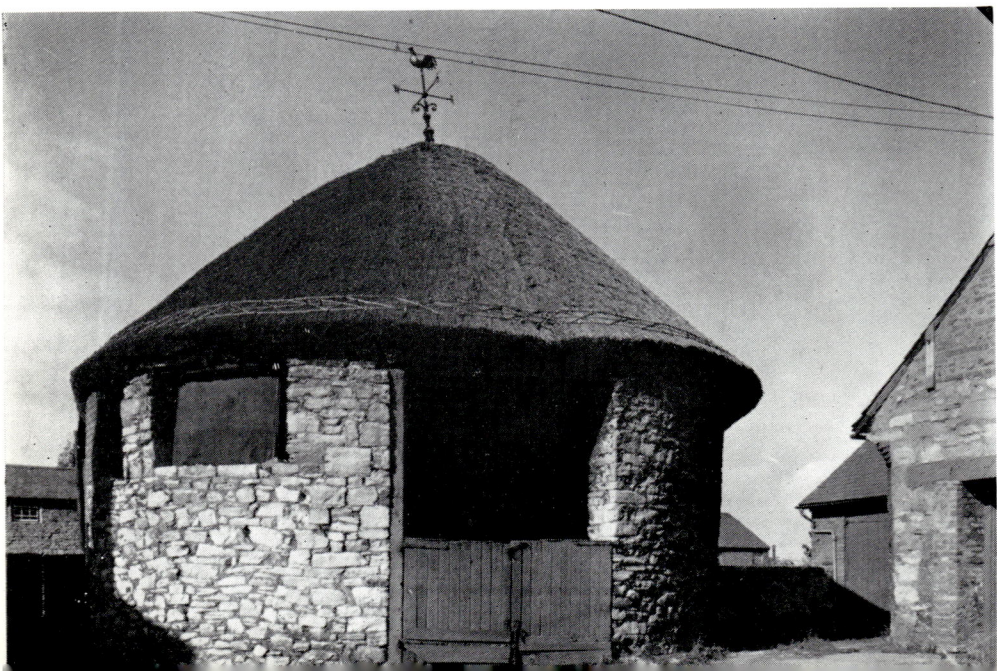

16. *Above left*. The Cock Pit, by William Hogarth, 1759. The interior of a cockpit, with a ticket in the border of the print. The appeal of cockfighting probably lay as much in its opportunities for gambling as in its savagery.

17. *Left*. Denbigh, cockpit at the Hawk and Buckle Inn. Cockpits were often provided inside inns; one survives today in the roof of the Angel, Kendal. This building, which may date from c. 1700, stands free in the inn yard.

18. *Above*. The Yarmouth Dutch Fair, by George Vincent (1796–1836). The Dutch Fair originated in the great autumn herring fair in the Middle Ages, when the fishing fleets congregated at Yarmouth, and the whole gathering of fishermen and merchants fell under the jurisdiction of the Cinque Ports for 40 days. The Dutch began to dominate the fisheries in the fifteenth century, and were not displaced by the Scots until after the Napoleonic Wars, but the character of the Yarmouth fair changed in the eighteenth century, when it became a general fair on the Denes and a local holiday of the traditional sort ⟨127⟩. This painting, appropriate to a town where the merchants' collections of paintings invited comparison with those in the Dutch towns, was made a few years before the Dutch made their last appearance at Yarmouth.

119. *Above.* Chester, Ceremonial Banner of the Smiths', Plumbers', and Cutlers' Gild, 1773. Trading communities under the name of gilds survived to a late date in some boroughs, and at Carlisle controlled the admission of freemen (pp. 57–8). Their duties at Chester included an annual contribution to the city's racing plate. (*By courtesy of Chester Corporation.*)

120. *Left.* Dalkeith, Badge of the Incorporated Trades, *c.* 1750. A carved badge from the loft or private gallery of the Incorporated Trades of the burgh of Dalkeith, formerly in the parish kirk.

121. *Right.* Liverpool, The Town Hall, 1748–1811. Liverpool commissioned a new Town Hall and Exchange from John Wood I, which was finished in 1754. In 1795 the building was gutted by fire and was then remodelled and sumptuously refitted by James Wyatt and John Foster, a local surveyor. The dome and portico are also Wyatt's work and were added in 1802 and 1811.

122. *Above*. Westminster Bridge, by Antonio Canaletto, *c.* 1747. Westminster Bridge, built between 1739 and 1750 to designs by Charles Labelye, a Swiss engineer, and demolished in 1861, was the first bridge over the Thames at London after London Bridge itself. Its elegant lines were not matched by any substantial works on the banks, and the abbey and medieval palace of Westminster are surrounded by a clutter of later houses in this view. The only other bridge built in London in the eighteenth century was Blackfriars Bridge, finished in 1760, and the river remained a great highway for passengers for many years afterwards; the craft shown here include two state barges. (*By courtesy of H.M. the Queen.*)

123. *Above right*. London, The Adelphi, 1771 onwards. The Adelphi was the grandest and most enterprising of the Adam brothers' ventures. It comprised a central block, the Royal Terrace, flanked by two streets of houses with pedimented ends on the Strand and the riverside, and the whole supported by a substructure of warehouses opening on to a wharf, the first effective embankment of the Thames. The scheme was a financial failure and had to be redeemed by a lottery, while the buildings were first mangled in the nineteenth century and then largely demolished in 1937.

124. *Right*. London, Somerset House and St. Mary-le-Strand, 1797. Somerset House was built to designs by Sir William Chambers to house a number of government offices and learned societies on the site of the great palace begun by Protector Somerset. Chambers's building was the first major public undertaking of its kind; the block fronting the Strand, one of its most successful features, was begun in 1776 and completed in 1780.

125. *Above.* Inveraray, Argyll, burgess ticket of William, Earl of Panmure, 1749. Burgess tickets were certified extracts from the burgh register of admissions, which proved a burgess's claim to his privileges, and the exclusiveness of the Scottish burghs kept them in circulation longer than similar documents in England. By the seventeenth century noble patrons and others were admitted to the freedom for the sake of past and future favours, receiving increasingly less impressive tickets at the clerk's hands. In 1767 Edinburgh resolved to limit the honour to those "signalised . . . in the service of the country or this city", and so instituted honorary freedom in the modern sense.

126. *Left.* Wolverhampton, Silver Tea-kettle, 1750. Not all eighteenth-century corporation plate took the form of punch-bowls and drinking-cups, or even of snuff- and tobacco-boxes. As tea-and coffee-drinking spread, tea- and coffee-pots appeared on public tables, while Liverpool, a temperate city by the standards of the age, had a silver cake-basket. The Wolverhampton tea-kettle has a tripod-stand containing a spirit lamp.

127. *Below right.* Coventry, Lammas Day, by David Gee, 1830. Coventry's arable fields were opened on August 1 each year for common grazing, like those of any village. The poorer citizens' interests helped to keep the practice alive, although not as disastrously as at Nottingham (p. 67), and the occasion remained a general holiday into the nineteenth century.

28. *Above left*. Bridlington, Yorkshire, shop-front. Although the term "shop-window" is medieval, the semi-permanent display of goods behind glass is a much later feature. Even in the eighteenth century shopkeepers relied on signs as much as on their windows to identify their shop, and displayed their goods outside when they were open. By that time, however, the double-fronted shop was well established ⟨131⟩, although until plate-glass was generally available the window panes were small, and the effect of a large window rather odd. The shop behind the car in this picture has narrow sheets of machine-rolled glass, an economical step towards the plate-glass window.

29. *Above right*. Cheltenham, 1 Montpellier Walk. Shops were an important feature of the Regency spa, and although this row is treated monumentally the shops are not disguised. The window blinds, which darkened the shop less than an arcade, are incorporated in the design.

130. Worcester, The Severn Bridge. Most improvements in eighteenth-century London were private; municipal activity was often slow and unwilling. The provinces generally had a better record, and most towns inaugurated schemes for paving, street-lighting, the upkeep of waterfronts and the like. The bridge over the Severn at Worcester was built in 1780 by public subscription, led by the city's M.P.s, to join the city to the fashionable suburb of St. John's. This picture also shows the river embankments tidied as much for the sake of their appearance as for use and safety: a new conception of public responsibilities.

131. *Below.* Salisbury, the demolition of the bishop's gildhall, 1788. An early and unusual view of demolition work; the medieval gildhall at the south-east corner of Salisbury market place was taken down in 1788 to make way for the present Council House. The picture also shows, besides two of the cutlers' shops for which the city was known at this time (right), the Parade Coffee House (across square, on left), and the open canals by which the low-lying site of the city was drained. These were eventually replaced after a severe outbreak of cholera in 1849.

32. *Below.* Tremadoc, Caernarvonshire: The Square. A private venture in town planning, Tremadoc was built by William Maddocks on land reclaimed at the mouth of the Glaslyn between 1800 and 1811. The little town hardly grew beyond the lines of its square, as local traffic was drawn to the harbour built at Portmadoc, a mile away.

133. *Above*. Edinburgh, Cowgate. A street scene in the Old Town, ramshackle and squalid. The wooden galleries and stone stairway were also features of the taller apartment blocks ⟨64⟩.

134. *Below*. Edinburgh, the new High School, from the Canongate churchyard. The High School, built in 1825–9 to designs by Thomas Hamilton, was the last major building in the New Town (p. 47). In the background the National Memorial on Calton Hill, which was never completed, is shown in scaffolding.

135. *Above*. Edinburgh, St. George's Church from George Street. St. George's in Charlotte Square ⟨136⟩ is the western terminal feature of the New Town, which was laid out about the axis of George Street.

136. *Below*. Edinburgh, Charlotte Square. Charlotte Square was projected as the chief feature of the New Town as early as 1768, but it was eventually built, after his death in 1792, to a general plan and elevations prepared by Robert Adam.

137. Edinburgh, Moray Place. The estates around the New Town were usually developed under single architects, each group of streets having some central feature, circus or crescent. In Moray Place, on the Earl of Moray's land, Gillespie Graham contrived to fit a regular and imposing inner façade on a most difficult site, but the houses on the north-west side turn their backs upon one of the best views that the city offers, across the Water of Leith. Few later architects would have resisted the temptation.

38. *Above*. Edinburgh, Moray Place, the western segment. The backs of these houses have elaborate substructures on the very lip of the valley, but even where the houses have garden plots behind them, their gardens were originally understood to be, as they are here, the central communal plot.

39. *Below*. Edinburgh, The University. The new building was begun in 1789 to a design by Robert Adam, but when work was suspended in 1793 the side shown here was unfinished, and the court behind was completed after 1815 to a different plan.

140. *Above*. Edinburgh, Princes Street and the Castle from Calton Hill, by Thomas Miles Richardson (1784–1848). The two towns complete, before the intrusion of the railway and the clearance of the south side of Princes Street. The castellated building in the left foreground is the prison, built when the old gaol was demolished in 1817.

141. *Below*. Edinburgh, the New Town from the Mound, *c*. 1850. A view showing Princes Street gardens and the Glasgow railway line, from the North Bridge to the tunnel below the National Gallery, with the Scott Memorial (1840–44). The tunnel to Leith, under St. Andrew's Street, can be seen just to the right of the lower bridge. The railway was an unexpected addition to the gardens, and excited great but ineffective opposition.

Above. Edinburgh, Dean Bridge. Dean Bridge is one of Thomas Telford's most impressive works. It was built in 1832, and connects the New Town to what was then suburban parkland across the Water of Leith. Its four arches, which carry the roadway 106 feet above the stream, are seen to greatest advantage from the waterside footpath from Stockbridge to Dean Village.

Below. Bristol, Clifton Suspension Bridge. A fund was set up to build a bridge over the Avon at Clifton in 1752, long before there was any real demand for a crossing, and the bridge was eventually designed by I. K. Brunel as much in response to the aesthetic and technical challenge offered by the gorge as to any practical needs. Work stopped when the pylons were completed in 1841, and the bridge was not finished until 1864.

144.

Above. "The Prince Regent entering a bathing machine at Brighton", 1818. A happy example of the English passion for improvised ritual.

145.

Left. Ladies in the Assembly Rooms at Weymouth, 1774. A fashion plate showing the season's holiday dresses in a fashionable context.

146.

Above right. Brighton, The Pavilion. The Pavilion began as an ordinary house built in the 1780s for the Prince Regent; it began to take on oriental trappings in 1802, and then was remodelled by Nash from 1815 onwards. Nash's design was a series of characteristically able improvisations, and very well suited to George IV's Brighton; the sea-side could not have had a more striking mark of approval.

147.

Right. Brighton, The Chain Pier, by J. M. W. Turner. The Romantic imagination lends a rather sombre air to this picture, but demonstrates the pier's solid qualities. It was built in 1823 for cross-Channel packets, but from the beginning it supported benches, refreshment stalls, and a Camera Obscura: the trappings of a pleasure pier (p. 50).

148. *Above*. Hove, Brunswick Square, c. 1825. The fashionable resorts had to offer their visitors the kind of accommodation they would find in London; despite the Pavilion there was not yet much sense of a holiday style; except perhaps that the makeshift was more readily tolerated, as it had to be in growing resorts like Southport. Fully-developed Regency architecture was well suited to Brighton and Hove; it had the right air of elegance, yet materials like stucco made it fairly cheap, and the terrace and square made for economical use of expensive land. Rapid development has not often produced such handsome results.

149. *Below*. Beaumaris, Victoria Terrace, c. 1840. Beaumaris living up, not without dignity, to its reputation as "one of the most fashionable bathing places in North Wales".

Above. Cheltenham, The Queen's Hotel. The spas were largely responsible for the inn's metamorphosis into the hotel. The Queen's Hotel at Cheltenham was built in 1836, and cost £50,000; it is more nearly the essence of contemporary Cheltenham than the pump rooms themselves.

Right. Berwick-on-Tweed, epitaph of Captain George Younghusband, R.N. Captain Younghusband was invalided from the Navy, and died at Cheltenham when he was only 30; most residents of the spas lived longer and earned only a local memorial. The testimony of the insurance companies and the merchants of Barbados is an unconscious witness to an important change in social habits (pp. 11, 51).

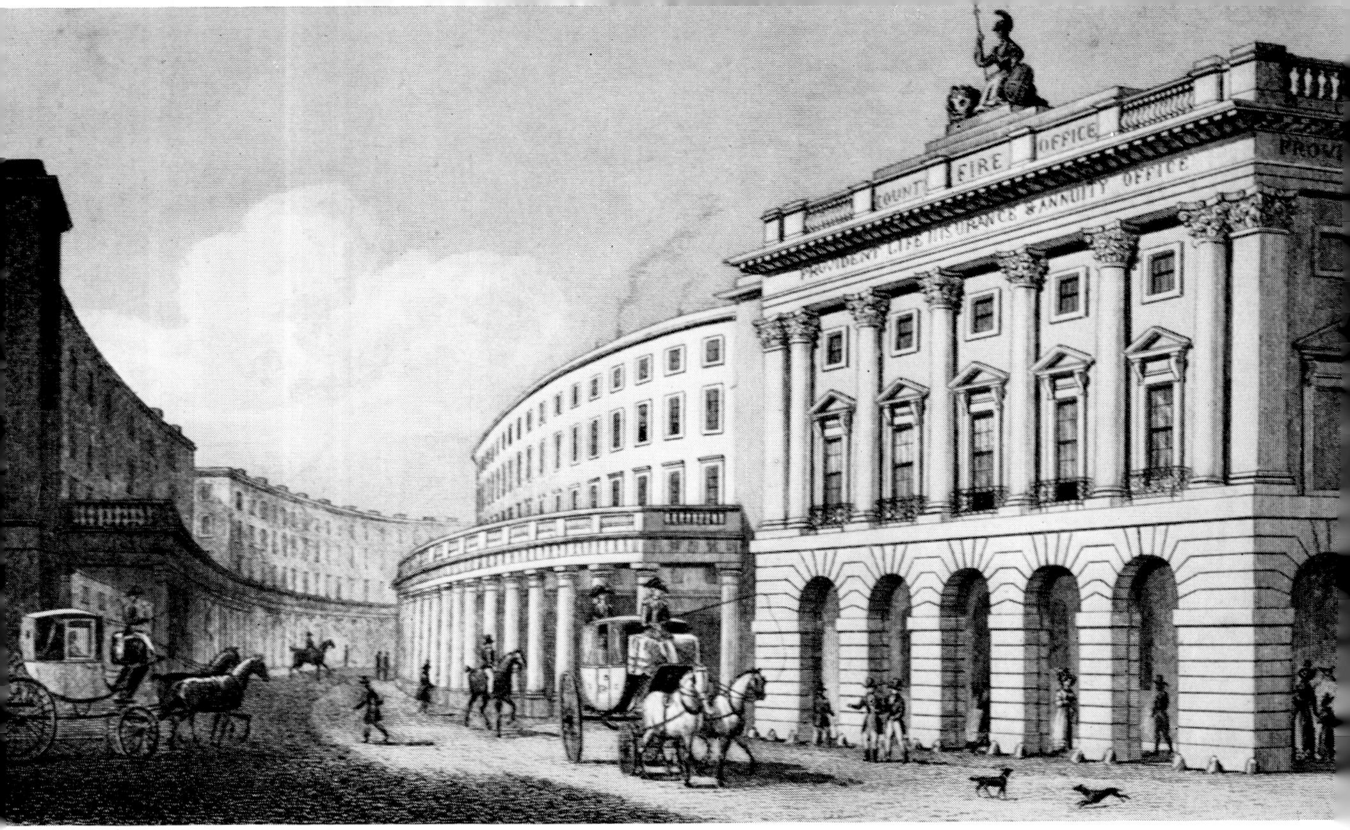
FIRE
OFFICE
PROVIDENT LIFE INSURANCE & ANNUITY OFFICE

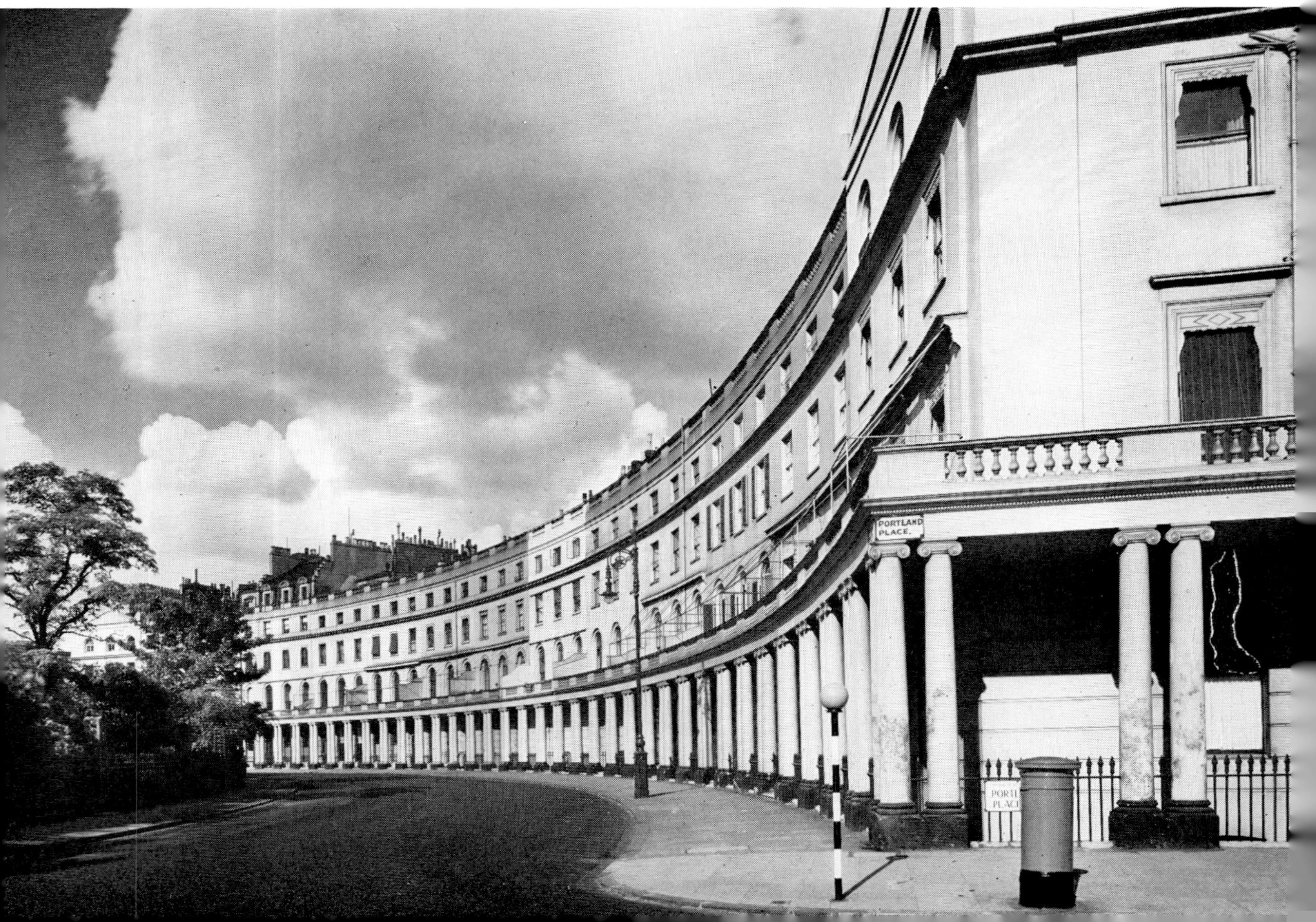
PORTLAND PLACE.

52. *Above left*. London, The Quadrant. The deliberately indirect line of Regent Street made its entrance to Piccadilly a critical matter: the Quadrant was an admirable device, but Nash had to build it at his own financial risk in order to control its details (p. 52). The gamble was fully justified. The arcades, an important part of the scheme, were removed in 1848.

53. *Left*. London, Park Crescent. "The key to Regent's Park", in Nash's own words, but the echo of the Quadrant is accidental; he first planned the Crescent as a circus, to carry Regent Street across the Marylebone Road.

54. *Above*. London, Regent's Park; Cumberland Terrace from the north. Nash's genius lay in planning rather than in architectural design, and his devices have an inspirational appropriateness. Regent Street was exactly the kind of road that the expanding West End needed, on aesthetic as well as practical grounds, while it served to dignify Regent's Park with a direct road to St. James's. The park was ingeniously planned (p. 52), but as the scheme was not realised in full some of its points are now obscured. Cumberland Terrace is the most theatrical of the terraces, an extraordinarily imposing design for a row of private houses. It stands in the middle of the west side of the park and was meant to face the *guingette* or pleasure pavilion that Nash planned for the Regent. The pavilion was never built, and Nash's elaborate architectural compliment is paid to strollers in the park instead.

155. *Above.* London, Regent's Park; the terraces from the Circular Road. The newly-planted trees and shrubs are too small to obscure the view from the roadway, which itself does not insulate the park as does an asphalt road full of motor cars.

156. *Below.* London, Regent's Park; Macclesfield Bridge. The Regent's Canal was eventually made to skirt the park on the north instead of winding through it (p. 52). Macclesfield Bridge is the north-west entrance to the park.

157. *Above*. Edinburgh, Holyrood House. An historic royal palace in a natural relationship with the capital burgh, reopened after long neglect for George IV in 1822; its setting between the King's Park and the city is extraordinarily fine, even by Edinburgh's standards.

158. *Below*. London, Buckingham Palace; Nash's original design, 1825–28. Regency London had no palace; George III lay mad at Windsor, and the Prince Regent lived at Carlton House, which Nash made the terminus of Regent Street. After his coronation George IV insisted on abandoning Carlton House, which was demolished, and commissioned a new house from Nash, a *pied-à-terre*, which Nash hoped to make his greatest work. The building was boldly planned but ill designed, and its defects were aggravated by the king's decision that it should serve after all as a palace. George's alterations made the work enormously expensive; the design's oddities were corrected by demolition and rebuilding, and on the king's death in 1830 Nash's plan was abandoned. The palace was finished, not very satisfactorily, by Edward Blore, but the present dull front was added by Sir Aston Webb in 1913.

159. Dunwich, Suffolk, from the north, *c.* 1750. Dunwich and Old Sarum are the two best-known examples of rotten boroughs. Both were important places in the early Middle Ages; Old Sarum was abandoned in the thirteenth century, while Dunwich was slowly washed away by the sea. Dunwich was the seat of a bishopric before the Conquest, and for some centuries probably the chief port on the Suffolk coast; by the end of the eighteenth century only one of its six parish churches and a handful of its houses remained, but it returned two Members to Parliament until 1832.

160. *Below.* "Freedom and Purity of Election; showing the Necessity of Reform in the close boroughs"; evictions at Tregony, Cornwall, 1820. Tregony was a decayed borough, incorporated in 1621, and returning two members until it was disfranchised in 1832. The constituency was frequently bought by the Treasury for Government candidates, and the tenants kept in debt to ensure obedience or legal eviction; the lord of the manor in 1820 was the Earl of Darlington.

61. *Right.* Manchester, "A View of St. Peter's Place". A contemporary drawing of the Peterloo massacre, 16 August 1819, when a peaceful reform meeting on the outskirts of Manchester was charged by two troops of yeomanry and hussars, who killed eleven people and seriously injured 500. The incident aroused great indignation outside the Government, and eventually served to discredit the current policy of repression.

2. *Below.* Nottingham, the Castle burning, 10 October 1831. The second Reform Bill was rejected by the Lords on 8 October 1831; the news provoked angry demonstration all over the country, and at Bristol there was a riot at the end of October which lasted for three days. The Duke of Newcastle, a borough-monger who argued that his parliamentary seats were his own property, had his windows smashed in London and his mansion, the Castle, burned in Nottingham.

163.
Above. Newcastle-under-Lyme, Staffs.; the election of the Mock Mayor, 1833. The mock mayors of Newcastle were elected in protest against the corporation's arrogation of the mayor's appointment (p. 59). When the free burgesses recovered their rights they chose Samuel Mayer as mayor in 1833. The mock elections were by that time a well-established tradition, and this commemorative picture was commissioned in 1833 by Joseph Mayer of Liverpool, Samuel's son, who presented it to Newcastle corporation. The mock mayor, dressed in a calf-skin coat and a sheep-skin wig, stands flanked by his two mace-bearers carrying cabbages. The clerk carries the charter of the mock corporation inscribed on a roll of hide, while the mayoress clings to a donkey below. On the right is Billy Punkey, a local idiot, who enjoyed yearly glory as marshal.

164.
Left. Boston, Lincs., the Borough Regalia. After the Muncipal Reform Act of 1835 the new corporations felt obliged to rid themselves of their predecessors' taints (p. 63). Corporation plate in particular aroused distasteful memories, and was often dispersed. Maces were generally kept, but at Boston the oar-mace (left, that on the right is a replica) was sold, besides the silver salver and the silver-gilt tazza (below). All have been recovered since.

165. *Right.* Thomas Burbidge, Town Clerk of Leicester, 1813–35. Burbidge was probably the most formidable champion of the unreformed municipal corporations, a cause which most people felt, with some justice, to be past defence. He took a leading part in opposing the Bill, and in organising and arguing a parliamentary petition against it, supervised the dispersal of his corporation's funds under the threat of imminent reform, and eventually secured compensation for losing his office, undoubtedly a substantial deprivation, from the new corporation.

166. *Below.* Leicester, Burbidge's valedictory entry in the Hall Book, 28 December 1835.

Memorandum

On Saturday the 26th day of December 1835 the election of Councillors for this Borough under the Act of 5th & 6th Wm 4th c. 76 took place and on Monday the 28th day of the said Month of December at one o'clock in the afternoon Richard Rawson, Esquire Mayor published and declared the names of the Councillors elected pursuant to the directions of the said Act of Parliament Whereupon and by virtue of the 38th Section of the said Act this Corporation which had existed from time immemorial was doomed to final *Dissolution*

Nevertheless God save the King and all that are put in authority under him.

167, 168.

Above. Exeter, the Cholera Epidemic of 1832; water-carriers at the dipping-steps ⟨167⟩, and men destroying infected clothing at the Shilhay ⟨168⟩. The first cholera epidemic came to England in the autumn of 1831; the disease reached Exeter the next summer, and between July and September killed 402 people there. The causes of the disease and infection were unknown, and only general precautions could be taken. Such sewers as there were discharged into the river, which was the commonest source of water in the city; water carriers drew water at the dipping-steps and elsewhere and sold it through the streets. When the epidemic began a system of quarantine and fumigation was imposed and special burial grounds opened. Infected clothing was burned by the quay on an open space called the Shilhay ⟨168⟩ normally used for tentering cloth; the racks can be seen in the background.

169.

Left. Coventry, The Provident Friendly Dispensary. One of many such institutions; the most effective steps towards improving public health were voluntary and private until the last quarter of the century.

170.

Right. Manchester, Reading the Riot Act at the Town Hall, 10 August 1842. The reforms of the 1830s created new political and economic problems: the working classes were disappointed by the Reform Act of 1832, and turned to Chartism (p. 64); municipal reform cleared the way for the incorporation of the industrial towns, but the government hesitated to entrust them with a police force. In the summer of 1842 Chartist strikes led to local violence; and at Manchester the mayor had to read the Riot Act to disperse a crowd. The Town Hall shown here was built for the town commissioners in 1822–25 by Francis Goodwin; its colonnade is now preserved in Heaton Park cf. ⟨182⟩.

171.

Below. Newport, Monmouthshire; the Chartist Revolt, 4 November 1839. The Chartists agreed on a general programme of reform but not on the means of securing it. The Physical Force party repeatedly threatened violence, but the only serious attempt at a rising occurred at Newport in 1839, when a local leader, John Frost, a J.P., led a pathetic attack on a small force of soldiers holding the Westgate Hotel. Fourteen Chartists were killed, and Frost and other leaders were later transported.

172.

Left. Newcastle-upon-Tyne, "Demolition of Houses on the Site of Collingwood Street", by William Nicholson (1781–1844). Newcastle is one of the few cities in England with a fine site ⟨175⟩ that has not been spoiled by greed and muddle. It was wealthy enough in the early nineteenth century to remodel its historic centre while architecture was still disciplined by an assured taste, and its commercial district could be planned and built for commerce unashamed. By 1800 the city was already well-built and improving rapidly, but towards the end of the Napoleonic Wars dressed stone was widely substituted for brick with happy results. The greatest improvements were the work of two men, John Dobson and Richard Grainger (p. 68), between 1825 and 1840.

173.

Below. Newcastle-upon-Tyne, Grainger Street. An entrance to the chief market, a block of alleys and an iron-and-glass-roofed hall between Grainger Street and Clayton Street.

Above. Newcastle-upon-Tyne, Grainger Street, by T. M. Richardson, *c.* 1840. A painting showing the triangular block of the Central Exchange, which once housed the Art Gallery and Reading Room, with the memorial column erected to Earl Grey in 1838. This area is the hub of the city; the colour of the stone is in interesting contrast to today's ⟨173⟩.

Below. Newcastle-upon-Tyne, The High Level Bridge. This bridge was designed by Robert Stephenson and John Dobson and was opened in 1849; the roadway (opened 1850), runs under the railway line. The whole work is as impressive a spectacle as the river demands.

176. Sheffield, *c.* 1850, by William Ibbitt. Although Sheffield had a medieval core and needed a new church Paul's, on extreme left) in the eighteenth century, it was largely created in the nineteenth. Unlike Newca

ad no local genius to impose order upon it, and it grew helplessly and quickly. It is a town accumulated
ne can hardly say organised—for work; the best-ordered district in this view is round the station and the
rves, the rest is confusion.

177. Rothesay, Bute, c. 1825. The Clyde invited excursions from Glasgow, and the steamboat encouraged them; Rothesay was attractively placed, and far enough away to draw only the wealthier citizens. Its beach was reinforced by the timely discovery of a mineral spring, and the burgh expanded to accommodate a new industry.

178. *Above left*. Torquay, Devon, from Park Hill. Away from Brighton and Margate, the tone of the early sea-side resorts was romantic and primitive. They looked back to the earliest days of the spa, and Torquay deliberately turned its back upon Classical notions of urbanity, masking its buildings with trees and garden plots. This engraving is from a letter-head sold by a Torquay bookshop.

179. *Above right*. Tenby, c. 1835; the rustic pleasures of an old port turned watering-place.

80. *Above.* Oban, Argyll. Oban began in 1711 as a storehouse for trade with the Western Isles. By the early nineteenth century it was a port and a bathing place, but its modern career as a holiday centre began later as steamers and the railways opened the Western Highlands to tourists. The extraordinary building on the hill, like a zoëtrope, was paid for *c.* 1900 by John Stuart McCaig to relieve unemployment; a recurrent problem in holiday resorts not usually so resolutely faced.

81. *Below.* Douglas, Isle of Man, *c.* 1900. The late Victorian sea-side: looming hotels and boarding houses, open carriages and trams with open sides, dark serge suits on all who can afford them.

182. *Above.* Manchester, The Town Hall and Albert Square, 1877. The triumph of municipal Gothic; designed by Alfred Waterhouse to replace the old Town Hall ⟨170⟩ in King Street.

183. *Below.* Harwich, Essex, The Great Eastern Hotel, 1864. The railway came late to Harwich (1854), and raised the town's hopes of reviving the packet service until the continental quay was opened at Parkeston up-river. One result was this large and self-assertive building at the pierhead, entirely out of scale with the rest of the town, and now the Town Hall after serving as a naval hospital in World War I.

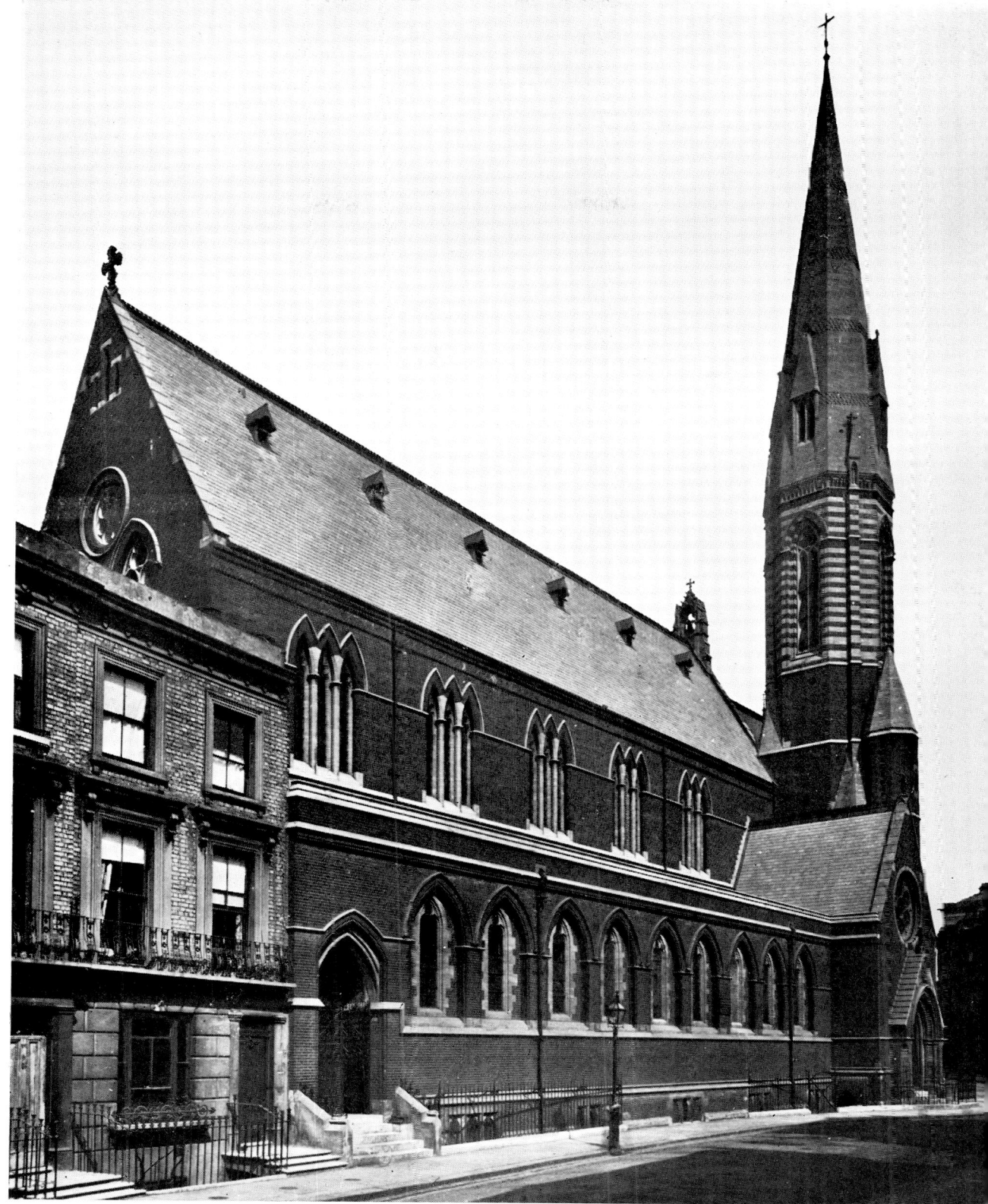

4. Paddington, St. Mary Magdalene, Woodchester Street, 1867–73. A town church by George Edmund Street, hard and gaunt, but lovingly served. Its clergy supervised a choir school, a penitentiary home and a working men's club, besides ordinary parish schools. Like some other highly successful churches in poor districts its services were conducted with an elaborate ritual; a source of warmth and colour in a district lacking both.

185. *Above*. Appleby, Westmorland, The Boroughgate in 1853, with the Moot Hall and St. Lawrence's Church. An early photograph of a small country town, looking much as the camera might have recorded it a century earlier—or, in some respects, today ⟨200.⟩
186. *Below*. Gorbals, Glasgow, Main Street, *c.* 1860. The hard, lowering face of a town overgrown and swamped by a city (p. 42).

187. *Above*. Glasgow, The Clothes Market. The second-hand clothes market probably clad the majority of a town's inhabitants in the nineteenth century; cheap, mass-produced clothes were a belated dividend from industrial progress. The market by Glasgow Green, stockaded like a North-West Mounted Police post, was an offshoot of the semi-permanent "rag fair" that choked the Saltmarket ⟨189⟩.

188. *Below*. Merthyr Tydfil. A queue at a Pawnshop, February 1875. Depression in the 1870s brought a long and bitter strike and lockout to the iron and mining towns in South Wales. Pawn-shops did well enough at the best of times; when no wages were paid at all they were the only source of money in the town.

189. Glasgow, a close in the Saltmarket, *c.* 1880. Slums are of two kinds: old houses that have deteriorated, and new houses built cheaply for a quick profit ⟨212⟩. The first kind are almost as old as towns themselves; the second became a serious and general problem in the nineteenth century; large towns had both in profusion. The Saltmarket was once Glasgow's most fashionable quarter; by the later nineteenth century it was an appalling warren.

190.

Right. Whitechapel, The People's Mission Hall, *c.* 1870. William Booth (1829–1912) opened his independent Christian Mission in 1865, and named the movement that it generated the Salvation Army in 1878. At first he was simply a revivalist preacher, but, as he said later, "in order to reach the people whom we could not reach by any other means, we gave the hungry wretches a meal, and then talked to them about God and eternity". The Salvation Army's great social work grew from these beginnings.

191.

Below. A picnic for slum children in Epping Forest, organised by the Salvation Army, *c.* 1900.

192. *Above.* Saltaire, Yorkshire, a view of Salt's alpaca worsted factory and the model town, *c.* 1860. Titus Salt opened his factory beside the Leeds and Liverpool Canal in 1853, and declared the model town complete in 1871, when he opened the ornamental park there (p. 69). The factory, which employed 3,000 hands, dominated the town, but the quality of the houses and of the town's amenities was very high by the standards of the time.

193. *Right.* Sir Titus Salt (1803–76). Salt was Mayor of Bradford and Liberal M.P. for the town as well as one of the leading cloth manufacturers of his day. He received a baronetcy for his work at Saltaire in 1869.

194. *Right*. Aberdeen, Queen Victoria turning on the new water supply, 10 October 1866.

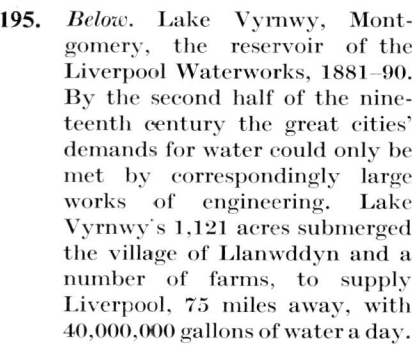

195. *Below*. Lake Vyrnwy, Montgomery, the reservoir of the Liverpool Waterworks, 1881–90. By the second half of the nineteenth century the great cities' demands for water could only be met by correspondingly large works of engineering. Lake Vyrnwy's 1,121 acres submerged the village of Llanwddyn and a number of farms, to supply Liverpool, 75 miles away, with 40,000,000 gallons of water a day.

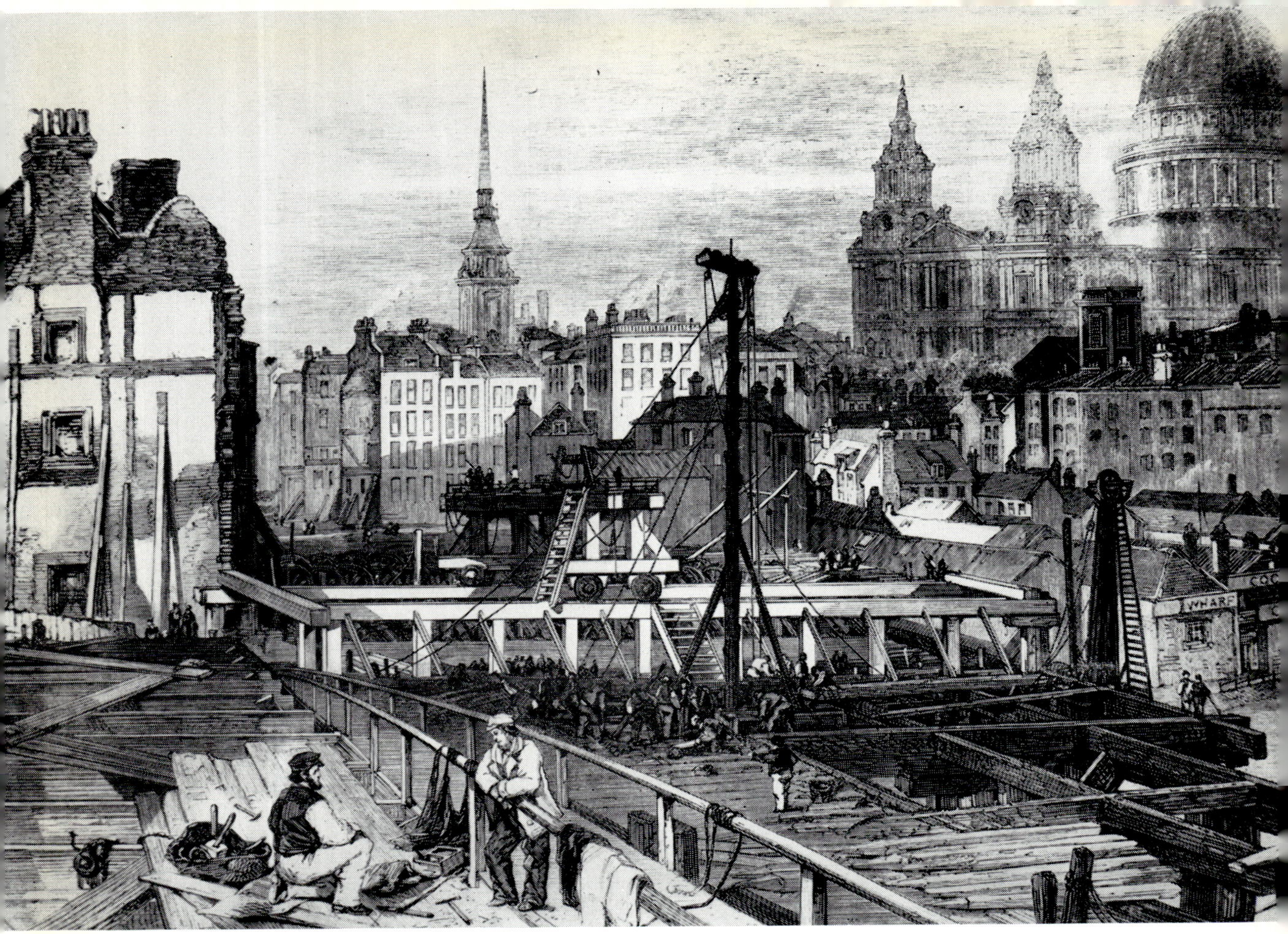

196. *Above*. London, work on the London, Chatham & Dover Railway's line from Blackfriars Bridge to Ludgate Hill and Holborn, 1864. The metropolitan works of what *Punch* called the "Goths and Vandals Railway" turned more than 3,000 people out of their houses. The railways helped workmen and others to live on the healthier fringes of the town, but at a very heavy cost in damage and dislocation at the centre, which they made less wholesome than ever.

197. *Below*. Barrow-in-Furness, a steam-tram, c. 1890. The steam-tram had a comparatively short life between the horse-drawn and the electric tram. Trams and their tracks were a nuisance to other traffic, but they offered the first chance to mechanise public transport inside the towns and were gratefully exploited.

198. *Right.* Birmingham, The Bull Ring, 1905. The heart of a city with the pedestrian still in control of the street. Morphologically speaking, this is the same area as Selby market ⟨11⟩ or the lower Boroughgate at Appleby ⟨185⟩—the commercial space in front of the principal church. Here the town has grown uncontrollably around it, but motor-traffic has not yet swamped the scene.

199. *Below.* London, Piccadilly Circus, *c.* 1895. A segment of Nash's work, riddled with offices and their important announcements, and choked by the bustling disorder of the Victorian city.

200. *Above*. Appleby, Westmorland, the Jubilee celebrations in Boroughgate, 1897. The same street as in 1853 ⟨185⟩ but this time part of the modern world. The restored Moot Hall has the hard edges appropriate to a mechanical age; the clothes, like the occasion, look old-fashioned to our eyes, but not archaic. The fire-brigade steam engine, perhaps, lies betwixt and between.

201. *Below*. Kirkcaldy, Fife, The Fire-Brigade, 1898. A volunteer brigade, of which seven men were building-workers. Fire-fighting was now a public service, and the brigades better equipped than ever before, although they had some years to wait for motor engines. In recent years the development of telephones and short-wave radio, together with the increasing cost of equipment, have produced a centralised service, largely managed by the counties; the Kirkcaldy brigade passed under county control in 1948.

202. *Above*. Westminster, Millbank Gardens, August 1905. An early London County Council housing scheme (1897–1902), remarkable because it is the first of its kind that does not advertise, however high-mindedly, its praiseworthy purpose. The blocks are large, but are planned and designed simply as large blocks of flats, not as Model Dwellings for the Industrious raised at public expense.

203. *Below*. Wandsworth, opening the Bathing Lake on Tooting Common, 28 July 1906. A newly-improvised ritual for a new occasion; municipal baths are older than municipal parks, but the swimming pool is a late arrival.

204. *Above.* The Upper Rhondda Fawr, Glamorgan. By 1914 the Rhondda Valley was the centre of the Welsh steam-coal industry, and had a population of more than 110,000 people scattered along its floor. Its houses took a respectful second place to industrial sites along what level ground there was, and as elsewhere in South Wales the settlements were entirely contained by the valley, with almost no communications across the hills. The Rhondda Urban District Council was set up in 1897, but its progress was checked by the depression after 1918, and the townships became a borough only in 1955. Since World War II the potentialities of the site have been intelligently exploited, but there are still many reminders of the fearful short-sightedness of Victorian industry.

205. *Above*. Liverpool from the Mersey. The waterfront at Liverpool is a monument to the great days of the Atlantic trade, and to the city's emergence before 1914 as the largest British port after London. The central trio of buildings comprises the domed Dock Offices (1907), the Liver Insurance building (1910), and between them the square block of the Cunard Offices, finished in 1916: an appropriate and impressive introduction to the cosmopolitan city behind.

206. *Below*. Liverpool, the Landing Stage; *c*. 1890. The half-mile landing stage in front of the quays at Liverpool has always been something more. It is a promenade, and a place where office workers can sit and eat, or stroll at midday: the natural focus of interest in a city that lives by shipping.

207. *Above*. Reading, a food-queue during World War I. Britain took longer to order its economic than its military resources in World War I, and there was no civilian rationing scheme until the German submarine campaign brought the country within sight of starvation in the winter of 1917–18. Food supplies were short, and were often inefficiently distributed. This grave oversight was partly responsible for the heavy loss of life in the influenza epidemic of 1918, and its lesson was remembered when the government had again to plan for war in the 1930s.

208. *Below*. Brighton, Earl Beatty unveiling the War Memorial, 1922. Although some ports on the north-east coast were shelled from the sea, and places in the south bombed, Britain's experience of World War I's crushing violence was indirect, and came through the casualty lists. There were hardships for the civilian population ⟨207⟩, but they could not remove the uneasy knowledge that the armed forces lived and died in a world awesomely apart. The war memorials that were raised all over the country after 1918 therefore had two functions. That avowed was to commemorate the dead, and their companions who survived; the other was to propitiate them, and to bury an intolerable memory under decent stone.

9. *Above*. Leeds, Quarry Hill. The greatest change induced in the towns by World War I was the appearance of municipal housing. The "council houses" sanctioned by the Housing Act of 1919 appeared everywhere, usually too quickly and too cheaply to be of more than mediocre quality. The flats at Quarry Hill are an interesting exception. They were designed in 1935, and deliberately avoid the characterless uniformity of the semi-detached housing estate, but their scale is very large and their site, though self-contained with its own shops and gardens, is rather bleak.

10. *Below*. London, the General Strike, May 1926; an escorted food-lorry entering Hyde Park. Either the Government or the strikers had to feed the towns during the Strike; in London the Government equipped a deliberately impressive depôt in Hyde Park. The emergency gave road transport an impetus it has not lost since.

211. The blight of the depression; a street corner in Wigan in the 1930s.

Nottingham, Kentons' Square, Edward Street, c. 1931. One of the courts, by no means the worst, cleared by Nottingham corporation under its rehousing scheme. Nottingham's housing problem was acute, for local and historical reasons (p. 67); the depression only underlined it.

213. *Above.* Professional football: supporters of West Ham United at Wembley, April 1923. Professional Association Football was a well-established popular sport by the 1920s, but it was essentially a townsman's sport: a weekly source of companionable excitement, and a relief from the sober demands of everyday life.

214. *Below.* Bedford, Marks & Spencer's store, *c.* 1932. The chain store appeared before 1914, but it made its greatest impression on the town between the wars. Despite the depression it brought abundance and the promise, gradually redeemed since 1945, of better quality for popular goods.

215. *Above*. Birmingham, the Gaumont Palace Cinema, *c.* 1945. The cinema became an essential part of the town after 1918. It offered excitement and an atmosphere of luxury when many people's lives were drab and anxious and, in 1939–45, even dangerous. Its façades yawn to impress and draw in the audience.

216. *Below*. Kentmere, Westmorland, the market-day omnibus, April 1960. Kentmere is a lonely fellside hamlet 10 miles above Kendal, but on Saturdays it has its own transport to the excitements of Kendal market, a luxury unthinkable even in the railway's most optimistic days.

Left. London, the Elephant and Castle Underground Station, 1940. Many of the assumptions made before the war about the effects of bombing were ill-founded, from want of experience. It was not possible, and in the event it proved unnecessary, to evacuate people from the larger towns on the scale proposed in 1938 and those who obstinately stayed proved much more resilient when in danger and discomfort than any cautious man could have supposed. The use of the Underground Railway stations as air-raid shelters, which was not originally an official policy, underlined the fact that a great town's resources, both human and material, were more adaptable than they seemed.
Above. A barrage balloon in a London park, *c.* 1942. The elements of this picture, the sheep, the balloon, and the park itself, make sense only in their relation to the invisible city.
Below. London. Oxford Street, 1940. The damage inflicted on British towns from 1940 onwards was greatly exceeded in Germany, and in Japan, but the winter of 1940–41 saw the first attempt in the history of war to reduce a country by aerial bombardment. The attempt failed, but it was one which could be conceived only in terms of a complex economy: towns provided both the weapons and the target. The monumental waste of material that ensued—though not the waste of life—is exemplified in this scene of squalid destruction.

220 *Above.* Plymouth, Royal Parade. Plymouth was one of the towns so badly damaged by bombing that their first concern after the war was simply to survive. Its planning was unusually urgent, but it could also afford to be bold. Royal Parade is a new street, which continues the line of the nineteenth-century Union Street across the devastated area. It opposes new shops and commercial buildings to the fifteenth-century parish church, St. Andrew's, and the Victorian Guildhall (1870-74), both gutted in the air-raids and now very happily refitted. The Parade is too open for the pedestrian's comfort, but it takes in the church and Guildhall in an ingenious and satisfactory way.

221 *Below.* Plymouth, Sutton Pool. The decay of the town's oldest districts is a problem not confined to Plymouth, but it was aggravated there, as at Yarmouth, by bombing. These flats in Woolster Street, fitted between a nineteenth-century (right) and a sixteenth-century house, mark the successful rehabilitation of the area round the original harbour. The new waterfront shows clearly the advantages of filling gaps and repairing old property, rather than razing a site that is sentimentally and aesthetically valuable to the town.

222. *Above.* Cwmbran New Town, Monmouthshire; Two Locks. In 1946 (p. 82) Cwmbran was a mining and steel town that had attracted new industries since the depression, and its Development Corporation had to provide housing on an intricately circumscribed site. The plan disposes a series of 'neighbourhoods', about an entirely new centre. Two Locks is a close of family houses, less extravagantly spaced than semi-detached houses, but still consciously rejecting the worst features of the past ⟨212⟩.

223. *Below.* Glenrothes New Town, Fife; Woodside, a local shopping centre, comprising a court of shops with flats above, and a community hall. Glenrothes is intended partly to control the development of the East Fife coalfield, and partly to draw off people from Glasgow, although the New Towns at East Kilbride and Cumbernauld are designed more specifically for that purpose.

224. *Above*. Crawley New Town, Sussex; Queen's Square. One of the most successful of the New Towns' centres, Queen's Square reacts in part against the Garden City, and also against the idea that the true end of town planning is to encourage motor traffic. The square is paved, and so can be walked on in all weathers, and most of it is closed to vehicles. The shops stand together, sheltering the passer-by without dominating the square, and the general simplicity is alleviated by the patterned pavement, the trees, and the Victorian bandstand.

225. *Below*. Corby New Town, Northamptonshire; Woodnewton Way Infants' School.

226. *Above*. Birmingham, Elmdon Airport, 1956. The smallness of Britain and the heavy competition from other kinds of transport have discouraged an elaborate system of domestic air-services. The first regular helicopter service between British cities was run experimentally by British European Airways between Birmingham, Nottingham and Leicester, with international connections at Birmingham, in 1956. This picture shows an S.55 helicopter landing at Elmdon from Nottingham.

227. *Below*. Liverpool, the Kingsway entrance to the Mersey Tunnel. The Mersey Tunnel was opened in 1934; it has an hourly capacity of 4,000 vehicles, but it opens on to streets that were not designed for motor traffic. The picture shows a stationary queue of cars in St. John's Lane.

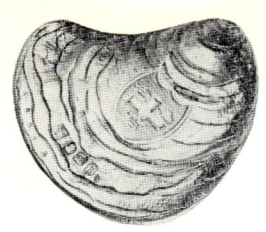

228. *Left.* Colchester, the opening of the Colne Fishery. Its rights in the Colne fishery extend the borough of Colchester's jurisdiction into the estuary of the river, and the oyster fishery there is opened annually by the mayor. This picture, taken in 1948, shows Alderman L. E. Dansie waiting for the oldest freeman on the river to open the first dredge.

229. *Above.* Colchester, Silver Oyster Gauge, 1804. This gauge, 2½ in. long, was used to check the size of oysters dredged and sold from the Colne fishery.

230. *Below.* Hawick, Roxburghshire, the Common Riding, 1960. Every year the boundaries of Hawick are ridden by the Hawick Cornet, carrying the town flag, which here is being dipped in the Teviot to mark a boundary-point. Similar ceremonies survive in other burghs, but the flag at Hawick is a copy of one captured from the men of Hexham Priory, Northumberland, in 1514, and appropriated as the town flag of Hawick. The original survived until 1704.

1. *Above.* Kendal, the Call Stone. This stone, once part of Kendal's Market Cross, is now built into the modern town hall, and is still used for special announcements: here for the proclamation of H.M. Queen Elizabeth II in 1952 by the mayor, Alderman W F. Pennington.
2. *Below.* Kirkwall, Orkney, The New Year's Day Ba' Game. Traditional games of football on fixed days, which are probably relics of pagan rites, survive in several places in Britain, but for obvious reasons they have lasted more readily in the country than in towns. The Kirkwall Ba' Game is a lively exception; the picture shows the throw-in at the Mercat Cross, about 1958.

233. London, the Lord Mayor's Show, 1959. The Lord Mayor's Show is one of the most famous pieces of civic pageantry in the world. In the Middle Ages the newly elected mayor rode in procession to Westminster after he had been sworn in at the Guildhall, to be presented to the Barons of the Exchequer, the government office to which municipal officers were primarily responsible. In 1459 the mayor went by water, and so inaugurated the river procession that remained the days' chief spectacle until 1849. Although London alone among English towns kept a Common Council that was democratically elected in the wards, the mayor's election, like admissions to the freedom of the city, lay with the companies, which therefore figured largely in the celebrations. During the nineteenth century the procession took on a different theme each year, usually inspired by the Lord Mayor's own associations, and in the twentieth it has been dissociated from the formal ceremony of admission (which now takes place before the Lord Chief Justice) to avoid choking the streets on a weekday. The Lord Mayors represent, as they have always done, a wide variety of industrial and commercial interests, and the Show's theme is more often topical than traditional. In 1959, however, the Lord Mayor, Sir Edmund Stockdale, was a farmer, and for a few hours town and countryside were as close together as when burgesses counted common grazing among their privileges, or when FitzStephen praised London's arable fields as "not parched and rough, but rich as the plains of Asia".

Bibliographical Note

THERE are more histories of British towns than there are towns in Britain; they begin with medieval chronicles and books of memoranda ⟨21⟩, and increase enormously in number from the sixteenth century onward ⟨53⟩. There are some thousands of books on London alone, and Great Yarmouth, one of the best-documented provincial towns, has a long succession of histories starting with those of the Henry Manships, elder and younger (edited by C. J. Palmer in 1847 and 1854), the earlier of which was written in Elizabeth I's reign. Apart from more specialised books, most English towns have been covered by the older county histories—such as John Hutchins's *Dorset* (1774), or *Westmorland and Cumberland* (1777) by Joseph Nicholson and Richard Burn— which often contain extracts from local records, besides depicting the towns on the eve of the great changes of the Victorian age.

The only critical survey of this great volume of work is Charles Gross's *Bibliography of British Municipal History* (1897). Gross—whose *Gild Merchant* (1890) is also a standard work, although it should now be read in the context of Emile Coornaert's "Les Gildes Medievales" (*Revue Historique*, 1948)—was chiefly interested in municipal institutions, and he compiled his bibliography just as a great generation of scholars began to explore the subject. The best guide to their work is James Tait's *Medieval English Borough* (1936), a deeply learned book which has suffered even in scholarly esteem from Tait's habit of making difficult subjects seem difficult. The only substantial addition that can be made to its bibliography is Martin Weinbaum's *British Borough Charters, 1307–1660* (1943). Like Gross, Tait was concerned with constitutional matters and only incidentally with ordinary life in towns: that subject necessarily took second place to the absorbing questions of origins and definition, and it has also suffered from the abundance of material, and perhaps from an English distaste for abstractions. There is nothing for England to compare with E. A. Lewis's admirable *Medieval Boroughs of Snowdonia* (1912), or with W. M. Mackenzie's *The Scottish Burghs* (1949), which treat their subjects in comprehensive terms.

Much of the material for a history of English towns is still buried in their muniment rooms. The *Reports* of the Royal Commission on Historical Manuscripts (1874– listed in H.M.S.O. Sectional List No. 17) are useful guides to borough archives, although their extracts are usually on a smaller scale than the solid volumes of the Scottish Burgh Records Society (1868–1911). Some towns have published part of their records: more than twenty volumes have appeared from the City of London's archives, many of them edited by R. R. Sharpe, Corporation Records Clerk from 1876 to 1913. Nottingham and Leicester each have a series, begun respectively by W. H. Stevenson and Mary Bateson, in which modern volumes are being prepared. Other places, like Southampton (1909–) and Bristol (1929–), have record societies which have produced some distinguished volumes. Social and economic historians have hardly begun to use this material. Stuart and Georgian Exeter is now quite thoroughly documented by a number of studies, of which the latest is W. B. Stephens's *Seventeenth-Century Exeter, 1625–88* (1958). Alice Green's *Town Life in the Fifteenth Century* (1894), which is based on the reports on Historical Manuscripts, is still useful, while in a highly specialised study of the same period Sylvia Thrupp's *Merchant Class of Medieval London* (1948) examines the London merchant and his family in remarkable detail.

Surveys of that kind are rare; in Britain more energy has gone into histories of particular towns, often with a strong legal and constitutional bias. Some are embedded in a wider subject, like the brilliant study of Cambridge in F. W. Maitland's *Township and Borough* (1898), or cover more topics than their titles imply, as does James Tait's *Medieval Manchester and the Beginnings of Lancashire* (1904). The most solidly informative are often old, like H. Owen and J. B. Blakeway's *History of Shrewsbury* (1825), but the little volumes of Longmans's series on *Historic Towns* (1887–1906) contain some interesting material. Two notable modern works are C. Gill and A. Briggs's *History of Birmingham* (1952), the first large-scale history of an industrial city, and J. W. F. Hill's history of Lincoln, of which two volumes, *Medieval Lincoln* (1948) and *Tudor and Stuart Lincoln* (1956), have so far appeared. *Stratford upon Avon*, by Levi Fox (1953), is an excellent study of a kind that is oddly rare: a brief history of an ancient town which is of both local and general interest. Ruth Fasnacht's *History of the City of Oxford* (1954) deals succinctly with the municipal history of a city usually overshadowed by its university; it also stands in entertaining contrast to the 100-odd volumes of the Oxford Historical Society, which has dealt most admirably with the history of the same place since 1884. The *Victoria County Histories* cover a number of towns, but at present only one, Leicester, has been accorded a volume to itself (1958), although others will follow.

Among social and economic histories, J. A. R. Pimlott's *The Englishman's Holiday* (1947) contains a valuable discussion of holiday resorts, since reinforced by E. W. Gilbert's *Brighton* (1954). J. D. Marshall's *Furness and the Industrial Revolution* (1958) describes the rise of Barrow-in-Furness. W. H. Chaloner's *Social and Economic Development of Crewe, 1780–1923* (1950) also falls in this category, and so does John Summerson's illuminating architectural survey: *Georgian London* (1948). The historic architecture of towns is discussed in some instances by the *Reports* of the Royal Commission on Historical Monuments, which as yet cover only a large handful of counties; the volume on Edinburgh (1943) also contains a valuable historical commentary. These are among the latest in a long line of official publications, which include such specialised matter as the reports on *Municipal Corporations* (1835) and *Municipal Boundaries* (1837), and the returns of the decennial *Census of the United Kingdom* which are in themselves a skeleton-history of the modern town.

INDEX

The figures in italics refer to the illustrations on p. 85 onwards.

ABERAVON, 20
Aberdeen, 21, 48, 73, *65, 194*
Abingdon, 12
Adam, the Brothers, 43
—, Robert, 46, 47, 54
—, William, 47
Allen, Ralph, 45
Appleby, 49, 58, *109, 185, 200*
Arnside, 73

BARROW-IN-FURNESS, 70–71, 75, *197*
Bath, 16, 33, 41, 45, 48, 51, 61, 71, 73, *91–98*
Beaumaris, 14, 22, 71, *149*
Bedford, *214*
Bentham, Jeremy, 44, 56, 65
Bere, Merioneth, 14
Berwick-on-Tweed, 15, 22, 26–27, 36, *151*
Birkenhead, 66, 70
Birmingham, 24, 28, 36, 43, 57, 59–60, 62, 63, 64, 74, 76, 82, *198, 215, 226*
Blackpool, 48, 73, 80
Blandford, Dorset, 54, *86*
Boston, 41, *164*
Boulton, Matthew, 43, 60
Bournemouth, 50, 72, 73, 81
Bournville, 70
Bradford, 36
Bridgnorth, 36
Bridlington, *128*
Brighton, 46, 48, 49, 50, 61, 73, 75, *144, 146–147, 208*
Bristol, 15, 17, 18, 23, 30, 36, 40, 41, 54, 62, 65, 74, *19, 21, 29, 30, 57, 99, 112*. See also Clifton
Bruton, Somerset, *82*
Burbidge, Thomas, 63, *165*
Burford, 24
Burghs, Convention of Royal, 21, 27, 41
Burton, Decimus, 54
—, James, 53–54
Bury St. Edmunds, 12, 13, 15, 23, *78*
Buxton, 33, 46

CADBURY, GEORGE, 70
Caernarvon, 9, 14, 22, 71, *1*
Calais, 21, 25

Cambridge, 14, 15, 24, 59, *43*
Canterbury, 11, 18, *32*
Cardiff, 12, 78
Cardigan, 12
Carlisle, 14, 22, 26, 57–58, 79, *14, 35, 48*
Carmarthen, 88
Chadwick, Edwin, 65, 67
Chantries, 23–24
Chard, Somerset, 38
Chartism, 64, 72, *170, 171*
Chatham, 40, *75*
Cheltenham, 51, 61, 62, *129, 150*
Chester, 14, 15, 23, 26, 28, 29, 56, 58, 67, *119*
Chichester, *13*
Chipping Campden, 34
Cholera, 67, *167, 168*. See also Public health
Churches, 13, 16, 17, 23, 32, 34, 35, 36, 49, 54, 69, 76–77, *3, 5, 11, 29, 40, 72, 86, 88–90, 135, 184, 185, 198, 220*
Cinemas, 80, 83, *215*
Cinque Ports, 12, 14, 30
Cirencester, 14
Clifton, 54, *143*
Colchester, 11, 13, 15, 24, 25, 29, 36, 43, 57, *100, 228, 229*
Congleton, Cheshire, 26
Conway, 14, 22
Corby, Northants, *225*
Corn laws, 61, 62, 64
Corporations, municipal, 17–18, 20–21, 37–38, 47–48, 57, 58–60, *125*
—, Act (1835), see Municipal Corporations. See also Mayors, Regalia and plate
Coventry, 17, 18, 19, 20, 24, 36, 81, *44, 127, 169*
Crawley, Sussex, *224*
Crewe, 69
Criccieth, 14
Cwmbran, Mon., *222*

DALKEITH, 120
Dalton-in-Furness, 71, *12*
Defoe, Daniel, 34, 42, 48
Denbigh, 30, 36, 60, 66, *117*
Derby, 59, 62, 70
Devonport, 40
Dingwall, 13, 41
Doncaster, 59
Dorchester-on-Thames, 11

Douglas, Isle of Man, 52, *181*
Droitwich, 51
Dumbarton, 42
Dundee, 41, 47
Dunwich, 57, *159*
Durham, 23, 36, 74
Dysart, Fife, 28

EDINBURGH, 13, 15, 21, 27, 41, 46–47, 53, 56, 57, 65, 82, *45–46, 64, 133–142, 157*
Elections, parliamentary, 18, 29–31, 57–58, 62, *108–111, 159, 160*
Elgin, 13, 49
Epsom, 33, 34, 40, 45, 48
Exeter, 19, 23, 48, *167, 168*
Exmouth, 48, 49

FAIRS, see Markets
Falkirk, 43
Falmouth, 40
Faversham, 19
Fire, 39, 54, *70–71, 84–86, 200, 201, 219*
Football, 79, *213, 232*. See also Sports

GARDEN CITIES, 70, 78
Gatton, Surrey, 18, 30, 57
General Strike, 80, *210*
Gilds and companies, 13, 16, 20, 23–24, 26, 58, *22, 23, 47, 119, 120, 233*
Glasgow, 13, 21, 40, 41, 42, 47, 48, 65, 76, 80, 82, *63, 186–187, 189*
Glastonbury, *31*
Glenrothes, Fife, *223*
Gloucester, 11, 17, 23, 26, 36, *38*
Grange-over-Sands, 73
Grantham, 18
Gresham, Sir Thomas, 32

HADDINGTON, 21
Hadleigh, Suffolk, 26
Halifax, 36
Hanley, Staffs., 59. See also Stoke-on-Trent
Harlech, 14
Harrogate, 33, 51
Harwich, 15, 57, *76, 183*
Hawick, *230*
Hedon, 18
Holidays, 26, 56, 72–73, 80, *163*. See also Pilgrimages, Seaside resorts
Holt, Norfolk, 54
Hospitals, 44–45, 49, *91, 169*. See also Public health legislation
Housing, 68, 71, 76, 77, 80, 82, 83, *202, 209, 212*. See also Town planning
Hove, 50, *148*
Howard, Ebenezer, 70, 78
—, John, 44, 56
Hull, 14, 18, 36, 81

IMPROVEMENT COMMISSIONS, 55, 60–61, 72, *130*
Inveraray, Argyll, *125*
Inverness, 13
Ipswich, 11, 23, 25, 35, 57, *42*

JONES, INIGO, 32, 43. See also Town planning

KELSO, 9
Kendal, 16, 22, *231*
Kirkcaldy, Fife, *201*
Kirkwall, Orkney, *232*

LANCASTER, 40
Leamington, 51
Leeds, 16, 34, 36, 62, 74, *209*
Leicester, 19, 35, 63, 75, *24, 165, 166*
Leith, 27
Letchworth, 78
Lever, W. H., 1st Viscount Leverhulme, 70
Lincoln, 11, 13, 18, 24, 25, 29, 35, 36, *51*
Liverpool, 9, 29, 30, 40, 42, 57, 59, 63, 65, 67, 76, *83, 121, 195, 205, 206, 227*
Llanvaes, Anglesey, 12
London, 12, 13–14, 15, 17, 20, 22, 23, 25, 26, 30, 31–34, 35, 36, 38–40, 41, 42, 43–44, 52–54, 56, 62, 74, 76, 80, 81, 82, *8, 39, 50, 53, 54, 61, 62, 69–72, 85, 87, 101, 103, 104–107, 123–124, 152–156, 158, 184, 190, 191, 196, 199, 203, 210, 213, 217–219, 232*. See also Westminster
—, County Council, 68, *202*

Looe, Cornwall, 59
Lostwithiel, *81*
Lowther, James, 1st Earl of Lonsdale, 59
—, Sir John, 40
Ludlow, 18, 22, 28, *23*
Lynn, King's (Bishop's Lynn), 14, 25, 36, 40, *18*

MALMESBURY, 23
Manchester, 10, 14, 36, 40, 55, 57, 59, 60–61, 62, 63, 65, 67, 73, 74, 76, *161, 170, 182*
Margate, 48, 50, 52, 73
Markets and fairs, 9, 11, 12, 13, 14, 16, 22, 26, 27, 28, 32, 34, 36, 40, 52, 53, 54, *9–14, 22, 26, 55, 57, 78, 118, 127, 131*. See also Holidays
Marlborough, 79
Mayors, 13–14, *21, 163, 228, 231, 233*. See also Corporations
Melrose, *36*
Merthyr Tydfil, 62, 66, *188*
Middlesbrough, 70
Mistley, Essex, 54
Montgomery, 12
Montrose, 47
Motor transport, 66, 80, 82, 83, *216, 227*
Municipal Corporations Act, 63

NASH, JOHN, 44, 46, 52–53
Nash, Richard, 41, 45, *92*
Nevin, 12
New towns, 11, 12, 13, 14–15, 16, 27, 33–34, 46–49, 69–72, 78, *1, 5, 60, 71, 77, 132, 133–142, 192, 197*. See also Fire, Seaside resorts, Spas, Town planning
New Towns Act (1946), 82, *222–225*
Newark, 37
Newbury, 35
Newcastle-under-Lyme, Staffs., 59, *163*
Newcastle-upon-Tyne, 15, 17, 18, 40, 68–69, *52, 172–175*
Newmarket, 34, *102*
Newport, Mon., 64, *171*
Newton, Dorset, 14
Newton, Lancs., 30
Nonconformists, 35, 37, 38, 56, 58, 60, 61–62, *87, 89*
Northampton, 54
Northleach, 16, *25*

Norwich, 12, 15, 18, 23, 25, 29, 35, 55, *9, 40*
Nottingham, 12, 18, 62, 67, 75, *162, 212*

OBAN, Argyll, *180*
Owen, Robert, 64, 69, 78
Oxford, 13, 14, 17, 23, 24, *27, 28*

PARKS, 68, 70
Perth, 41
Peterborough, 23
"Peterloo", 61, *161*
Pilgrimages, *31–34*. See also Holidays
Plague, 16, 31, 38, 39, *69*
Plymouth, 18, 28, 36, 40, 81, *220–221*
Poole, Dorset, *89*
Poor Law Commission, 65
Poor relief, 19, 24–25, 44, 65, 77–78, *47, 50, 82, 83, 190, 191*. See also Public health legislation
Population, 15, 16, 18, 21, 31, 40, 65, 71, 74, 82
Port Glasgow, 42, *113*
Port Sunlight, 70
Portsmouth, 40, *115*
Preston, Lancs., 37, 40, 57, 62, 73
Priestley, Dr. Joseph, 60
Public health legislation, 67, 68, 76. See also Cholera, Hospitals, Poor relief
Pwllheli, 12

QUATFORD, Shropshire, 12
Queenborough, Kent, *111*

RAILWAYS, 65–66, 71, 83, *141, 175, 176, 196*
Ramsgate, 48
Ravenser Od, Yorks., 14
Rawtenstall, 69
Reading, 23, 36, 38, 75, *207*
Reform Act (1832), 62, 64
Regalia and plate, 19, 59, 63, 75, *18, 20, 21, 48, 49, 66, 79–81, 126, 228, 229, 231*
Renfrew, 47
Rhondda Valley, *204*
Rhuddlan, 12
Richmond, Yorks., *49*
Rothesay, Bute, 48, *177*

ST. ALBANS, 23, *7*
St. Andrews, 13, 21, 73

St. Leonards-on-Sea, 54
St. Neots, 11
Salford, 65
Salisbury, 15, *131*
Salt, Sir Titus, 69, *193*
Saltaire, Yorks., 69, 70, *192*
Salvation Army, 78, *190, 191*
Scarborough, 24, 33, 36, 41, 48, 61, 73, *37, 114*
Schools, 20, 24, 35, 41, 75, *23, 41, 42, 50, 82, 83, 134*
Seaside resorts, 48–50, 71–73, 80, 81, *144–149, 177–181*. See also Holidays, Spas
Selby, 11
Sheffield, 24, 74, 75, *176*
Shepton Mallet, *10*
Shrewsbury, 28, 55
Sidmouth, 49
Smith, Adam, 42–43
Southampton, 19, 22, 75, *4*
Southend-on-Sea, 48, 73
Southport, 49, 50, 73
Southwold, Suffolk, *84*
Spas, 33–34, 40–41, 45–46, 48, 50–52, 54, *73–74, 91–98, 114, 150, 151*. See also Holidays, Seaside resorts
Sports and recreations, 55, 56, 59, 66, 68, *48, 102, 103, 116–117, 203, 213, 232*. See also Holidays, Markets, Parks, Theatres
Stamford, 11, 19
Stirling, 13, *2*
Stoke-on-Trent, 69
Stourport, 54
Strathpeffer, 48
Suburbs, 68, 71, 81, 83
Sudbury, Suffolk, 57
Swindon, 69

TELFORD, THOMAS, 47
Tenby, 73, *179*
Tewkesbury, 23
Thaxted, Essex, *22*
Theatres, 32, 49, 55, *54, 99–100*
Thetford, 11, *80*
Torquay, 69, 71–72, 73, *178*
Totnes, 16–17
Town halls, 75, *15–17, 63, 121, 131, 182, 183, 220*
Town planning, 13, 14–15, 28–29, 32–33, 38, 43, 45–47, 49, 51, 52–54, 68–72, 76, 78, 82, *1, 5,*

6, 56, 58, 59, 60, 61–62, 71, 72, 77, 93–97, 132, 133–142, 148, 152–158, 172–175, 178, 192, 197, 202, 209, 220–221. See also Housing, Markets, New towns, Public health legislation
Trade unions, 72, 79. See also General Strike
Tramways, 66, *181, 197*
Tregony, Cornwall, *160*
Tremadoc 54, *132*
Tunbridge Wells, 33–34, 45, 48, 49, 69, *74*

UNEMPLOYMENT, 80, *211*
Universities, 14, 21, 24, 27, 47, 74, *27, 28, 45, 46, 139*

VYRNWY, LAKE, Montgomeryshire, *195*

WALTON-ON-THE-NAZE, 50
War, 11, 12, 14, 19, 22, 27, 36, 79, 81, *35–37, 207–208, 217–219*
Warrington, 14
Water supplies, 15, 29, 32, 67, 69, 76, *26, 43, 67, 68, 167, 194, 195*. See also Public health legislation
Warwick, 47
Watt, James, 42–43, 60
Wells, Somerset, *6, 26*
Welwyn Garden City, 78, 82
Wesley, John, 56
Westminster, 13, 23, 31, 52, 62, *110, 122, 202*
Weymouth, 49, 62, *145*
Whitehaven, 40, 42, 77
Wigan, *211*
Winchelsea, 14, 61, *5*
Wick, 13
Wolverhampton, *126*
Wolverton, Bucks., 69
Wood, John, junior, 46
—, senior, 45–46
Worcester, *130*
Wren, Sir Christopher, 39
Wymondham, *55*

YARMOUTH, GREAT, 18, 28–29, 55, 82, *15, 59, 90, 118*
Yarmouth, Isle of Wight, 30
York, 11, 13, 14, 15, 18, 22, 28, *3, 16, 17*